£3.85 7L

STUDIES IN ENGLISH LITERATURE

Volume XXXVI

MIDDLE ENGLISH PROSE STYLE

Margery Kempe and Julian of Norwich

by

ROBERT KARL STONE

The University of Wisconsin-Milwaukee

1970

MOUTON

THE HAGUE · PARIS

LIBRARY OF CONGRESS CATALOG CARD NUMBER: 69-10748

Printed in The Netherlands by Mouton & Co., Printers, The Hague.

For Shirley, Bill, and Bob

ACKNOWLEDGMENT

The late Professor John J. Parry of the University of Illinois first introduced me to *The Book of Margery Kempe* a number of years ago, my interest initially being centered on Margery's psychology. With the passage of time the stress has shifted to her prose style, an element much more in keeping with my present knowledge, interests, and professional duties.

Throughout the planning and writing of this study, Professor Roland M. Smith, late of the University of Illinois, provided searching and helpful comments and criticism. To that kind, wise man, a good friend, I owe more than I can say. His death was a great loss, personally and professionally.

Several other people provided me with help, advice, and encouragement during various stages in the development of this work: Miss Eva Fay Benton of the English Library, University of Illinois; Miss Isabelle Grant, formerly Rare Book Librarian, University of Illinois; John H. Smith, Brandeis University.

I owe most to my wife, whose laborious typing of my frequently indecipherable longhand, especially my copy from microfilmed manuscript, would have been endured by no one else. Without her help and encouragement, this study would not have been completed.

University of Wisconsin — Milwaukee 1969

TABLE OF CONTENTS

I

INTRODUCTION

With recent editing of Middle English manuscripts, modern researchers have been calling more and more for study of the hitherto largely overlooked area of medieval prose style. Thus, we find statements that "analysis of individual works is vital if we are ever to be able to speak with any authority on medieval prose".[1] In commenting on the desirability of more editions of Middle English texts, one scholar declares that with such editions "we shall at last be in a position to make useful generalizations on the style and content of ME devotional prose".[2] Discussion of prose style is sparse for most periods of literary study, and such analysis seems certainly to be both needed and valuable not only to students of the medieval period but also to those specializing in the times that followed it. Tracing the development and continuity of English prose is important to the field of linguistic and literary history. On another level, early writing has use as a model in the study of prose technique: to determine what "medieval style" is, what "bad" elements provide lessons for modern writers, and what values should be remembered. The present study is an attempt to contribute to further knowledge of that style by examining intensively two late Middle English devotional works: *The Book of Margery Kempe* and the *Revelations of Divine Love* by Dame Julian of Norwich. The former work will recieve the greater stress. The original intention was to concentrate on Margery Kempe alone because of the greater interest her work has for the modern reader.

[1] Elizabeth Zeeman, review of *A Litil Tretys on the Seven Deadly Sins, MLR*, 52 (1957), 581.
[2] S. S. Hussey, review of *The Chastising of God's Children* and *The Treatise of Perfection, MLR*, 53 (1958), 231-232.

But because Julian of Norwich provides such an excellent sounding board by which Margery's prose can be analyzed more meaningfully, both works have been considered together.

It is fitting that the writings of Margery Kempe and Dame Julian should be compared and contrasted, for they have much in common. Although their work was classified by R. W. Chambers under "the ordinary medieval prose of pious instruction", he significantly said of this type: "Yet much of it is exceedingly beautiful; for instance the *Revelations of Divine Love* of Dame Julian of Norwich."[3] Writing before the full text of Margery was known, he called her work "noble fragments".[4] Apparently the two women were on the same level of evolution in the development of English prose: it was their type of homiletic and devotional writing that kept English prose alive during the years following the Norman Conquest, when French became the official language and, with Latin, threatened to squeeze out English entirely. Furthermore, the devotional prose of the thirteenth and fourteenth centuries contained a body of writing addressed particularly to women. "For the first time", says Chambers, "we come across a fact which is the cause of the composition of so much English prose: the fact that women recluses would not be expected to be as familiar as men would be with Latin."[5] Julian and Margery go one step farther: they are the most prominent female *writers* of Middle English devotional prose, women who "break a long tradition of feminine silence in England".[6]

---

[3]   *On the Continuity of English Prose*, EETS, 191A (London, Oxford University Press, 1957), p. cxvii. An extract from the Introduction to Nicholas Harpsfield's *Life of Sir Thomas More*, edited for EETS by E. V. Hitchcock and R. W. Chambers in 1932.

[4]   His knowledge of the full text has caused some modification of this view. In his introduction to W. Butler-Bowdon's modernized version of *The Book of Margery Kempe* (New York, Devin-Adair, 1944), Chambers says that the work may "shock the reader" and must be "painful" to "those who had hoped to find a new *Scale of Perfection*" (p. xvii).

[5]   *Continuity of English Prose*, p. xciii.

[6]   *The Book of Margery Kempe*, ed. Sanford B. Meech and Hope Emily Allen, EETS, 212 (London, Oxford University Press, 1940), p. lxii. This edition will hereafter be referred to as "Meech and Allen". References to the text itself will be in the form of *page* and *line* numbers (e.g., 42/10-12), and generally will not be footnoted, but will follow the quotation immediately.

Other similarities are perhaps even more striking. Margery Kempe's Lynn and Julian's Norwich are both in Norfolk, not more than forty miles apart. Margery was born approximately at the time of Julian's "shewings" in 1373, and the two women met personally at least once for a period of "many days".[7] According to their own accounts, both women were illiterate, "cowde no letter",[8] and therefore made use of amanuenses.[9] Likewise, both showed the typical medieval stress on the Passion: "... a genuine intuition of the joyful aspects of the Passion was conditional on a full appreciation of its physical awfulness".[10] In both cases, also, the writing was going on approximately twenty years after the mystical experiences began,[11] although Margery continued to have visions of a consistent pictorial type throughout this intervening period while Julian, after her initial sixteen "Corporeal and Imaginative visions", experienced only "Intellectual visions or illuminations" during her long period of contemplation.[12] And both writers had the same avowed goal, to help others to achieve greater knowledge and appreciation of God's ways through understanding: "Here

[7] Meech and Allen, 42/7-43/20.

[8] *Revelations of Divine Love*, ii/2. Quotations from Julian's *Revelations* are made directly from a microfilmed copy of Sloane 2499 (see discussion of texts later in this chapter). References are to *chapter* numbers and *line* numbers. The latter may vary slightly according to texts used; lines here are numbered from *Revelations of Divine Love*, ed. Dom Roger Hudleston (London, Burns Oates, 1952). For Margery's illiteracy see Meech and Allen, 3/25-27, 39/25, 111/20-22, 143/25. Julian's illiteracy has been contested, notably by R. M. Wilson, "Three Middle English Mystics", *Essays and Studies* 1956, n.s. 9, pp. 87-112. Wilson does not accept "cowde no letter" too literally, believing the phrase to mean merely that Julian had never had conventional training in Latin rhetoric and composition (p. 97). Eric Colledge, *The Mediæval Mystics of England* (New York, Charles Scribner's Sons, 1961), also mentions this meaning, but goes on to say: "... those who are unwilling to take her words literally forget those mediæval spiritual works showing familiarity with. ... Scriptures and ... other writings and also a great command of the language, which were dictated by women who could neither read nor write — St. Catherine of Siena ... and Margery Kempe" (p. 85).

[9] Meech and Allen, pp. vii-viii.

[10] R. H. Thouless, *The Lady Julian* (London, S.P.C.K., 1924), p. 32. For examples of "Passion" writing, see Meech and Allen 191/4-194/24 and *Revelations* vii/11-28.

[11] Meech and Allen, 3/28 ff. *Revelations*, li/100 ff.

[12] Hudleston, *op. cit.* (above, note 8), p. xviii.

begynnyth a schort tretys and a comfortabyl for synful wrecchys, wher-in þei may haue gret solas and comfort to hem and vndyrstondyn þe hy & vnspecabyl mercy of ower souereyn Sauyowr Cryst Ihesu" (1/1-4). "For trewly I saw & understode in our Lords mening þat he shewid it for he will have it knowen more than it is" (lxxxvi/7-9). Margery and Julian, of course, were mystics in the sense that both allegedly experienced personal visions of and discussions with God or His agents, in each case the mystical occurrences beginning after an illness. Their writings, the products of the same eastern county of England at approximately the same time, provide many areas for comparison.

Although these striking similarities do exist, there are also outstanding differences, caused primarily by the distinct personalities and responses of the authors. Anyone reading the two works will be struck by some of the contrasts in character. Obviously Julian thought much more deeply about her experiences than did Margery in the intervening years before writing took place. The more studious, contemplative nature and response of Julian are evident throughout her work, her more moderate and quiet though vivid presentation contributing much to this impression. Julian can give "reasoned reflections possible only to high intelligence".[13] Julian's humility and her work in general appear sincere; in Margery's work the reader feels much more strongly the possible motive of self-glorification. When our view in the *Book* moves from Margery to Julian (42/7 ff.) we sense, as one reviewer puts it: "a change from the self-occupied fervours of the devotee to the calm objectivity of the saint".[14] But some of Margery's characteristics make her work more interesting to the reader: her book is manyfaceted; Julian's is unrelievedly concentrated. The extreme and eccentric behavior of Margery makes her character fascinating. Her quickness and alertness, her presentation of non-religious matters, and her emotional responses are probably more appealing to most readers than is the studious, single-minded religious tone of

[13]   E. Mackinnon, "Studies in Fourteenth Century English Mysticism", unpub. diss. (University of Illinois, 1934), p. 301.
[14]   Evelyn Underhill, "Margery Kempe", *The Spectator*, 157 (October 16, 1936), 642.

Julian. Above all, *The Book of Margery Kempe* gives us autobiography where Julian gives us no details of her own life beyond
the circumstances of her "shewings". It is the more casual, extra-
neously detailed autobiographical tone and the accompanying
view of the life of the time which serve to distinguish Margery's
work from Julian's, to give it its unique flavor, and to make it an
object of general interest to the reader of today.

Brief accounts of their works, lives, and experiences point up
these essential differences. The contents of the *Revelations of
Divine Love* may be summarized rapidly. The revelations appeared
to Julian in May, 1373,[15] during the crisis of an illness which
threatened her life. Some time before her illness Julian had desired
"three gifts of God": mind of His Passion; bodily sickness in youth,
at thirty years of age; three wounds — of very contrition, of kind
compassion, and of wilful longing toward God. At the age of
thirty and a half, Julian experienced the illness that she desired. At
the crisis, unable to speak, "dede fro the middis downewards",[16] she
fastened all her attention on the crucifix held before her by her
curate. Just when she thought she would die, all her pain disap-
peared. She then remembered her second wound, compassion and
the desire to suffer with Jesus. The crucifix seemed to come to life,
and the visions commenced.[17] The first fifteen of the revelations
followed continuously for about five hours, but then Julian's own
sufferings returned, causing a temporary lack of faith in what she
had seen. Falling asleep at last, she dreamed of the devil, who tried
to strangle her. After awakening and experiencing smoke, heat,
and stench apparent to no one else in the room, she blessed God
and immediately lost all sense of illness. Her faith in the truth of
her visions returned, and that night Julian experienced the sixteenth
and last revelation. Her descriptions of these "shewings" and her
exposition of their meanings after twenty years of contemplation
form the *Revelations of Divine Love*.

---

[15] *Revelations*, ii/2-3. Sloane 2499 gives the date plainly as May 8; the Paris
MS (see discussion of texts later in this chapter) says May 13.
[16] *Revelations*, iii/21-22. Chapters ii and iii give general information leading
up to the revelations.
[17] The following summary is taken from Chapters lxv-lxvii.

Although Julian gives very little information about her life, certain facts do appear in the *Revelations*, in the scribe's preface to the Amherst MS (1413), and in contemporary documents. She was a "recluse atte Norwyche and yitt ys on lyfe" in 1413.[18] Her recluse status is affirmed by bequests in a contemporary will (May 19, 1404) "to Julian an anchoress at St. Julian's Church, Norwich 12d. and 8d. to Sara living with her", and also by a record of a twenty shilling legacy to "Julian, recluse at Norwich".[19] The latter information is contained in Archbishop Chichele's register for 1416, indicating Julian to be alive at an age of seventy-four. From her age at the time of her revelations, we may assume that she was born in 1342. The Amherst MS (ch. x) tells us also that her mother was present during her daughter's illness, and we have already noted that Julian "cowde no letter". During her lifetime she evidently had considerable renown, as Margery Kempe herself indicates: "[Margery] was bodyn be owyr Lord for to gon to an ankres in þe same cyte whych hyte Dame Ielyan" (42/7-9); "þe ankres was expert in sewch thyngys & good cownsel cowd ȝeuyn" (42/16-17); "Mych was þe holy dalyawns þat þe ankres & þis creatur haddyn be comownyng in þe lofe of owyr Lord Ihesu Crist many days þat þei were to-gedyr" (43/18-20). Not everyone that Margery meets comes off so well in the pages of her book. These are the only facts known to date about Julian's life.

But *The Book of Margery Kempe* is quite different, giving us much more information about the author herself. Margery seems to have advanced through some of the commonly accepted steps to the mystical union with God, sharing one of them, illness, with Julian. After the birth of her first child she was out of her mind for eight months, tormented by an unconfessed sin. Then came her first vision and after it a recovery of health and a superficial religious awareness. She remained vain and proud, and only after being humbled by business failures did she turn wholly to God.

---

[18] This quotation is from the scribe's preface to the much shorter version of the *Revelations* found in the Amherst MS (British Museum Add. MS 37790). For fuller information, see materials on texts later in this chapter.
[19] *Revelations of Divine Love*, tr. James Walsh (New York, Harper, 1961), p. 2.

The cumulative effect of Margery's series of misfortunes finally accomplished her conversion to what she would have called "contemplation" or "perfection". The period of penance which followed is typical of the first stage in the mystic's initiation. This Purgation, in Margery's case, seems to have been followed "in schort tyme" (2/20) by the supernatural experience of 11/12 *sq.* (cp. 11/20 *et n.*), which may be said to belong to the mystic's second period, Illumination.[20]

As an effect of her first illumination she acquired three characteristics: a desire for chastity, continual talk and thought of heaven, and the habit of tears. Margery had visions of the Passion, held conversations with God, was orthodox in various matters of faith such as belief in indulgences and in the Sacrament. Uniquely, her conversations with God (and the Saints) are exceedingly frequent, detailed, and personal. In her visions Margery herself becomes involved in Biblical events: "... her personal mysticism seemed to reach its most characteristic form in a queer sort of self-transference to remote periods of time".[21] In addition Margery "seems to have been endowed with a supernatural insight or foresight".[22] Thus in Capitulum 12, having received divine information, she reproves a wicked monk, who reforms and becomes sub-prior. Similarly, she is given foreknowledge of the troubles she will encounter in Jerusalem, of deaths to come, and of recoveries from sickness: "sche knew & vndyrstod many secret & preuy thyngys whech schuld beffallen aftyrward" (2/36-37).

We have said earlier that both Margery and Julian had the same goal, to instruct others. Margery naturally says nothing herself about desiring glory — indeed one of the conditions necessary to achieve the mystical state was a humbling of her pride and her desire for worldly glory. A sympathetic critic takes as fact, then, that "the specific object of her book is to show the mercy of God".[23] The didactic purpose of the book is stressed further by Miss Cholmeley:

[20] Meech and Allen, p. 260 (note on 11/4). For other passages which mention Margery's conversion, see Miss Allen's note on 2/1 (p. 256).

[21] B. G. Brooks, "Margery Kempe", *The Nineteenth Century and After*, 132 (July, 1942), 30-32.

[22] Katherine Cholmeley, *Margery Kempe: Genius and Mystic* (London, Longmans, 1947), pp. 109-110.

[23] Cholmeley, p. 12.

The narrative was written to show how she was drawn from sin and fickleness into the way of high perfection. The revelations enjoin that this way lies in contemplation, in the life of love, the unitive life. Not much fasting, not heavy penance, not a multiplicity of devotions, not abundant alms giving in itself, but a life centered and hidden in God.[24]

and by another reviewer:

Her experience she saw as a revelation of the goodness of God, which it was her duty to share in order that others might be brought to a livelier realization of that goodness and so to their salvation.[25]

Margery had great faith in her mission as an agent of intercession, and God himself tells her that her prayers will save thousands (20/10-12) and that her writing pleases him (3/30-4/2).

But despite her renunciation of wordly glory, the direction of her spiritual conversations tends constantly to present her in a good light: as an agent of intercession; as a highly chosen person who willingly suffers abuse and sorrow; as a brave, energetic, witty woman. Margery seems honestly to have thought herself to be free of desire for worldly glory, for she probably "intended in general to keep the book a secret in her lifetime".[26] Despite this intention we feel her desire for posthumous fame in her frequent quotations of God's affection for her personally: "'& so schal l ben worschepyd in erth for þi loue, dowtyr, for I wyl haue þe grace þat I haue schewyd to þe in erth knowyn to þe worlde þat þe pepil may wonderyn in my goodnes'" (206/18-21); and "'þu hast be despysed for my lofe, & þerfor þu xalt be worshepyd for my lofe'" (52/20-21).[27] At any rate, her statements of purpose and the attitude shown in her writing appear at times to be in disagreement.

In addition to the many facets of character that appear in her work and provide a portrait worthy of detailed study, Margery also gives a vivid background of personages and pilgrimages in a panorama of contemporary life. Indeed, Chambers, evidently disturbed by some of the less spiritual elements in Margery's mysticism, believes the chief value of the book to consist in the light thrown

[24]   Cholmeley, p. 105.
[25]   Helen C. White, "Margery Kempe of Lynn", *Commonweal*, 39 (1943), 164-165.
[26]   Meech and Allen, p. 258 (note on 4/7).
[27]   See also 52/19-20, 156/19-30, 183/19-22, 186/13-15.

upon fifteenth-century life.[28] Reflecting an uncloistered life, Margery gives views of virtues and faults of the people, both lay and secular. She provides accounts of her trials for heresy with brief, fascinating glimpses of the people involved. Particularly interesting are the details of medieval wayfaring life — food, lodging, customs, companionship, and dangers — that emerge as she goes about on extensive travels. It is the constant movement from place to place, occurrence to occurrence, and person to person that

gives her book that variety which is to seek in most M.E. prose "tales" — Chaucer's Parson's occurs to us at once — and we can now see that the fictional method of "Robinson Crusoe" and "Moll Flanders", so far from being a new one, or a legacy from seventeenth century criminal narrative and the Elizabethan "Iacke Wilton", has its roots in the spiritual autobiography, one more instance of the continuity of literary forms.[29]

The Book of Margery Kempe, then, has merit and interest not only as a work of mysticism but also as history and autobiography as well as literature.

But before going on to a closer study of the "literary forms" of Margery's *Book* and Julian's *Revelations*, it is necessary to make some observations concerning the texts themselves. Margery Kempe had the help of an amanuensis in writing her book; we have noted some opposition to the idea of Julian's illiteracy (see footnote 8). The question arises: how much of these writings is actually the mystics' own? Where do Julian and Margery end and the amanuenses enter? It is generally impossible to tell, of course. Julian may not have had any; in her case, we are more in the dark than we are about Margery. We may say, however, that if Julian dictated her work, many of the points made to support Margery's control of composition apply to her also. In the case of Margery Kempe, it is apparent that her amanuensis did have considerable work to do involving revision of parts, at least. The *Book* begins by recounting the priest's tribulations in attempting to revise an earlier edition of Margery's text:

---

[28] Butler-Bowdon, *op. cit.* (above, note 4), p. xxiii.
[29] Anon., "Among the English Classics: The Autobiography of Margery Kempe", *LTLS*, 35 (1936), 805.

þe booke was so euel wretyn þat he cowd lytyl skyll þeron, for it was neiþyr good Englysch ne Dewch, ne þe lettyr was not schapyn ne formyd as oþer letters ben ... þan he cownseld hir to gon to a good man whech had ben mech conuersawnt wyth hym þat wrot fyrst þe book ... þis good man ... cowd not wel fare þerwyth, þe boke was so euel sett & so vnresonably wretyn ... þan sche gat a-geyn þe book & browt it to þe preste wyth rygth glad cher ... he red it ouyr be-forn þis creatur euery word, sche sum-tym helpying where ony difficulte was. Thys boke is not wretyn in ordyr, euery thyng aftyr oþer as it wer don, but lych as þe mater cam to þe creatur in mend whan it schuld be wretyn. ... And þerfor sche dede no þing wryten but þat sche knew rygth wel for very trewth. (4/14-5/18)

The main stress here is on the handwriting itself; significantly, Margery exercised close supervision over the copy. We may conjecture that generally we do have Margery's own words before us, that the strong-willed woman dictated these words to the man who faithfully wrote them down. We still may wonder whether the priest might not have helped Margery, perhaps unconsciously, by conversations about the topics as well as by possible rephrasings. Particularly in her scenes with her examiners, where she meets all questions perfectly with extensively quoted scriptural details and parable and where the illiterate witness gives Latin quotations, is the question of possible priestly assistance most obviously raised. While Margery quotes Latin from the Psalter to excuse herself against a monk (235/35 ff.) and makes some use of the language at other times (88/25, 248/7-9), elsewhere she maintains she cannot understand Latin:

þe Styward a-non, as he sey hir, spak Latyn vn-to hir, many prestys stondyng a-bowtyn to here what sche xulde say. ... Sche seyd to þe Stywarde, "Spekyth Englysch, yf ȝow lyketh, for I vndyrstonde not what ȝe sey." (112/34-113/4)

However, with her religiosity and perhaps *because* of illiteracy — because of the need to remember without recourse to books or notes — Margery could be expected to have thorough knowledge and recall of oral Church teachings. Her memory was probably very good: although a long period of time intervened between the writing down of her experiences and their actual occurrence, Margery relates her visions and activities with great detail; she gives long quotations and dialogue from her conversations with God and people. The reader may feel doubt: could Margery be exaggerating her experiences? Many people do exaggerate when repeating a story. After twenty or so years of living and reliving her experiences, might not Margery be giving an expanded or even changed account? The firmly devout might cite St. Theresa's opinion on the traits of true revelation: "Divine auditions express meaning so clearly and impress themselves on the memory so deeply, that one cannot forget the slightest syllable ..."[30] A critic who has commented extensively upon this matter strongly supports the veracity of the accounts:

Margery's revelations are, in some instances, of great length. Can she be credited with an exact and perfect memory of divine locutions? On consideration, it is hardly to be doubted. She is, in the first place, obviously one of those whose memory is retentive of particular circumstances and detail. The faculty that made her so observant of the external world made her observant of the interior also ...

She could not read. Her mind was not cluttered with shreds and tatters of a heap of written matter only vaguely or imperfectly remembered, if indeed consciously remembered at all. Her locutions were evidently so clear and emphatic as to make a profound and enduring impression on the mind and soul: to be engraven upon them. Nor that alone. She did not keep them to herself. She sought counsel of this one and that, recounting them to confessors, recluses, and various priests, from whom she desired counsel and guidance; for, though she does not express astonishment at being the recipient of vision or revelation, she was both wise and humble enough to dread the deceit and craft of the Devil. She sought advice continually, and must have retailed her revelations over and over again, so it would not be impossible to record them after the lapse of some twenty years.[31]

Miss Allen reinforces this:

I think that Margery's "'dread' for illusions" was a motive which trained her to an accuracy of expression (as to external events) quite exceptional in the Middle Ages.

. . .

Margery's series of interviews must have had the effect of clarifying

---

[30] J. H. Leuba, *The Psychology of Religious Mysticism* (London, Kegan Paul, Trench, Trübner & Co., 1925), p. 180 (note).
[31] Cholmeley, pp. 101-102.

her narrative of her spiritual history and fixing her revelations in her
memory, which otherwise she would be inclined to forget.[32]

If we accept these ideas, Margery's remarkable memory makes the
ability to quote Latin and make use of church teachings seem
possible.

In addition to the priest's own words about Margery's control of
the writing and to the plausibility of her use of unexpected material,
three other points are pertinent in an attempt to give Margery
credit for the work which bears her name. First, the manner of
the work — its organization and presentation — is probably not
representative of a priest. Indicating Margery's responsibility, the
amanuensis tells us that the book is poorly organized, "not wretyn
in ordyr, euery thyng aftyr oþer as it wer don, but lych as þe mater
cam to þe creatur in mend" (5/12-14). Similarly, in a note to a
specific passage, Miss Allen says:

The loose phraseology in this passage gives one example of such seemingly impromptu expression on Margery's part as seems to indicate her
control of the dictation of the book.[33]

Second, although Margery normally uses the third person ("þe
creatur ... sche"), perhaps following German women's books of
revelations,[34] she occasionally slips into use of the first person: "I
purpos to wrytyn" (14/7-8); "þe Bysshop dede no mor to us at þat
day, saue he mad us rygth good cher and seyd we wer ryght wol-
come" (34/25-26).[35] Finally, we have Margery's own character,
which, as we shall see, emerges in a way which could not be likely
if the priest, and not Margery, were controlling the writing. Although the problem of who wrote what will probably never be
completely solved,[36] it cannot detract from the pertinence of val-

[32] Meech and Allen, p. 257 (notes on 3/8, 3/10-13).
[33] Meech and Allen, p. 331 (note on 175/29).
[34] Meech and Allen, p. 255 (note on 1/27). Julian refers to herself as "creature" in the opening lines of Chapter ii, but ordinarily uses the first person.
[35] In some cases, however, the first person may conceivably refer to the
amanuensis: 44/17-18, 214/23-24, 230/21-22. Miss Allen, in her note on 1/27,
makes no distinction.
[36] Although impossible to substantiate, some passages seem to me to be
"amanuensis flavored" because of content, attitude, or wording: the poem
(see 5/30), 55/6 ff., 70/22-71/15, 72/20 ff., 152/29-154/20, 162/17-21, 199/9-15,
219/33-220/24, 221/1 ff.

uable medieval texts to the study of the prose of the period. The important fact remains that, whether by amanuensis or mystic, we have Middle English prose: "in reference ... to the ... seven or eight centuries before, say 1450, the subject of enquiry ... is not what they intended to do, but merely what they did".[37]

What these writers *did* do — and we shall call them Margery and Julian no matter who set pen to paper — is available in several forms. The text of *The Book of Margery Kempe*, extant only in a single manuscript owned by Colonel W. Butler-Bowdon, has been ably edited with excellent apparatus by Sanford B. Meech and Hope Emily Allen for the Early English Text Society, as already noted.[38] A projected second volume to the EETS edition has not appeared, but the text itself is presented complete in the first volume. The second volume, planned to present further notes and appendices, has been delayed by the unfortunate death of Hope Emily Allen.[39] While we may hope that this long-anticipated work will

[37] George Saintsbury, *A History of English Prose Rhythm* (London, Macmillan, 1922), p. 103.

[38] The text is also available in the previously cited modern version by W. Butler-Bowdon. This version is not reliable for scholarly study of Middle English literature: spelling has been modernized and many words have been replaced by modern equivalents (p. xxv). The following examples (with the Meech-Allen edition in parentheses) indicate some of the losses in alliteration: "reward and merit" ("mede & meryte" 48/32-33), "hinder me in loving" ("let me to lofe" 49/8-9), "unknown and uncertain" ("vnsekyr & vncerteyn" 55/9). Similarly, modern "'I must get on with my job and beg my living'", loses much of the effectiveness of the original "'I must gon on with my purchase & beggyn my leuyng'" (77/22-23).

[39] In a personal letter to me dated February, 1957, Miss Allen expressed both her hopes to complete the second volume with the help of Dr. Mabel Day and her difficulties in doing so: "There has been no time when I have not worked to some degree on BMK II. But I have never been strong and BMK I was an exceeding [sic] exhausting enterprise for me, leaving me not very fit for quick synthetic composition. ... I was found in 1950 to have arthritis ... and had to alter my entire mode of life. ... One thing and another since then has aggravated this condition. ... I am not allowed to sit to the typewriter more than very short periods — this is a permanent state and I find it hard to find here typists able to manage my vocabulary. And I write very illegibly. I am going to try to improve that —" Miss Allen also enclosed a notice sent to "Research in Progress", indicating her efforts: "Masses of copy from 15th century N. [sic] English translations from St. Bridget of Sweden, and other foreign women mystics, have been copied for me and edited for text and linguistics by Dr. Mabel Day of EETS. I have much new material also on early medieval English mystical

someday appear, its absence does not affect the scope of this study.

Four manuscripts of Julian's *Revelations of Divine Love* exist. In order of antiquity they rank as follows:

(1) British Museum Add. MS 37790, sometimes called *Amherst MS*, dated 1413. This MS contains, in addition to a series of medieval devotional works, a version of the *Revelations* which is much shorter (thirty-six pages compared to Sloane 2499's 110 pages) than that given in the other MSS and which stands outside their tradition.[40]

(2) Paris Bibl. Nationale, MS Anglais 40, from the sixteenth century. This MS is the basis for the latest "translation" of the "long version", by Father Walsh, who believes that it "represents more nearly the MS tradition".[41] In this he follows Sister Anna Maria Reynolds, editor of the shortened version,[42] feeling that her conclusion is borne out by the discovery of a late fifteenth-century *Florilegium* in the Westminster Cathedral Library containing extracts from Julian's *Revelations* which favor Paris MS readings against

(3) British Museum MS Sloane 2499. This early seventeenth-century MS has been the basis for the two other most recent editions of the long version, by Dom Roger Hudleston (1952) and Grace Warrack (first published in 1902 but now in its 14th edition).[43]

(4) British Museum MS Sloane 3705, of the late seventeenth or early eighteenth century,[44] may be a copy of Sloane 2499 but is considerably modernized in spelling and language.[45]

---

piety prepared, and the last year have added a good deal on Hilton and Julian of Norwich. ... My selections [from "immense ME anthologies from St. Bridget"] are designed to give the exceptional background of medieval mystical piety in the England of MK's time, and later." The foregoing excerpts testify to the courage, dedication, tribulation — and kindness — of a sorely missed scholar.

[40] Walsh, p. v (note). In a note on p. 1, Fr. Walsh speaks of the general agreement among scholars that this MS is not an abridged version of the longer text but rather a type of first "edition".

[41] Walsh, pp. v-vi.

[42] *A Shewing of God's Love* (London, Longmans, 1958).

[43] My references to this work will be to the 4th edition: *Revelations of Divine Love* (London, Methuen, 1911).

[44] Walsh, p. v; Hudleston, p. vi.

[45] Hudleston, p. vi.

At the time this study began, Sloane 2499 was the basis for all modern printed editions and was the logical choice as the basic MS to follow. The appearance of Father Walsh's translation with its dependence on the Paris MS does not seem to me to alter the situation. First, although Father Walsh collated both the Paris and Sloane MSS, his translation can in no sense be considered a definitive edition for scholarly purposes. He gives no apparatus whatsoever and the text of the *Revelations* is free of footnotes, although it is not a literal copy of the MSS at all:

Wherever I felt the reader would understand the archaic word, expression or construction without too much difficulty, the original has been retained; but punctuation and spelling have been modernized throughout. Absolute consistency, even where it is possible, has been considered undesirable, since some archaic forms act as an irritant to the modern reader.[46]

The modernized Hudleston and Warrack editions of Sloane 2499, similarly not definitive texts, at least provide some scholarly apparatus, frequently, for example, noting MS words and spelling where modern equivalents are used or changes occur. A case in point is chapter headings, which occur only in Sloane 2499 and "are presumably the work of the transcriber".[47] Hudleston says (p. viii) that he prints these headings "with some curtailment, however, especially after Chapter 50, when they tend to become inordinately long". Father Walsh states (p. vii) that the chapter headings are taken from the Sloane MS, but he makes no mention anywhere that he has renumbered and divided the headings for Chapters 65-73 to fit the Paris MS, which separates content into chapters at points differing from the Sloane divisions. Without note of emendations and variant readings, with modernized spellings, and with changes in the text itself,[48] Father Walsh's study

---

[46] Walsh, pp. vi-vii.

[47] Hudleston, p. vii.

[48] These changes sometimes result in real loss. Note the increasing balance and rhythm as we go to the various readings of li/25: (Walsh) "he attended only to his last feeling of woe"; (Hudleston) "he gave intent to his feeling and endured in woe"; (Sloane 2499) "he entended to feling and indured in wo". Likewise, alliteration may be lost, as in xxv/21: (Walsh) "I am not taught to long to see"; (Hudleston) "am I not learned so long to see"; (Sloane 2499) "am I not lerid to longen to see".

loses much value for the examination of Middle English prose. Still lacking a scholarly edition of Julian's *Revelations*, the study of her style continues to require individual MS reading.

Second, Father Walsh's reliance on the Paris MS stems from fifteenth-century "extracts" that "favour" Paris MS readings against Sloane readings. Nowhere, however, does he indicate the scope of the extracts, on which he bases his decision. Similarly, when he says (p. vi) he has "never scrupled to substitute a reading from Sloane whenever this seemed superior, either linguistically or textually", there is no indication of the extent to which Sloane "seemed superior". But even more important than this lack of crucial information is the basis for preferring Paris to Sloane readings: "My choice of readings has been governed largely by what appear to me to be the principles of Julian's spiritual theology."[49] Contrasted to this reason for choosing a basic MS is the opinion of Dom Hudleston:

This leaves us, however, in the unsatisfactory position of having no manuscript of the entire work earlier than the Paris codex, which belongs to the sixteenth century — two hundred years or so later than the date of the actual Revelations ... — though both the Paris MS and Sloane 2499 appear to derive from a fourteenth century original, the spelling and dialect of which they have retained. This lost archetype seems to have been written in a mixed East Anglian and Northern dialect, and, of the two copies, Sloane 2499 is perhaps nearer to the original text. Unless, therefore, the lost fourteenth-century original of the longer version is found, we are not likely to obtain a better text of this than appears in Sloane 2499, which has accordingly been used as the basis of the present edition.[50]

Until a scholarly collation with proper application to language and literalness appears — and the need for such a work becomes more and more obvious — we must go to the text itself to make interpretations. Sloane 2499 is the only MS with published texts based entirely on it — texts that provide some indication of MS form

---

[49] Walsh, p. vi.
[50] Hudleston, p. xi. Similarly, Warrack, *op. cit.* (note 43, above), p. xi: "The English of the Fourteenth Century seems on the whole well preserved in both [Paris and Sloane 2499], especially perhaps in the later Manuscript [Sloane 2499], which must have been copied from one of mixed East Anglian and northern dialects."

when emended. More important, until more fully documented language study proves the Hudleston-Warrack position wrong, Sloane 2499 remains the MS in which language, not theology, has been stressed as the basis for judging nearness to the original. I have therefore retained the Sloane MS as a basis for study of Julian's Middle English prose style.

In using quotations from both Julian and Margery,[51] I have tried to change my texts as little as possible. Margery's quotations from the Meech and Allen edition have been changed by eliminating the italics used by the editors to indicate forms originally abbreviated. Occasionally, I have also used the editor's insertions without the square brackets used to indicate such inserts. Quotations from Julian's *Revelations* come from a microfilm made from the Modern Language Association rotograph deposit of Sloane 2499 at the Library of Congress. The MS is sometimes very difficult to read; I have indicated readings that I believe differ considerably from those given in published versions of Sloane 2499. Quotations from Julian have been changed in the following ways:

(1) Punctuation — negligible in the MS — has normally been added to aid the reader.

(2) Julian's abbreviation for *and* has been changed to an ampersand to match Margery's use.

(3) Double *ff* spelling has frequently been modernized to a capital letter.

(4) Capital letters have been used to introduce sentences.

(5) Various abbreviations have been put into full form, the change being indicated by italics: "pañe"="pan*n*e."

(6) The use of the scribal *y* with raised *e* or *t* to represent the older thorn and spelling of certain words (y^t=þ*at*) is not regular, but where it occurs it has been normalized to the thorn and expanded spelling of the Margery text.

As Father Walsh has quite rightly said, "Students of Middle English literature have spoken of the high quality of her [Julian's] prose, but never more than in very general terms, or in passing."[52]

---

[51] See notes 6 and 8 above for additional information on my use of references.
[52] Walsh, p. 10. In a note to this passage Father Walsh refers to the "brief

Margery's prose likewise has received little attention. The only significant study to date that has considered the prose style of both has been a brief analysis by R. M. Wilson[53] that also considered Richard Rolle, but more remains to be said. Besides tracing the threads of prose continuity visible in the works and isolating some of the values that early writing can contribute to modern technique, I also hope to clarify the important stylistic relationships between Margery and Julian, disagreeing in some cases, especially in the last two chapters, with the implications of the Wilson study. To these ends, the works of both mystics will be studied closely but not exhaustively. For example, although the texts have been examined completely with some care, only every *fifth* chapter has been studied with what could be considered intensive thoroughness. At times, several successive chapters (for example, the beginnings of both works) have received such attention as have chapters like Julian's fifty-first, which are obviously impressive as sources for discussion material.

The first step in the study will be the detailed examination of character, particularly Margery's. Next will come an analysis of three main areas of style: "words and the senses", alliteration, and syntax, with special stress on elements of balance and variety. In these general areas will be found most of the individual habits, devices, and techniques that combine to form the elusive quality known as "style".

·

---

but illuminating discussion of Julian's prose style" in the shorter version of the *Revelations*, Reynolds, *op. cit.* (note 41, above), pp. xxii ff.
[53]   "Three Middle English Mystics", *op. cit.* (note 8, above).

II

INTROVERSION AND EXTRAVERSION

Contrast in character is apparent to any reader of Margery Kempe and Julian of Norwich. The work of Julian is strikingly intellectual. She is an *analytical* mystic[1], carefully examining her visions, her conclusions, and her questions about the conclusions. Characteristically, she views problems in enumerated parts: "In this litil thing I saw iij properties. The first is that God made it; þe second is that God loveth it; the iij þat God kepith it" (v/17-19). There is a single-mindedness in her work, a preoccupation with religious matters that excludes the worldly. The work of Margery Kempe, on the other hand, is basically non-intellectual. There is little or no analysis, little or no examination of philosophical causes, effects, or questions. Instead, we find a primarily emotional reaction, personalized, focusing on Margery herself: *her* feelings, reassurances from God about *her* own worth, *her* involvements with the most sacred personages of Christian theology. Also, the world is much with her. As the center of attention and as a non-recluse, Margery of necessity must deal with worldly matters. What we get from her, therefore, is mainly emotional autobiography. Basically her work is narrative; Julian's is more purely expository — explanatory and analytical. Where in Julian we feel that the self is subordinated to the examination of basic religious questions, in Margery we feel no such philosophical concern but rather an interest mainly in her own self, a bolstering of her own worth.

The essential difference in character between Julian and Margery may be expressed in the terms "introversion" and "extraversion":

---

[1] Warrack, p. xlix.

These two types of rhetoric [discursive = thought, exposition, intellectual assent; non-discursive or symbolic = sensibility, persuasion,
emotional assent] ... may be related to opposed directions of mental
activity — the two directions of psychic energy which Jung has called
'extraversion' and 'introversion.' ... one can quite generally 'describe
the introverted standpoint as one that under all circumstances sets the
self and the subjective psychological processes above the object and the
objective process, or at any rate holds the ground against the object —
the extraverted standpoint, on the other hand, sets the subject below the
object, whereby the object receives the predominant value'. He adds that
'every human being possesses both mechanisms as an expression of his
natural life-rhythm. ... But the complicated external conditions under
which we live, as well as the presumably even more complex conditions
of our own individual psychic disposition, frequently favour the one
mechanism and restrict and hinder the other; whereby a predominance
of one mechanism naturally arises. If this condition becomes in any way
chronic, a *type* is produced, namely an habitual attitude, in which the
one attitude permanently predominates; not, of course, that the other
can ever be completely suppressed, inasmuch as it also is an integral
factor in psychic activity. ...'

Just as certainly as these psychic conditions produce a *type*, so as
certainly they produce a *style*. ...[2]

As the personalities of the authors affect the content, so do they
affect the prose style. The "extraversion" of Julian — seen in her
stress on the object, her submerging of self-glorification, her questioning of the meaning behind the visions — is reflected in a calm,
studious, generally polished and restrained prose style. Margery's
"introversion" — seen in her subjectivity, her vanity, her pettiness,
especially in her possible motive of self-glorification — is reflected
in a flamboyant, careless, unrestrained style. Despite their fitness
as examples of the two types,[3] however, both Margery and Julian
also provide support for the idea that the predominant feature
will never completely suppress its opposite.

No one who reads *The Book of Margery Kempe* can help feeling
the impact of the author's individuality on the way in which

---

[2]   Herbert Read, *English Prose Style* (Boston, Beacon Press, 1961), p. 84.
The quotation from Carl Jung in this passage is from *Psychological Types*
(London, Kegan Paul, Trench, Trübner & Co., 1938), pp. 12-13.

[3]   The common idea of the "extrovert" as a "show-off", one who acts rather
than thinks, does not apply to Julian, just as the common idea of the "introvert"
as one who tends to think rather than act, does not apply to Margery.

thoughts are expressed. The character and personality of Margery Kempe are, indeed, the distinctive features of her *Book*, and a discussion of its merits as literature would have to include the ways in which these qualities emerge. Practically all critics have commented upon some mental aberrations in Margery at one time or another. Illustrating this opinion is a comment upon her first vision and recovery from illness:

The experience undoubtedly marks a stage of recovery and a real reintegration of personality. But it is just as obvious that she never recovered normality, and remained throughout her life profoundly psychopathic, though in most respects she was shrewd in practical matters and often revealed a unique insight and wisdom.[4]

It is important to note here a dichotomy in Margery: she is "psychopathic" but has a "unique insight and wisdom". A number of elements besides her already mentioned overall lack of organization contribute to the idea of disorder in Margery.

One characteristic often taken as indicative of abnormality is the desire to suffer. Julian, of course, states explicitly that she desired sickness, mind of Christ's Passion, and the three "wounds" of compassion, contrition, and wilful longing towards God (Chapter ii); her stress on suffering in her accounts of the Passion is also evident, as passages later in this section will show. But Julian intellectualizes about suffering and probes the underlying need:

But I saw not synne; for I believe it hath no manner of substance, ne no party of being, ne it myght not be knowen but by þe peyne þat it is cause of. & thus peyne it is somethyng, as to my syte, for a tyme, for it purgith & makyth us to knowen our selfe & askyn mercy (xxvii/30-35)

Margery shows little thought about her delight and personal involvement in suffering:

it was to her in a maner of solas & comfort whan sche sufferyd any dysese for þe lofe of God & for þe grace þat God wrowht in hyr. For euyr þe mor slawnder & repref þat sche sufferyd, þe mor sche incresyd in grace & in deuocyon of holy medytacyon of hy contemplacyon (2/27-31)

[4] Rufus M. Jones, *The Flowering of Mysticism* (New York, MacMillan, 1940), p. 229.

Throughout the text Margery gives examples of this desire.[5] Although it is a noble trait that one should suffer or give up something for another, there is something wrong when this desire becomes excessive or something to exult in.

Than she teld hir confessowr how gret desyre she had to kyssyn laӡerys, & he warnyd hir þat sche xulde kyssyn no men, but, ӡyf sche wolde algetys kyssyn, sche xuld kyssyn women. þan was sche glad, for sche had leue to kyssyn þe seke women & went to a place wher seke women dwellyd whech wer ryth ful of þe sekenes & fel down on hir kneys be-forn hem, preyng hem þat sche myth kyssyn her mowth for þe lofe of Ihesu (177/4-13)

The characteristic also has another side, one that has a bearing on Margery's introversion:

Certain aspects of the behavior of the great mystics, especially their professions of humility and obedience and their apparent readiness to suffer anything, however offensive, has led to an altogether wrong interpretation of their character. They have been assimilated with the humble and purposeless. This is a misunderstanding; they are, on the contrary, determined not only to be worth while but also to be recognized as such; they will not tolerate the "inferiority complex". Their light shall not shine under a bushel. They show the firmest purpose and accept no influence that does not lead where they want to go.[6]

Certainly one does not have to read far in Margery to begin feeling contradictions to the modesty of the appellation "þis lityl tretys" (1/12).[7]

Closely connected with her desire to suffer is a possible persecution complex. Throughout her book mention is made of people who insult, annoy, slander, or discomfit her.[8] In one place Margery

[5]   For example, 104/31ff., 107/23-24, 120/2-9, 123/18-21, 131/16-23, 137/5-10, 181/12-15, etc.

[6]   J. H. Leuba, *The Psychology of Religious Mysticism* (London, Kegan Paul, Trench, Trübner & Co., 1925), pp. 120-121.

[7]   Such self-deprecation, of course, has been a frequent occurrence in literary introductions, e.g., Chaucer (*Gen Prol*, 746) and the florid prefaces to some eighteenth century works. But when Margery assumes a humble tone, either praise from others is usually forthcoming (18/31-33) or the humility becomes so overdone as to seem false (141/5 ff.).

[8]   For example, 10/34 ff., 12/29, 61/15-62/22, 63/7-14, 66/14-17, 67/2 ff., 80/13 ff., 104/24-25, 107/13-17, 109/17 ff., 110/15-18, 111/25-112/2, 119/9-10, 119/24-25, etc.

speaks out against her persecutors in regard to "a manner of proverb against her":

> þe forseyd wordys wer neuyr of his spekyng, neyþyr of God ne of good man, þow so wer þat it wer leyd to hir, and sche many tymys & in many placys had gret repref þer-by. Þei wer fowndyn of þe Deuyl, fadyr of lesyngys, fauowryd, maynteynd, and born forth of hys membrys, fals invyows pepil, hauyng indignacyon at hir vertuows leuyng, not of powyr to hyndryn hir but þorw her fals tungys (243/22-30)

Margery shows some deviation from normal sexual patterns. In at least some of her attitudes she was typical of many female mystics: "Usually Christ became to the mediæval nun or anchoress a husband or lover."[9] Throughout early sections of her book she openly shows her attempts to avoid sexual relations with her husband. She continually stresses her devotion to the "manhood of Christ" and, in a most interesting section (Capitulum 35), marries God. Leuba's general description of mystics[10] fits Margery well: she desired to be chaste after her conversion; she was excited by "spiritual" love; and she was attracted to persons of the opposite sex in the form of confessors.[11] Also, the overwhelming delight she feels at times can be traced to a sexual source. Ellis, quoted by Leuba (p. 141), points out such a connection: "In many hysterical and psychically abnormal women, auto-erotic phenomena and sexual phenomena generally, are highly pleasurable, though they may be quite innocent of any knowledge of the erotic character of the experience." Other possible expressions of sexual frustrations may be seen in Margery's tears at the sight of male children (86/26 ff.; 94/11 ff.); in her confessions of delight in thoughts of carnal pleasures (pp. 144-145); in her obsessive fears for her chastity (even at the age of sixty) (236/32 ff., 241/7-13, 112/15);[12] and in her offer to show her love for Christ: "And I wolde, Lord, for þi lofe be leyd nakyd on

---

[9] Mackinnon, p. 293.

[10] Leuba, p. 143.

[11] On the last point, see especially 217/1 ff.

[12] A few lines preceding the 236/32 ff. passage is a reference to Margery as "Englisch sterte" (236/29-30). In a note to this term (p. 305), Professor Meech traces the meaning from "either MLG. *stert* 'tail', or MDu. *stert* 'tail', cognate with OE. *steort* 'tail', used as a term of abuse for an English man or woman in allusion to the old accusation that Englishmen had tails. The earliest previously recorded instance of such use in English is in 1673." Although the term may not necessarily have had any sexual allusions, it is interesting to note the con-

an hyrdil, alle men to wonderyn on me for þi loue" (184/19-21).[13]
Additional symptoms of possible mental disorder appear. Her
glorified interpretations of even the simplest experiences could be
the product of wish fulfillment. God often gives her support in
their conversations: constant affirmation of her status as a "chosen"
person; constant statements of love and regard for her; denuncia-
tion or criticism of people whom Margery dislikes;[14] constant
reassurance that no harm will befall her. The tendency to take
almost anything (such as rain at a certain time or crossing the
sea safely) as a miracle sent by God can also be considered part of
the desire to have conscious of subconscious wishes fulfilled. Even
the most important matter of all to Margery, God's love, can be
taken in this light: "to be loved by God gratifies in a perfect way
the need for self-respect and self-affirmation."[15]

Closely connected to wish fulfillment is auto-suggestion. Jones
makes the flat statement that "Many of the incidents in her life
are unconscious imitations of the auto-suggestive type."[16] A
specific example is cited by Cholmeley:

The actual form or vesture of her visions and "contemplations" would
seem, at least on occasion, to have been derived from, or suggested by,
pictures or carvings that she had looked upon. As she knew Norwich,
she must almost certainly have looked at the retable in the cathedral
with its Passion scenes. The memory of that may have limned for her
the contemplation in which she saw "Our Lord Jesus Christ bound to
a pillar, and His hands bound above His head."[17]

---

text of the word "taillynge" in Chaucer's pun "Taillynge ynough unto oure
lyves ende" (*Sh T*, 1624), where the word may refer only to dealing by tally, on
credit, or again may have a smutty meaning. Since the *Shipman's Tale* may
have been originally composed for the Wife of Bath, the parallel is even more
interesting, for Margery shows other similarities to Alice, as shall be noted.

[13]   Margery's "showmanship" here also shows some resemblance to Chaucer's
Wife of Bath, who boasts "I hadde the best *quoniam* myghte be" (*WB Prol*, 608)
and who is not averse to being looked at: "I wol runne out, my borel [coarse
wool clothing] for to shewe" (*WB Prol*, 356).

[14]   See in particular 45/16 ff., 85/23-33, 155/18-25.

[15]   Leuba, p. 120. William James, *The Varieties of Religious Experience* (New
York, Collier, 1961), p. 275, is much more outspoken about "proofs of God's
partiality" in his discussion of the "paltry-minded recital" of the thirteenth-
century Benedictine nun St. Gertrude.

[16]   Jones, p. 230.

[17]   Cholmeley, p. 109.

But hysteria is the trait commentators see most frequently in Margery.[18] The customary outward manifestations of Margery's mystical experiences are tears, cries, and falling, "which have all the appearance of violent hysteria".[19] White gives a good analysis of the situation:

The difficulty is to be found in certain personal limitations which affect the account of her experience and her expression of it. In the main these limitations are of two types. The first is to be found in the basic character of her mental and physical make-up. Three elements went into that, an extraordinary sensibility, a complete literalness of imagination, and an unusual physical responsiveness to the impulses of feeling and imagination. The result is that the usual sermon ... produced in Margery an uncontrollable hysteria of crying and weeping.[20]

Miss Allen, in her EETS preface (p. lxv), cites Father Thurston, who convincingly labels Margery's temperament as hysterical, basing his statement upon the definition of hysteria as "'before everything else a mental disease consisting chiefly in an exaggeration of suggestibility'". Thus, he can say "'That Margery was a victim of hysteria can hardly be open to doubt'" and can speak of her "'terrible hysteria'" and "'the hysterical temperament revealed in every page'". That these "attacks" were not epileptic in nature can be shown by Margery's retention of consciousness during them and also by the occurrence of similar symptoms in other cases of hysteria.[21]

It should not be forgotten, of course, that at one time Margery was definitely out of her mind. The illness from which her conversion rescued her was largely mental. Margery's recovery can be interpreted from a completely psychological viewpoint. If we assume, as Leuba does, that many of the great mystics had illnesses or other difficulties based primarily on social maladjustment, a sufficient remedy is any means by which inhibitions and repressions

[18]   For other discussions not mentioned in the paragraph see: Jones, p. 232; Leuba, pp. 192 ff.; S. Undset, "Margery Kempe of Lynne", *The Atlantic Monthly*, 164 (1934), 236.
[19]   Dom Justin McCann, "The Book of Margery Kempe", *Dublin Review*, 200 (1937), 110.
[20]   White, 165.
[21]   Leuba, p. 192.

can be worked out. A remedy which releases pent-up forces will bring about "a transformation similar to that achieved by the love of God". According to Leuba, love of man or God is the most effective of all liberators, for it satisfies the "most fundamental and irresistible of all physiological functions and innate cravings: the sex functions, the tendencies to self-affirmation and self-esteem, and the desire for the peace of inner unity and of affectionate trust".[22]

It is important to notice that, in spite of all these symptoms, Margery still received (and receives) strong support from others. In her book she tells us of important personages who supported her and apparently believed her reports to be authentic. Among her supporters are Thomas Arundel, Archbishop of Canterbury; Richard Caister, Vicar of St. Stephen's Church, Norwich; Philip Repyngdon, Bishop of Lincoln; parish priests of St. James' and St. Margaret's, both in Lynn; and various friars, confessors, and lay folk. It is to be expected that the clergy would be patient in dealing with very pious lay folk, but Margery's actions in disturbing the congregation must have been quite annoying. White explains the continued tolerance on the basis of clerical familiarity with the "Liturgical use of tears" and the accompanying hesitancy "to risk obstructing Grace".[23] The support of Margery by young priests may have a more natural basis: younger priests may have attached themselves to an older, possibly inspired woman whom they called "Mother".[24] After all, modern churchmen support Margery also, in the persons of Father Vincent McNabb and Father Gumbley, who consider Margery "perfectly genuine".[25]

As mentioned above, this tolerance of Margery in her own day was furthered by her following, in her own degree, the powerful church tradition of worship by weeping. Indeed, there is the possibility of auto-suggestion based upon her knowledge of other mystics.

The reminiscences of earlier visionaries are numerous — especially

---

[22] Leuba, p. 299.
[23] White, 165.
[24] Undset, *op. cit.* (note 18, above), 239.
[25] Cholmeley, pp. viii-ix.

St. Mechthild of Hackeborn, St. Bridget of Sweden [frequently mentioned as Brigypt or Bryde in Margery's *Book*], St. Catherine of Siena — and show Margery Kempe as possessed of a very active and suggestible sub-conscious mind, always ready to turn to personal use any suitable material that came to hand. Thus the account in Chapter 35 of her "spiritual marriage" appears to derive from St. Catherine of Siena, whose life was well known in England by the opening years of the fifteenth century.[26]

Likewise, confirmation of her gift of tears could be found in the history of such a saint as St. Mary of Oignies (d. 1213);[27] Rolle could be taken as the model for the flame of love around her heart and the sweet melodies in her ears; the pseudo-Bonaventure[28] for her "devout meditation on the life of Our Lord". "But her supreme model, in her Pilgrimages, contemplations, and revelations, is the great fourteenth-century mystic, St. Bridget of Sweden. The influence of *St. Bride's Book* is manifest throughout and Margery evidently conceived herself as another St. Bridget."[29]

We know that Margery was familiar with English mystical works. With Rolle she shares the enjoyment of sensory visions, while having an actuality of physical sensation denied by Rolle,[30] and practicing physical austerities disapproved by him.[31] Hilton recommended frequent shrift, a habit practiced by Margery. On the other hand, Hilton's attention was directed towards making clear the means to attain a good life and with it contemplation, while Margery's efforts cannot really be considered in the light of teaching. Hilton also refutes the devotion of God to the individual soul, and generally would disapprove of Margery's form of mysticism.[32] Indeed, when compared with the most respected

---

[26] Evelyn Underhill, "Margery Kempe", *The Spectator*, 157 (1936), 642. In a note on 212/21 (p. 339), Miss Allen likewise refers to St. Bridget, St. Mechthild, and other sources as showing similarities to Margery's idea of "I receyue euery good wyl as for dede", a statement "highly characteristic of medieval English mysticism".

[27] Margery's amanuensis (152/29-153/37) tells how his reading of "Maria de Oegines" changed his antagonism and disbelief to support of Margery.

[28] See note on 143/28 and, especially, Miss Allen's note on 187/19 *sq.*

[29] McCann, 112.

[30] Brooks, 30.

[31] Meech and Allen, p. 261 (note on 12/29).

[32] Meech and Allen, notes ðn 39/23, 44/22, 87/13, 156/26.

mystics of her time, "One cannot put Margery Kempe on the same high spiritual level as one would put *The Cloud of Unknowing*, or Walter Hilton. She was at best a 'broken vessel', and carried through life a somewhat 'shattered' mind. ..."[33] The *Cloud* also stresses the point that God is "absolutely Other than man-wise", a point evidently rejected by Margery. Like Hilton, the author of the *Cloud* would have disapproved of much of Margery's mysticism.[34]

Still, and for this reason, Margery is an interesting character, and many more facets of her personality emerge. She is annoying (221/ 23-25, 228/20-22), generous with the belongings of others (92/14-21), smug (45/16-22, 47/25-27, 49/1-34, 140/29-33, 143/20-25, etc.), nasty (46/7-13, 45/16-24, 243/26-30), outspoken and critical (108/27-35, 109/12-16, 111/15-18, 116/1-16, 120/24-29, 122/16-25, etc.); she tells the Virgin Mary what to do (189/14-20), dares argue with the Apostles (175/8-13) and is not above enjoying revenge (103/1-27). She may have been attractive (113/10 ff.) and at times attracted the pity of contemporaries (93/25-94/7, 98/37-99/6, etc.). Attitudes of others towards her are especially revealing (33/10-20, 151/7-13, 221/23-25, 228/17-22). To sum up, she certainly is "petty, neurotic, vain, illiterate, physically and nervously overstrained, devout, much-travelled, forceful, and talented".[35] In character, Margery remains a contradictory and puzzling figure, a "mixture of piety and violence meekness and egotism, love and hatred; sometimes quiet and submissive, at others boisterous and arrogant; but always, in all her story, vivid, vital, and interesting".[36]

Two specific illustrations of Julian's character appear that are in distinct contrast to Margery's. The latter opposes Church practices and direction by citing Christ as an authority. Christ tells her:

"dowtyr, I wyl þow leue þi byddyng of many bedys and thynk swych thowtys as I wyl putt in þi mend." (17/26-27)

"& I am wel plesyd wyth þe, dowtyr, for þu stondist vndyr obedyens of Holy Cherch & þat þu wylt obey þi confessowr & folwyn hys cownsel,

33   Jones, p. 233.
34   Meech and Allen, notes on 44/22, 87/29, 156/26.
35   Meech and Allen, p. lxiv.
6   McCann, 113.

whech thorw auctorite of Holy Cherch hath asoyld þe of þi synnes &
dispensyd wyth þe þat þu schuldist not go to Rome ne to Seynt Iamys les
þan þu wyl þin owyn selfe. Not-wythstondying al þis, I comawnde þe
in þe name of Ihesu, dowtyr, þat þu go vysite þes holy placys & do as I
byd þe, for I am aboue al Holy Cherch & I xal gon wyth þe & kepyn þe
rygth wel." (72/35-73/6)

"ȝyf þu seydest euery day a thowsand Pater Noster, þu xuldist not
plesyn me so wel as þu dost whan þu art in silens & sufferyst me to speke
in thy sowle." (89/21-25)

"Ther is no clerk can spekyn a-ȝens þe lyfe whech I teche þe, &, ȝyf he
do, he is not Goddys clerk; he is þe Deuelys clerk." (158/12-14)

Similarly:

& so it was long tyme þat þis creatur herd no mo of þis mater. Aftyrward owyr Lord Ihesu Crist seyd to þis creatur, "þat thyng I bad xuld
a be don for þe sowle it is not don. Aske now þi gostly fadyr." & so
sche dede, & he seyd it was not don. Sche seyd a-ȝen, "My Lord Ihesu
Crist teld me so rygth now."[37] (47/9-14)

Accusations of being a Lollard (112/1 ff., 124/1 ff., 135/15 ff.) may
be further evidence of certain unorthodoxy on Margery's part.
Julian, however, is clear-cut in her acceptance of Church supervision:

But in al thing I leve as holy church levith, preachith, and teachith,
for the feith of holy church, the which I had afornhand understonden &
as I hope by the grace of God wilfully kept in use & custome, stode
continually in my sight, willing & meneing never to receive ony thing
that might be contrary therunto. (ix/24-29)

Further testimony to Julian's meekness and orthodoxy is clear:

And yet in this I desired as I durst þat I myte have had ful syte of helle
& purgatory, But it was not my mening to maken privy of any thyng
that longyth to the feith. For I levyd sothfastly þat hel & purgatory
is for þe same end þat longith to my feith. ... For thow þe Revelation
was made of goodnes in which was made litil mention of evil, yet I was
not drawne therby from any poynt of þe feith þat holy church techyth
me to lovyn. ... but I saw not so propirly specyfyed þe Jewes þat deden
hym to ded. Notwithstondyn I knew in my feith þat þei wer accursid &
dampny[d] without end, savyng those that converten be grace. And I

---

[37]   For other examples citing Christ as an authority opposed to the earthly
church, see 103/20-27, 155/18-25, 227/1-6.

was strengthyd & lered generaly to kepe me in the feith in every pointe[38]
(xxxiii/1-28)

therwith I am wele paid, abyding our Lords will in this hey mervel. And
now I yeele me to my moder holy Church as a simple child oweth
(xlvi/53-56)

The other contrast lies in the differing concepts the two writers
have of themselves in relation to God's love. Margery evidently
believes herself to be a favorite, a recipient of special attention and
approval, for Christ tells her:

God louyth þe specyaly ... þu art a synguler louer, & þerfor þu xalt
have a synguler loue in Heuyn, a synguler reward, & a synguler worshep
&, for-as-mech as þu art a mayden in þi sowle, I xal take þe be þe on
hand in Hevyn & my Modyr be þe oþer hand & so xalt þu dawnsyn in
Hevyn[39] (52/17-29)

Julian, on the other hand, does not appear to expect to "dawnsyn
in Hevyn" in a pre-eminent role: seeking little personal credit, she
exemplifies humility, an attitude much different from that of
Margery:

For sothly it was not shewid me that God lovid me better than the lest
soule that is in grace, for I am sekir that there be many that never had
shewing ner sight but of the comon techyng of holy church that loven
God better than I. For if I loke singularly to my selfe I am right nowte;
but in general I am in hope, in onehede of charite with al myn evyn
Cristen (ix/5-12)

& that I say of me I say in the person of al myn even-Christen, for I am
lernyd in the gostly shewing of our Lord God that he menyth so. &
therefore I pray you al for Gods sake & counsel you for your owne
profitt that ye levyn the beholding of a wretch that it was shewid to, & ...
behold God that of his curtes love & endles godenes wolde shewen it
generally in comfort of us al, for it is Gods will that ye take it ... as Jesus
had shewid it onto you all (viii/37-46)

& thys shewyng I toke singularly to my selfe, but be al the gracious
comforte tha[t] folowyth as ye shal seen I was leryd to take it to al my
even-Christen, al in general & nothing in special. Thowe our Lord shewid
me I should synne, by me alone is vnderstode al (xxxvii/4-8)

---

[38] For Margery's detailed ("propirly specyfyed"?) description of Jews and
the Passion, see 190/2-192/40.
[39] Miss Allen's note to 52/27 *sq.* (p. 283) refers to a similar vision of St.
Mechthild and also to the celestial dance of virgins in *Hali Meidenhad.*

And all this leryng [Hudleston: *believing*] in this trew comfort it is
generall to all myn even-Cristen as it is afornseid, & so is Gods will
(lxviii/21-23)

Julian also clearly indicates lack of the special knowledge that
Margery frequently receives:

And whan God Almyty had shewid so plentevously & so fully of his
godenes, I desired to wetyn a certeyn creature that I lovid if it shuld
continue in good lyvyng, which I hoped be the grace of God was be-
gonne. And in syngular desire it semyd þat I lettyd my selfe, for I was
not taught in this tyme. & than was I answerid in my reson as it were
be a freindful mene: "Take it generally & behold the curtesy of the Lord
God as he shewith to the, for it is mor worship to God to behold hym
in al than in any special thyng." I assentid & therewith I leryd þat it is
more worship to God to knowen al things in general, than to lyken
onythyng in special (xxxv/1-12)

Humility is also shown in Julian's self-criticism, which seems more
sincere than Margery's "modesty" (see note 7, above):

This [showing] I levid sothfastly for the tyme þat I saw him, & so was
than my will & my mening ever for done without end, but as a fole I let
it passyn fro my mynd. A, lo, I wretch [Hudleston: "wretch that I am"].
This was a gret synne, grete onkindness, that I for foly of feling of a
litill bodily peyne so onwisely lost for the time the comfort of all this
blissid shewing of our Lord God. Here may you sene what I am of my
selfe (lxvi/27-34)

Even in a situation where Christ appears to give Julian special
favor, she does not take it personally. The shift in pronoun number
is especially significant:

Than seyd Jesus our kinde Lord: "If thou art payde I am payde. It is
a joy, a blis, an endles lekyng to me that ever suffrid I passion for the; &
if I myht suffre more I wold suffre more."
In this felyng my understondyng was lifte up into hevyn, & there
I saw thre hevyns ... the first hevyn, that is the plesyng of the fader,
shewid to me as an hevyn, & it was ful blisfull; for he is ful plesed with
al the dedes that Jesus hath done aboute our salvation. Wherefore we
be not only his be his beying, but also by the curtes geft of his fader;
we be his blis, we be his mede, we be his worshippe, we be his corone —
and this was a singular mervel & a full delectable beholdyng that we be
his corone. And in these words, "If that I might suffre more I would suffer more", I saw sothly that as often as he myght deyen so often he wold
... [remainder of chapter continues to analyze the quotation] (xxii/3ff.)

In general, however, Julian does not enter into her writing in the way that Margery does, and not as clear a case can be made to demonstrate her personality. The reader cannot know her as a person: he can only make inferences from her method of examining and relating her experiences. Her work is analytical, soul-searching, dispassionate; her objectification of experiences while examining them is almost scientific:

And after this I fel into a sadhede & seid: "I se iii things: game, scorne, & arneste. I se game that the fend is overcome; I se scorne that God scornith him & he shal be scornyd; and I se arneste that he is overcome be the blissfull passion & deth of our Lord Jesus Criste, þat was done in ful Arneste & with sad travelle" (xiii/38-44)

Her ability to discuss her particular revelations without turning them to self-glorification suggests a freedom from psychological problems or deficiencies which might color her interpretations. Other previously mentioned qualities such as sincerity, intelligence, and a questioning curiosity also emerge from her work. The most outstanding characteristic is that Julian tends to think deeply about the intrinsic meaning of her revelations, to stress the object. Margery tends to act or react subjectively, to stress her role in all experiences. These differences in the women account for much of the contrast between their works, especially in the single-minded, religious subject matter of Julian and the more varied, peripatetic view of medieval life given by Margery.

Julian's personality leads her naturally into a quiet, restrained prose style. One way that she achieves this tone is through extensive use of understatement. The term as used here includes two forms: litotes (affirmation by denying the contrary) and a more general type in which descriptions are more modestly worded than the experiences would lead us to expect. Through its reflective, sub-dued effect, understatement may be "one of the principal sources of power" in English prose as John Ciardi believes it to be in English poetry.[40] Certainly the device strengthens Julian's prose, and might have been used more by Margery with great profit.

To stress Julian's use of understatement, however, is not to

[40] John Ciardi, "How Does a Poem Mean", *An Introduction to Literature* (Cambridge, Mass., Houghton Mifflin, 1959), p. 672.

indicate that she could never show emotion or passion, or that she could never even go to an excess in these matters. Both works contain examples of flamboyant writing, although they occur more frequently in Margery. Typical of medieval mystics is Julian's picturing of Christ's crucifixion, with its near delectation in physical details and suffering:

In this sodenly I saw the rede blode trekelyn downe fro under the garlande hote and freisly and ryth plenteously (iv/1-2)

I saw the bodyly sight lesting of the plentious bleding of the hede. The grete dropis of blode fel downe fro under the garland like pellots, semand as it had cum out of the veynis; & in the comeing out it were browne rede for the blode was full thick; & in the spredeing abrode it were bright rede; & whan it come to the browes than it vanyshid; not withstondyng, the bleding continuid till many things were sene & understondyn. The fairehede & livelyhede is like nothing but the same. The plenteowshede is like to the dropys of water that fallen of the evys after a greate showre of reyne that fall so thick that no man may numbre them with bodily witte; & for the roundhede it were like to the scale of heryng in the spreadeing on the forehead. These iij came to my in the tyme: pellotts, fer roundhede, in the comynge out of the blode; the scale of heryng in the spreading in the forehede for roundhede; the dropys of evys for the plentioushede inumerable. This shewing was quick & lively & hidouse & dredfull, swete & lovely (vii/10-30)

And after this I saw beholding the body plentiously bleding in seming of the Scorgyng as thus: The faire skynne was brokyn ful depe into the tender flesh with sharpe smyting al about the sweete body. So plenteously the hote blode ran oute þat there was neither sene skynne ne wound, but as it were al blode. And whan it come wher it should a fallen downe than it vanyshid. Notwithstondyng the bleding continued a while til it myt be sene with avisement. & this was so plenteous to my syt þat me thowte if it had be so in kind & in substance for that tyme it should have made the bed al on blode and a passid over aboute (xii/1-11)

Although Margery also enters into lengthy descriptions of the Passion (e.g., 190/2 ff., 207/15 ff.), typical of Julian is her generalizing from the details given above. Again, emotion is notable:

The dereworthy blode of our Lord Jesus Criste as verily as it is most pretious as verily it is most plentious. Beholde & se the pretious plenty of his dereworthy blode descendid downe into helle & braste her bands & deliveryd al þat were there which longyd to the curte of hevyn. The pretious plenty of his dereworthy blode overflowith al erth & is redye

to wash al creaturs of syn*n*e which be of gode will, have ben & shal ben.
The pretious plenty of his dereworthy blode ascendid up into hevyn to
blissid body of our Lord Jesus Criste, & there is in him bleding &
praying for us to the father, & is, & shall be as long as it nedith. And
evermore it flowith in all hevyns, enjoying the salvatio*n* of al mankynd
that arn there & shal ben, fulfilling the number that failith (xii/21-34)

These passages certainly cannot be called understated. Although
such paeans are uncommon in Julian's work, they are there, and,
because of the contrast to the subdued tone, are extremely striking
and effective. Julian, moreover, appears to use rhetorical devices
to further the emotion of such passages.[41] Notable in the preceding
example are alliteration, parallel structure, balance and repetition —
devices which will be examined in more detail later. In another
passage, excitement is conveyed through the use of imperatives and
an interrogative:

And al this shewid he ful blisfully, meneing thus: "Se! I am God;
se! I am in al thing; se! I doe al thyng; se! I lift never myne hands of myn
werke ne never shall withoute ende. Se! I lede al thing to the end I
ordeynd it to from withoute beginnyng be the same might, wisdam, and
love þat I made it. How should any thing be amysse?" (xi/56-61)

Again, repetition and balance play an important part in the emphasis developed in the passage.

   Far more characteristic of Julian, however, is her use of understatement. Litotes abounds: "take no harm", "he hath no despite
of that he hath made", "it is not other than the faith", "he doeth no
sin", "there was no thing unknown to him", "I felt no pain",
"something that is no lack in his sight", "make all well that is not
well", "that which is impossible to thee is not impossible to me",
"I was not drawn ... from any point of faith", "he perished not", "he
may not be wroth", "the Father is not man", "in the Godhead may
be no travail". Such extensive, almost habitual use of this device
would appear to be highly appropriate:

Whoso calls the Absolute anything in particular, or says that it is *this*,
seems implicitly to shut it off from being *that* — it is as if he lessened it.
So we deny the "this", negating the negation which it seems to us to

---

[41] As does Margery. For an example of a detailed description involving
alliteration, see 208/10-23.

imply, in the interests of the higher affirmative attitude by which we are possessed. The fountainhead of Christian mysticism is Dionysius the Areopagite. He describes the absolute truth by negatives exclusively.

> The cause of all things is neither soul nor intellect; nor has it imagination, opinion, or intelligence; nor is it reason or intelligence; nor is it spoken or thought. It is neither number, nor order, nor magnitude, nor. ...

But these qualifications are denied by Dionysius, not because the truth falls short of them, but because it so infinitely excels them[42]

In keeping with her character, Julian significantly also makes much use of the second, general type of understatement: the quiet, subdued presentation of material that is more modestly worded than we would expect. It would be difficult to find in Margery's work a pronouncement so condensed yet so pregnant with meaning as Julian's "And after this I saw God in a poynte, that is to sey, in myn understonding, be which sight I saw that he is in al things" (xi/1-3).[43]

Grace Warrack, in her still extremely valuable study of Julian, makes an interesting comparison:

> Of a little child it has been said: "He thought great thoughts simply", and Julian's deepness of insight and simplicity of speech are like the Child's. "For ere that he made us He loved us, and when we were made we loved Him" (liii). "I love thee, and thou lovest me, and our love shall not be disparted in two" (lxxxii)[44]

An earlier critic also makes some pertinent comments:

> Once again she [Julian] touches the same octave, condensing in a single phrase which has seldom been transcended in its brief expression of the possession that leaves the infinity of love's desire still unsatiated: 'I saw Him and I sought Him, I had Him, and I wanted Him!' Fletcher's tenderness, Ford's passion, lose colour placed side by side with the utterances of this worn recluse. ...
> Strange too is it, in an epoch when the physical hell of fire and torture — such hells as that of Teresa's later vision, 'with long narrow lane,

---

[42]   James, *op. cit.* (note 15, above), pp. 326-327.
[43]   For a discussion of the word "point" in this context, see Warrack, p. 26 (note). For a similar geometric usage in Dionysius the Areopagite see Sister Anna Maria Reynolds, "Some Literary Influences in the *Revelations* of Julian of Norwich", *Leeds Studies in English*, 7-8 (1952), 24.
[44]   Warrack, pp. xliv-xlv.

low and dark and close, with mire of reptiles and contracting walls'–
had branded itself upon the orthodox, to read Julian's quiet words:
'To me was showed none harder hell than sin; hell was as sin to my sight;'
and from sin she gives sad assent to the inexorable law of human weakness, 'we may not in this life keep us'.[45]

There is an abundance of examples of understatement in the
Revelations, ranging from the philosophical quietness of some of
the above examples to the subdued pathos of "And in youngith yet,
I thought great sweeme to dye" (iii/8-9).

Understatement is less frequent in Margery and is found not in
the retelling of her religious experiences, where excess is the general
rule, but rather in the accounts of her worldly adventures, or her
affairs with typical human beings. A delightful example of such
understatement occurs in Capitulum 11, where Margery and her
husband argue about her desire to be chaste. In this scene, notable
also for its use of rhythm and alliteration, Margery shows some of
the narrative gifts of Chaucer's Wife of Bath, to whom Margery
seems similar in other ways also.[46] Margery carries a bottle of beer
in her hand; her husband has a cake in his bosom. As Margery
tells him that she would rather see him slain than return to sexual
contact with him, he says what must certainly be considered one of
the prize examples of understatement, "ʒe arn no good wyfe".
After this litotes, Margery finally gets her way, but not before the
not-so-stupid husband has won his point of having Margery pay his
bills.

The following examples show Margery's use of understatement
(examples 1-6) and also her specific use of litotes (examples 7-12).

(1)   þis lytyl tretys (1/12) (Cf. 1/1, "a schort tretys," and note 7 above.)

---

[45]   Anon., "Catholic Mystics of the Middle Ages", *Edinburgh Review*, 184
(1896), 319-320.

[46]   In addition to the similarities observed in notes 12 and 13 above, Margery,
like Alice of Bath, traveled widely, visiting Rome, Jerusalem, Germany, and
Spain. Margery's eventual mastery over her husband in the episode also is in
complete agreement with the Wife's fundamental beliefs about marriage and
the husband-wife relationship. The earthiness and, in a way, the crudeness of
character shown are also reminiscent of the Wife's traits. Alice, however,
would not have been as tearful, pleading, or subservient as Margery. In other
places Margery shows an outspoken, blunt nature that is more akin to Alice's.
See the discussion of Margery's character earlier in this section.

(2) Oþer days whan sche was not purueyd sche beggyd hir mete fro dore to dore (94/5-7) (This example gains emphasis because of its position as the last sentence of Capitulum 38.)

(3) Sche had ful greet envye at hir neybowrs þat þei schuld ben arayd so wel as sche (9/25-26) (This example is understated in its context.)

(4) Sche thowt þat sche louyd God mor þan he hir (13/36-14/1)

(5) sche fond alle pepyl good on-to hir & gentyl saf only hir owyn cuntremen (75/17-18)

(6) þan the Meyr alto-rebukyd hir & rehersyd many repreuows wordys & vngoodly, þe whiche is more expedient to be concelyd þan expressyd[47] (115/23-26)

(7) I schal not byndyn ȝow soor. I pray ȝow beth not dysplesyd wyth me (19/21-23)

(8) But ȝet sche left not þe world al hol (10/10)

(9) She leuyd þe Deuelys suacyons & gan to consentyn for be-cause sche cowde thynkyn no good thowt (15/9-11)

(10) Sythen þis creatur dede alle oþer ocupacyons as fel for hir to do wysly & sadly j-now, saf sche knew not veryli þe drawt of owyr Lord (9/3-6)

(11) þe booke was so euel wretyn þat he cowd lytyl skyll þeron, for it was neiþyr good Englysch ne Dewch (4/14-16)

(12) what grace þat he werkyth in any creatur is ower profyth yf lak of charyte be not ower hynderawnce (1/8-10)

Some direct comparison may show more clearly the different techniques of Julian and Margery. Early in both books there are passages detailing the first meeting with Mary, mother of Jesus. Julian ends Chapter iv with the following account:

In this he browght our blissid Lady to my understondyng. I saw hir ghostly in bodily likeness: a simple mayde & a meke, young of age & little waxen above a child, in the stature that she was wan she conceived with child. Also God shewid in party the wisedom and the trueth of hir soule, wherein I understood the reverend beholding that she beheld hir God & Maker, mervelyng with greate reverence that he would be borne of hir that was a simple creature of his makeyng. And this wisdom

[47] Both Julian and Margery frequently make a point of refusing to narrate, a device which of course emphasizes the material supposedly omitted. Julian: ix/35-39, xvii/54-55, xxvi/11-17, xxxvii/10-12, lxxii/6-7. Margery: 61/34-35, 73/21-22, 133/30-32, 145/29-30, 172/7-10, 177/23-24, 191/31-32, 199/10, 201/33-38, 214/23-24, 219/12-13. William James considers "the incommunicableness of the transport" to be "the keynote of all mysticism" (p. 318). Although Julian's refusals center on religious experiences, many of Margery's concern human actions against her.

& trueth — knowyng the greteness of hir maker & the littlehede of hir selfe that is made — caused hir sey full mekely to Gabriel, "Lo me, Gods handmayd!" In this sight I understoode sothly that she is more than all that God made beneath hir in worthyness & grace; for aboven hir is nothing that is made but the blissid [Hudleston inserts *Manhood* here] of Criste, as to my sight. (iv/27-41)

The following are excerpts from Margery's description of her first meeting with Mary:

And þan a-noon sche [Margery] saw Seynt Anne gret wyth chylde, and þan sche preyd Seynt Anne to be hir mayden & hir seruawnt. & anon ower Lady was born, & þan sche besyde [= busied] hir to take þe chyld to hir & kepe it tyl it wer twelve ȝer of age wyth good mete & drynke, wyth fayr whyte clothys & whyte kerchys. And þan sche seyd to þe blyssed chyld, "Lady, ȝe schal be þe Modyr of God." The blyssed chyld answered & seyd, "I wold I wer worthy to be þe handmayden of hir þat wuld conseive þe Sone of God." Þe creatur [Margery] seyd, "I pray ȝow, Lady, ȝyf þat grace falle ȝow, forsake not my seruyse." The blysful chyld passyd awey for a certeyn tyme, þe creatur being stylle in contemplacyon, and sythen cam a-geyn and seyd, "Dowtyr, now am I bekome þe Modyr of God." & þan þe creatur fel down on hir kneys wyth gret reuerens & gret wepyng and seyd, "I am not worthy, Lady, to do ȝow seruyse." "ȝys, dowtyr", sche seyde, "folwe þow me, þi seruyse lykyth me wel." ... And þan þe creatur fel down on kneys to Seynt Elyȝabeth & preyd hir sche wold prey for hir to owyr Lady þat sche mygth do hir seruyse & plesawns. "Dowtyr, me semyth", seyd Elysabeth, "þu dost ryght wel þi deuer". And þan went þe creatur forth wyth owyr Lady to Bedlem & purchasyd hir herborwe euery nyght wyth gret reuerens, & owyr Lady was receyued wyth glad cher. Also sche beggyd owyr Lady fayr whyte clothys & kerchys for to swathyn in hir Sone whan he wer born, and, whan Ihesu was born, sche ordeyned beddyng for owyr Lady to lyg in wyth hir blyssed Sone. And sythen sche beggyd mete for owyr Lady & hir blyssyd chyld. Aftyrward sche swathyd hym wyth byttyr teerys of compassyon, hauyng mend of þe scharp deth þat he schuld suffyr for þe lofe of synful men, seyng to hym, "Lord, I schal fare fayr wyth ȝow; I schal not byndyn ȝow soor. I pray ȝow beth not dysplesyd wyth me." (18/15-19/23)

Some striking differences emerge when we compare these two passages. Julian, supporting the authenticity of her vision, gives a detailed physical description of Mary where Margery gives none. In this physical description Julian uses words that are simple, basic, and, in themselves, quiet and understated. Words like "simple", "meke", "young", and statements like "little waxen above a child, in the stature that she was wan she conceived with child" bring about a diminution, a softening of the presentation that reaches a quietly eloquent and evocative climax in "... caused her sey full mekely to Gabriel: 'Lo me, Gods handmayd!'" Also typical of Julian is her cogitation over the vision, her reflective "In this sight I understoode sothly that she is more than all that God made beneath hir in worthyness & grace; for aboven hir is nothing that is made but the blissid Manhood of Criste, as to my sight." The overall impression is one of thoughtful humility on the part of the mystic: "she utters, by few and adequate words, a thought that in its quietness convinces of truth, or an emotion deep in life".[48] In the passage from Margery there is no thoughtful reflection about the significance of her experience; indeed, it gives a different impression altogether. Mary is not described at all. *Margery* becomes the central figure in her recounting; she is entering into the story — indeed, playing the main role. It is Margery Kempe (replacing Gabriel!) who tells the child Mary of her future role as mother of Jesus, Margery Kempe who is praised and approved by holy personages, Margery Kempe who provides for their needs and, in general, "runs the show". What many critics feel to be an excess of personal involvement gives Margery's passage its excitement, its hurried, foreshortened, almost hysterical, tone. The opposite of this — Julian's calm, quiet, and reflective detachment — results in the understated, but nonetheless effective, prose style of the *Revelations*.[49]

---

[48] Warrack, p. xliv.

[49] A number of similarities between Julian and Margery surround these parallel passages. Both make use of dialogue and give much the same speech to Mary: "'I wold I wer worthy to be þe handmayden of hir þat xuld conseive þe Sone of God'" and "'Lo, me, Gods handmayd!'" On the same page in Margery's text, Miss Allen notes a different parallel to Julian's work in the similarity of "Dowtyr, ȝe sowkyn euyn on Crystys brest" (18/2) to Julian's "The Moder may given her Child soken her mylke, but our pretious Moder Jesus he may fedyn us with himselfe & doith full curtesly & full tenderly with the blissid sacrament" (lx/35-38). Miss Allen makes no mention of the similar dramatic treatment of *Mary's* "handmaid" statement in both works, although in her note on 18/31 she mentions *Margery's* "conception of herself as the handmaiden of the Blessed Virgin". The "handmaid" statement has Biblical authority (Luke i.38,48), and Julian's use of "Lo" is similar to the Luke rendering (Luke i.38):

Although understatement is frequently considered an ally of humor, irony and sarcasm, such uses are lacking in the work of Julian. She presents a picture of faith and hope, without enlivening her message with any of the experiences or incidents, the "asides", that Margery gives. Julian's work is unrelievedly devout, sincere, analytical, thoughtful; humor is non-existent.[50] Although humor occurs in Margery's *Book* it seems mostly unintentional (the husband-wife scene or the irony of "þis lityl tretys", for instance) with both the amanuensis and Margery responsible. A litotes, apparently by the amanuensis, is ironic in the eyes of a modern reader who reads through the disorganized text: "Thys bok is not wretyn in ordyr" (5/12-13). The modern reader may also find that syntax unintentionally gives a humorous turn to an idea: "And, whan þis creatur saw Ierusalem, rydyng on an asse, ..." (67/16-17). Margery, on the other hand, recounts a full-fledged joke in an understated manner:

... o prest cam to hir whil sche was in þe seyd Mynstyr &, takyng hir be þe coler of þe gowne, seyd, "þu wolf, what is þis cloth þat þu hast on?" Sche stod stylle & not wolde answeryn in hir owyn cawse. Childer of þe monastery goyng be-syde seyd to þe preste, "Ser, it is wulle." (120/17-22)

A tongue-in-cheek effect is also achieved in other passages:

Than þe preste swor a gret othe, & be þe boke in hys hand, þat sche was as fals as sche mygth be & dispysed hir & alto-rebukyd hir. & so sche had euyr mech tribulacyon tyl sche cam to Iherusalem. &, er sche cam þer, sche seyd to hem þat sche supposyd þei weryn grevyd wyth hir (67/6-11)

"Forsoth Marie seide, Loo! the hand mayden of the Lord; be it don to me aftir thi word" (Wyclif). Although both women appear to be relying on a common tradition, Julian's "Lo me, Gods handmayd" provides a briefer, quieter, more evocative use of understatement than does Margery's presentation.
[50] William James (p. 273) equates such concentration with "feeble intellect", an accusation which is doubtful in light of Julian's analytical thoughtfulness: "In gentle characters, where devoutness is intense and the intellect feeble, we have an imaginative absorption in the love of God to the exclusion of all practical human interests, which, though innocent enough, is too one-sided to be admirable. A mind too narrow has room but for one kind of affection. When the love of God takes possession of such a mind, it expels all human loves and human uses."

Sche desirying to seylyn wyth hem to Douyr, nowt þei wolde helpyn
hir ne latyn hir wetyn what schip þei purposyd to seylyn in. Sche speryd
& spyid as diligently as sche cowde, & euyr sche had knowlach of her
intent o wey er oþer tyl sche was schepyd wyth hem, & whan sche had
boryn hir thyng in-to þe schip wher þei wer, supposyng þei xulde a
seylyd in hast sche wist not how sone, þei purueyd hem anoþer schip
redy to seilyn. What þe cawse was sche wist neuyr. (241/36-242/9)

Margery's relationship with her husband, her desire to live chaste,
provides ironic humor as we have observed in the scene already
described in which Margery finally wins her desire. Margery
recounts another incident that gives the modern reader humorous
insight into the feeling and attitudes of John Kempe, who seems
to have had a natural bent for irony, as well as, perhaps, a most
necessary philosophical forbearance.

oftyn-tymys þis creatur cownseld hir husbond to levyn chast, & seyd
þat þei oftyn-tymes, sche wyst wel, had dysplesyd God be her inordynat
lofe & þe gret delectacyon þat þei haddyn eyþer of hem in vsyng of
oþer, & now it wer good þat þei schuld be her boþins wylle & consentyng of hem bothyn punschyn & chastysyn hem-self wylfully be
absteynyng fro her lust of her bodys. Hir husbond seyd it wer good
to don so, but he mygth not ʒett, he xuld whan God wold. And so he
vsyd her as he had do befor (12/8-17)

Similarly, after Margery has been granted her desire to live chaste,
husband John ends the dialogue in Capitulum 11 on a tellingly
ironic note. Margery is summing up her request:

"... makyth my body fre to God so þat ʒe neuyr make no chalengyng
in me to askyn no dett of matrimony aftyr þis day whyl ʒe leuyn, & I
schal etyn & drynkyn on þe Fryday at ʒowr byddyng." Than seyd hir
husband a-ʒen to hir, "As fre mot ʒowr body ben to God as it hath ben
to me." (25/8-13)

III

STYLE: WORDS AND THE SENSES

All writing is made up of words, the basic materials by which meaning is communicated, and word choice can do much to aid or obstruct the effectiveness of what is said. As used here, the term "word choice" simply means the use of striking words alone or in combination. Some of the words used by Margery are striking because of their flavor: they seem learned, unexpected in the work of a person supposedly illiterate. In the works of both mystics other expressions are impressive in their own right: they fit the subject exactly and convey a meaning effectively and emphatically. Some of these strong words are especially noticeable in episodes of religious experience and exaltation.

Some of Margery's words are rare today and seem to have been so even in her time. When a word like "cotidianly" appears (69/13, 234/14), there may be a tendency to attribute it to a person more learned than Margery, to her amanuensis perhaps. Indeed, the *Middle English Dictionary*[1] records this form of the word as being used for the first time by Margery Kempe. But a similar form, "cotidian", had been used before Margery's *Book* (the *MED* lists two early fifteenth-century uses), and she conceivably could have known the word, perhaps hearing it from a reading of the Epistles of Paul, one of the earlier *MED* listings. The word, however, was clearly not common at the time, and it is interesting to note that the Wyclif version of the Epistles, according to the *MED*, did not use it. Some other seemingly unusual expressions had earlier uses in works that Margery may have heard read. The Middle English

---

[1] *Middle English Dictionary*, ed. Hans Kurath and Sherman H. Kuhn (Ann Arbor, University of Michigan Press, in progress).

Revelations of Saint Birgitta[2] and Wyclif, among others, made use of "alienyd" in the sense of "deranged" as did Margery in "alienyd of hir witte" (178/8). According to the *New English Dictionary*, "obediencer", in Margery's "sche was hys obediencer" (247/24-25), was first used in 1380 by Wyclif. The problem of Margery's illiteracy is always with us and never more so than in a study of her diction. It is possible that she was influenced by hearing the Wyclif version of the Bible, by hearing other readings, and by the amanuensis himself.

Some of the conclusions of Shozo Shibata, who has made a brief study of Margery's vocabulary, are pertinent here.[3] Mr. Shibata believes that, since the book was dictated, it should show colloquial features. In its use of "mystic 'jargon'", however, the text has a "fairly high proportion of 'hard' words of French and, particularly, Latin origin." He lists examples that date mostly from the fifteenth or late fourteenth century and that are technical, theological, scientific, or legal terms. His list includes the following (with earliest listed use in *MED*):

erroneous (132/24) first recorded use
exaltyn (40/11) 1420
excludyn (151/37) c1400 (in the sense of "debase")
excludyn (168/17) a1393 (in the sense of "prevent")
exercysen (1/17) c1384 (in the sense of "to practice")
                    a1425 (in the sense of "to train, drill")
exhortacyon (93/11) c1384
expedient (115/25) 1418
fervent (209/6) c1384

Although his examples are drawn only from words beginning with *e* or *f* "so that they may be easily checked" with the *MED*, Shibata feels that they present words "not yet established as part of the daily vocabulary".

In going beyond Mr. Shibata's findings, I have drawn examples

---

[2]   For mentions of St. Bridget in Margery's work see Meech's note to 39/24, p. 276. For a discussion of the "profound influence of 'Bridis boke'" on Margery, see Allen's note to 39/24, pp. 276-277.

[3]   "Notes on the Vocabulary of the *Book of Margery Kempe*", *Studies in English Grammar and Linguistics in Honour of Takanobu Otsuka* (Tokyo: Kenkyusha Ltd., 1958), pp. 209-220.

from the end of Margery's *a* glossary, from her *b* words, and from a sampling of her *c* words. A number of these words are recorded (*MED*) as used for the first time by Margery. For some words she is listed as the first and only recorder: "attyd", "a-wondyr", "choppyng" (gerund, "bargaining"), "compassif" (for two adjective meanings), "compassyfly", "contemptibly" (adverb, "disgracefully"), "cowche" ("hump"). For others, she is the first recorder, but is followed by others: "Austyn" (*b*: adjective, "Augustinian"), "awarde" (*c*: "custody"), "bannars", "belschyd", "berm", "bloberys" ("pustule"), "bolendinys" (recorded later only in a treatise on money), "cotidianly", "certifyin" (4: "to inform, tell"), "consentyng". Margery also provides early instances of recorded use for "autorys" (second entry, "auctour" 2*a*, earliest c1400), "babyl" (second entry, earliest c1390), "blo" (first with specific figure "as _____ as eni led"), "bonyr" (fourth entry, "bonair", with Margery's alliterative "buxum and bonyr" differing from Wyclif's "meke and bonere"), "bottumles" (third entry), "cawdel" (third entry, *b*: "pudding"), "chalengyng" (second entry, earliest a1402), "chanel" (fourth entry, 2: "gutter", earliest a1420), "confidens" (second entry, earliest a1425), "Confiteor" (second entry, *b*, earliest a1425).

Such findings indicate that *The Book of Margery Kempe* has considerable importance as a source of information concerning Middle English diction.[4] With the evidence that the *Book* provides a number of early uses of words, "hard" uses, and "original" uses, one may question the consistency of Mr. Shibata's position that the text "should show colloquial features", especially since he himself stresses words which are not "a part of the daily vocabulary". Such a view, of course, would seem to bear out the idea that the amanuensis controlled the writing. It must be remembered, however, that the *MED* is not complete, that much literature — like Julian's, for example — is not included, and that we really cannot be sure of the extent of "colloquial" language. Although the listings

---

[4] This statement applies also to Julian's *Revelations*. Lacking a scholarly edition and glossary, this text is much more difficult to examine than is Margery's, but I shall note unusual or interesting expressions as they occur. Julian's MSS are not included among the texts on which the *MED* is based.

may indicate some external influence, they do not impinge upon the points made in Chapter One concerning the problem of Margery's illiteracy and her use of an amanuensis. Indeed, it is noteworthy that Shibata's conclusions approximate those we reached earlier. After examining other words, he supports the idea of Margery's control: his study "bears out admirably our contention that the general nature of our text is colloquial in spite of all its non-colloquial paraphernalia and accretions" (p. 215), and "In short, the style of the text may be defined as that of sober colloquialism" (p. 219). The "hard" words listed by Shibata are scattered in the book, and the lack of heavy concentration appears to minimize priestly intervention. Thus, although "inkhorn" terms are occasional features of the style, they do not necessarily indicate control by an amanuensis. Nevertheless, a study of Margery's words raises some intriguing questions. The *MED* frequently indicates that Margery uses words in a manner similar to that of Wyclif, but Scriptural influences and commonplaces are also involved. Her personal knowledge of "hard" words and the extent of outside influence must remain conjecture. On the other hand, Margery's travels ("bolendinys"), business ("berm"), and worldly vision ("bloberys") appear to have had something to do with the "new" diction found in her *Book*.

Everyday expressions that seem natural to both mystics abound, but not always for the better. Obvious in both works, but more pronounced in Margery's, is the use of apparently hackneyed, often needless, terms that seem to be used automatically without much thought. The following are examples of these phrases, mainly transitional in nature, that occur again and again.

In Julian: "as to my sight", "as to my feleing", "as to myne understondyng", "and after this", "so far forth", "without(e) end(e)".

In Margery: "at þe last", "ryth wel", "as schal be seyd aftyr", "as kynde wolde", "wyth-owtyn ende", "boþe for-non(e) & aftyr-non(e)", "on a tyme", "wyth good wil", "as is wretyn be-forn".

In addition, both writers share three other types of clichés. One is the use of certain tautological pairs, a device which will be discussed under repetition rather than word choice. Other stereotyped expressions are certain alliterative phrases, frequently involving religious ideas, which will be considered more fully under alliteration. Finally, there is the jargon which occurs only in religious contexts and is common in devotional writings of the period: "wyth hy devocyon", "worschepyd (blyssyd) mote he be(n)", "for Goddys lofe", "as owr Lord wolde", "derworthy Criste", "our fader God".

Another very frequent element in word choice involves the use of active or passive verbs. Modern composition texts generally stress the active voice as leading to vigor and strength in presentation. Julian, who makes more striking use of passive constructions than does Margery, conceivably might be considered a weaker writer on this basis. On the contrary, however, her use of the passive, which contributes to a weighty, pedantic tone, is appropriate and effective: the extraverted Julian, despite her first-person presentation, is not as interested in herself as she is in what she has seen — the vision that was beheld and its significance. Thus in Julian there are many constructions like the following: "is comprehended" (li/246), "is understood "(li/251), "was this shewed, and it is spoken of" (lvii/60-61), "... man ... is loved" (lxv/2-3), "God is worshipped" (lxxx/2), "all-thing is done as it was then ordained before that anything was made" (lxxxvi/18-19). An attempt by Julian to avoid the overuse of "I" in a work in which she is stressing not herself but her observations, may also be a possible cause of passive constructions, while Margery, with the interchangeable third person "creatur ... sche" and her characteristic introversion, might naturally have been inclined to the more direct active voice in her account of travels, worldly experiences, conversations, and other actions in which she played the leading role.[5]

But whereas learned terms, overused words, and passive verb forms may be considered flaws in one way or another, both writers also make extremely effective use of words. Succinctness and concreteness of diction are two of their strengths which many modern writers might profitably seek to emulate. There are, of course, the wordy, repetitive sentences in which both works abound and which

---

[5] The playing of the leading role in visions and other religious experiences is also not "above" Margery. See Chapter Two on Margery's character.

will be considered in detail later, but in many briefer statements the apt phrase or word expresses the thought admirably. Some occasionally overlapping types of these effective usages are notable in both mystics. As will be true of almost any lengthy group of examples from either writer, commonplaces and Scriptural influences are present. Some examples also reveal the individual writer more than others do.

Examples of conciseness are found in both works, but do not seem as characteristic of Margery as they are of Julian.[6]

Julian:

(1) "Good Lord, may my living-no-longer be to thy worshippe" (iii/16-17)
(2) my eyen were sett up-right-ward into hevyn (iii/31-32)
(3) full lovesome to the soule (v/45)
(4) his goodness comprehendith all his cretures (v/47)
(5) for he is the endleshede (v/48-49)
(6) our onforsighte (xi/9) (Similarly, "onpeace", xlix/45)
(7) al this was shewid in a touch (xxvii/26-27)
(8) Rythfulhede is that thyng that is so goode that may not be better than it is (xxxv/30-31)
(9) for al this life & this langor þat we have here is but a poynte, & whan we arn taken sodenly out of peyn into bliss than peyn shall be nowte (lxiv/28-30)
(10) than shewid our good Lord words full mekely withouten voice & withouten openyng of lipps (lxviii/10-11)
(11) And thus be the syte of the less that our Lord shewith us, the more is wastid[7] which we se not (lxxviii/20-22)
(12) he lovith us endlesly & we synne customably[8] (lxxxii/12)

Margery:

(1) Þu art as sekyr of þe lofe of God as God is God (89/10-11)
(2) Þer is gold to-þe-ward (92/38-39)

---

[6] Other examples may be found in the earlier discussion of understatement.
[7] Hudleston replaces this word with 'reckoned'. In a footnote he cites the MS as "(probably) 'castid'", apparently following Warrack's footnote to the word in question: "S. de Cressy [editor of the earliest printed edition, published in 1670]: 'wastid' but the indistinct word of the Brit. Mus. MS is probably '*castid*' for 'cast', or '*casten*', = 'conjectured'". I cannot agree to the initial *c* reading of the manuscript; the first letter looks more like a *w* or a *v*, and *wastid* matches the clearly spelled "wastyd" of the Paris MS.
[8] Cf. "Here synne ys moche þe more, ȝyf þey synne custummably" (*MED* quoting Mannyng, *Handlyng Synne*, 2695).

(3) Also anoþer maistyr of diuinite had behestyd hir to a ben þer wyth hir, but he drow on bakke tyl he knew how þe cawse xulde gon, whedyr wyth hir or a-ȝen hir (121/32-35)

(4) sche hath a devyl wyth-inne hir (126/14-15)

(5) A, Lord, for thy gret peyn have mercy on my lityl peyne (137/33-34)

(6) he went forth ful mekely a-forn hem al modyr-nakyd (190/19-20)

(7) mor encresyd to-owr-Lord-ward (207/23)

(8) reualacyons be hard sum-tyme to vndirstondyn (219/33)

Both writers (but Julian more than Margery) also provide examples of effective connotation, gaining strength through the evocative power of certain words.

Julian:

(1) a ghostly sight of his homely loveing (v/1-2)

(2) For this sigte I lauhyd migtily, & that made hem to lavhyn that were about me, & her lauhyng was a likeing to me (xii/26-28)

(3) This lestenid but a while & I was turnyd & left to my selfe in hevynes & werines of my life & irkenes of my selfe, that onethis [= scarcely] I coude have patience to leve (xv/6-8)

(4) it was the most likyng word þat he might have gove me (xxv/40)

(5) synne is behovabil[9] (xxvii/13)

(6) In this nakid word "synne" (xxvii/16)

(7) me thowte it myte molten our herts for love & bresten hem on to for joy (li/149-150)

(8) we love our maker and like him (lviii/9)

(9) renewid by lygthings & tuchyngs (lxv/42-43)

(10) [we] fallen into our Lords brest as the child into the Moder barme (lxxiv/40-41)

(11) dredfully tremeland & quakand for mekehede of joye, mervelyng at the greatness of God the maker & of the litilhede of all that is made (lxxv/35-37)

Margery:

(1) Lady, us is wo þat ȝowr sone is ded (195/1)

(2) blamyd hir of hyr feerdnes (230/23)

(3) trustyng to ben an eyr of joy & blisse[10] (246/27)

---

[9] Julian here may be recalling the Psalter, Psalm xxxii. 5-7. The earliest *MED* entry for *bihoveable* is c1400 in the *Midland Prose Psalter* [Dub].

[10] It is interesting to note, in conjunction with the dropped *h* in *heir*, some other examples of spelling that seem to indicate pronunciation. Julian uses *hopinly* for *openly* (ix/36). Margery uses *abite* for *habit, clothing* (246/14); *ermyte* for *hermit* (226/23); *habundawntly* and *habundawnce* for *abundantly* and *abundance* (163/1 and 199/31 respectively); *eretyke* for *heretic* (29/1); *hogely* for *ugly* (126/32).

Finally, both writers also give examples in which concrete diction and homely terms are effective. The less intellectual, more colloquial Margery makes more vivid use of this type of expression.

Julian:

(1) uggyng [*fear*, Hudleston] of fiends (xix/4-5)
(2) in his benignite & in his buxumhede[11] (xlix/25-26)
(3) clothyng was a white kirtle, sengil, old, & al defaced, died with swete of his body, streyte fittyng to hym & short as it were an handful benethe the knee, bar semand as it shuld sone be weryd up redy to be raggid & rent (li/195-199)
(4) delvyn & dykyn, swinkin & swetyn, & turne þe earth up so downe (li/225-226)
(5) þe flesh was rent from þe hede panne, falland in pets into þe tyme þe bledyng failyd, & than it began to dryand agen, clyngand to þe bone (li/343-345)
(6) a bolned quave of styngand myre (lxiv/33)
(7) swifie and lively (lxiv/35)

Margery:

(1) He sett a peyr of spectacles on hys nose (5/22)
(2) deuelys opyn her mowthys al inflaumyd wyth brennyng lowys of fyr as þei schuld a swalwyd hyr in, sum-tyme rampyng at hyr, sum-tyme thretyng her, sum-tym pullyng hyr & halyng hir boþe nygth & day (7/24-27)
(3) A-non as it was noysed a-bowt þe town (10/34)
(4) "Wel", he seyd, "þan schal I medyl ȝow a-geyn" (24/19-20)
(5) sche sey a powyr man sittyng whech had a gret cowche[12] on hys bakke. Hys cloþis wer al for-clowtyd, & he semyd a man of L wyntyr age. (76/23-26)
(6) [people] born hyr on hande [= accused] (107/16, 145/2)
(7) Whan he had long jangelyd wyth hir (120/32)
(8) þu takyst ful lytyl heede how þu seyst þi Mateynes & þi seruyse, so it be blaberyd to an ende (127/18-19)

---

[11] The *MED* has no entry for *buxumhede* or for the similar form *bolnehed* (lxiv/36), which Hudleston and Warrack both give as "swollenness" without any notation. The Paris MS has *buxsumnesse* (Walsh: "kindliness") and *swylge* (Walsh: "bloated mass"). Still another similar form, *endleshede*, (v/48-49), listed fourth in Julian's preceding examples of conciseness, has an *MED* entry that antedates her work: ?c1400 (c1340) Rolle *Psalter*. Cf. note 9, above, for Psalter influence.

[12] "from the context, it would appear that *cowche* means a hump. No satisfactory etymology for the word suggests itself. Compare OD *Crouchback* and *Croche*, sb[1]" (note to 76/24, pp. 296-297).

(9) he turnyd childisch a-ʒen & lakkyd reson þat he cowd not don
hys owyn esement to gon to a sege, er ellys he wolde not, but as
a childe voydyd his natural digestyon in hys lynyn clothys þer he
sat be þe fyre er at þe tabil, wheþyr it wer, he wolde sparyn no
place (181/2-6)

(10) þei wolde not spare to luggen hys blisful erys and drawyn þe her
of hys berd (190/15-16)

(11) hys face wex ful of whelys & bloberys (222/11)

(12) þe good powr man, hogelyd[13] in hys clothys vn-sperd & vn-botenyd,
cam to þe dor (242/35-36)

In a way the examples of effective diction listed above can be loosely
considered to be forms of imagery, for they provide word pictures
that give sense impressions and emotional associations that will
vary from reader to reader. However, a more specialized way to
enrich meaning through an appeal to the physical senses is found
in both writings. Again, there is an overlapping of terms which
must be distinguished arbitrarily. Imagery has been defined as
"mental reproduction, without external stimulus except through
words, of things seen, heard, touched, tasted and smelled".[14] Images make an impression by appealing to the senses in eight ways:
color ("mauve"), form ("spiral"), auditory ("buzzy"), simple tactual
("soft"), thermal ("cold"), kinaesthetic ("squeeze"), gustatory
("sour"), olfactory ("pungent"). The examples listed above by
Edith Rickert (p. 32) are "simple" images; "complex" images
appeal to different senses simultaneously (e.g., "rubber tube"
would give form, color, tactual, and olfactory impressions). Miss
Rickert goes on to analyze methods.[15] She defines three types of
image development: *cataloguing* is the accumulation of a number
of images of details; *repetitive* development is the repetition of an
image in association with a different subsidiary image; *suggestive*
development uses a single image "to suggest a large number commonly associated with it in experience". Likewise, she finds three
methods of presentation: the *photographic* method presents an

[13] *hogylyd*: "this is probably related to OD *huggle*" (note to 242/35, p. 348).
The glossary defines the word as "hastily dressed".
[14] Edith Rickert, *New Methods for the Study of Literature* (Chicago, University
of Chicago Press, 1927), p. 24.
[15] Rickert, pp. 34-37.

image "ready-made", "by a word or group of words so commonly associated in experience as to make a unitary impression"; a *synthetic* presentation builds up an image step by step from words freshly associated by the author; a *dynamic* method presents an image in the process of changing or becoming. Miss Rickert makes some generalizations about these methods:

Of least value are the cataloguing and repetitive methods if the images are merely photographic. A long catalogue of these tends to weary the attention; repetition, to irritate it. One image after another is recognized, but before it can be constructed into a picture, it is supplanted by the next. The imaginative faculty is hampered by the number of details which must be fitted to its own memories of experience. Under the pressure of fatigue the images called up grow faint and blurred; and reading, instead of being the re-creation of life, becomes the mere following of words.

It should perhaps be added that, while these methods are the least effective in literature, they are the most certain to reach readers of limited experience and imaginative power. ...

Both the cataloguing and the repetitive methods, however, take on value when their images are presented synthetically or dynamically. If the reader is made, not merely to recall experience but to construct from it, out of details in themselves often unrelated, a new image, the creative imagination is kept active and alive, and reading is not the mere following of words but the re-creation of life.[16]

Both Julian and Margery make considerable use of cataloguing, but it is important to note that, although they both might be of "limited experience", they do have "imaginative power" as shown by their use of synthetic or dynamic images. Examples are not difficult to find. As is frequently the case with Julian, who analyzes each revelation over a number of chapters, vivid writing appears in a scene witnessing the Passion. Here we have a cataloguing of images presented synthetically, with the accumulated details building up a total picture step by step:

I saw the bodyly sight lesting of the plentious bledeing of the hede. The grete dropis of blode fel downe from under the garland like pellots, semand as it had cum out of the veynis, & in the comeing out it were browne rede for the blode was full thick, & in the spredeing abrode it were bright rede & whan it come to the browes than it vanyshid; not

16 Rickert, pp. 37-38.

withstondyng the bleding continuid till many things were sene & under-stondyn. The fairehede & the livelyhede is like nothing but the same. The plenteowshede is like to the dropys of water that fallen of the evys after a greate showre of reyne that fall so thick that no man may numbre them with bodily witte, & for the roundhede it were like to the scale of heryng in the spreadeing on the forehead. These iij came to my ["mind" inserted here by Hudleston] in the tyme: pellotts fer roundhede in the comynge out of the blode; the scale of heryng in the spreading in the forehede for roundhede; the dropys of evys for the plentioushede inumer-able. This shewing was quick & lively & hidouse & dredfull, swete & lovely. (vii/12-30)

Similarly, an example of synthetic cataloguing appears in a des-cription of the Passion by Margery, but there appears again a basic distinction between the two mystics: Julian gives the more careful, searching, penetrating examination; Margery the broader, apparently less thoughtful picture, with her own characteristic physical involvement.

it was grawntyd þis creatur to beholdyn so verily hys precyows tendyr body, alto-rent & toryn wyth scorgys, mor ful of wowndys þan euyr was duffehows of holys, hangyng vp-on þe cros wyth þe corown of thorn up-on hys heuyd, hys blysful handys, hys tendyr fete nayled to þe hard tre, þe reuerys of blood flowyng out plentevowsly of euery membre, þe gresly & grevows wownde in hys precyows syde schedyng owt blood & watyr for hir lofe & hir saluacyon, þan sche fel down & cryed wyth lowde voys, wondyrfully turnyng & wrestyng hir body on euery syde, spredyng hir armys a-brode as ȝyf sche xulde a deyd, & not cowde kepyn hir from crying, — and þese bodily mevyngys for þe fyer of lofe þat brent so feruently in hir sowle wyth pur pyte & compassyon. (70/9-22)

This view of the Passion is preceded in Capitulum 28 by two other noteworthy passages. In another example of synthetic cataloguing Margery builds up a most interesting picture of her manner of crying:

sche fel down þat sche mygth not stondyn ne knelyn but walwyd & wrestyd wyth hir body, spredyng hir armys a-brode, & cryed wyth lowde voys as þow hir hert xulde a brostyn a-sundyr, for in þe cite of hir sowle sche saw veryly & freschly how owyr Lord was crucifyed. Beforn hir face she herd and saw in hir gostly sygth þe mornyng of owyr Lady, of Sen Iohn & Mary Mawdelyn, and of many oþer þat louyd owyr Lord. & sche had so gret compassyon & so gret peyn to se owyr Lordys peyn þat sche myt not kepe hir-self fro krying & roryng þow sche xuld a be ded þerfor. And þis was þe fyrst cry þat euyr sche cryed in any contempla-cyon. (68/12-24)

And this passage is followed soon after by another synthetic cata-loguing which reveals the attitude of traveling companions towards this "krying & roryng":

as sone as sche parceyvyd þat sche xulde crye, sche wolde kepyn it in as mech as sche myth þat þe pepyl xulde not an herd it for noyng of hem. For summe seyd it was a wikkyd spiryt vexid hir; sum seyd it was a sekenes; sum seyd sche had dronkyn to mech wyn; sum bannyd hir; sum wisshed sche had ben in þe hauyn; sum wolde sche had ben in þe se in a bottumles boyt; and so ich man as hym thowte. (69/19-27)

Cataloguing in a dynamic method can be seen in Julian:

I saw his swete face as it was drye & blodles with pale deyand. And sithen more pale dede langoring; & than turnid more dede into blew & sithen more browne-blew as the flesh turnyd more depe dede. For his passion shewid to me most propirly on his blissid face, & namly on his lippis; there I saw these iiij coloures, tho þat were aforn freshe, redy, & likyng to my sigte. This was a swemful chonge to sene this depe deyeng. & also the nose clange & dryed to my sigte, & the swete body was brown & blak, al turnyd oute of faire lifely colour of hymselfe on to drye deyeng. (xvi/3-13)

Dynamic cataloguing is present in the work of Margery, but is not as easily found:

Whan þow stodyst to plese me, þan art þu a very dowtyr; whan þu wepyst & mornyst for my peyn & for my Passyon, þan art þow a very modyr to haue compassyon of hyr chyld; whan þow wepyst for oþer mannys synnes and for aduersytes, þan art þow a very syster; and, whan thow sorwyst for þow art so long fro þe blysse of Heuyn, þan art þu a very spowse & a wyfe (31/26-33)

Both mystics also develop their word-pictures repetitively. In one passage Julian uses repetitive images in such a way as to indicate both the step-by-step presentation of the synthetic method and the idea of change or becoming of the dynamic method:

And thus our good Lord answerid to al the question & doubts that I myte makyn, sayeing ful comfortably: "I may makyn al thing wele, I can make al thing wele, & I wil make al thyng wele, & I shall make al thyng well, & thou shal se thi self that al maner of thyng shal be well." That he seyth "I may", I understond for the fader; & he seith "I can",

I understond for þe son; & where he seith "I will", I understond for
the Holy Gost; & wher he seith "I shall", I understond for the unite of
the blissid trinite, iij persons & one trouthe. & where he seith "þu shal
se thi selfe" I understond the onyng of al mankynd þat sha [*sic*] be save
into the blysful trinite, & in thes v words God wil be onclosid in rest &
in pees. (xxxi/1-14)

In the same Capitulum 28 that provided three examples of cataloguing, Margery also gives a repetitive image that in its parts is
photographic but also builds up an impression that in its entirety
can be called synthetic.

&, whan sche come hom in-to Inglonde, fyrst at hir comyng hom it
[cryings] comyn but seldom as it wer onys in a moneth, sythen onys in
þe weke, aftyrward cotidianly, & onys sche had xiiij on o day, & anoþer day sche had vij, & so as God wolde visiten hir, sumtyme in þe
cherch, sumtyme in þe strete, sumtym in þe chawmbre, sumtyme in þe
felde whan God wold sendyn hem, for sche knew neuyr tyme ne owyr
whan þei xulde come. (69/10-18)

Despite the possible merits of such descriptive writing, however,
the modern reader of both Margery and Julian may be inclined to
agree with a further point made by Miss Rickert: "As a rule, the
cataloguing and repetitive methods, even when the images are
presented synthetically or dynamically, lose their effect if developed
at great length" (p. 40). Here is one of the basic flaws of both: the
excessive length and detail of such descriptions, frequently occur-
ring, soon become tedious. When this weakness is combined with
excessive coordination of sentence elements, excessive repetition,
and lack of variety in sentence structure or in subject matter, the
reader becomes aware of some of the shortcomings of medieval
prose.[17] Although found in later times also — including today —
these elements are the ones that most obviously weaken medieval
prose; along with the language barrier, they probably are the
reasons for the modern lack of popular interest in such writing.

More effective than the cataloguing or repetitive methods, according to Rickert (p. 40), is the suggestive method — a single
image used to suggest a number of associations. Much more common in poetry than in prose, of course, although prominent in the

[17] For further discussion of these weaknesses, see the chapter on syntax.

prose (poetry-prose?) of such moderns as Thomas Wolfe and James Agee, suggestive imagery might be expected to be rare in medieval prose. With the looseness of the Rickert definitions, however, such is not the case, for any single word that has much connotative meaning may be called a suggestive image. And even if the definition is taken to apply only to *groups* of words forming an image, both Julian and Margery still provide examples of this most effective type. Margery presents an idea that is both suggestive and dynamic: "sche was so raueschyd in-to contemplacyon wyth swetnes & deuocyon" (117/17-18). In another section, she recounts a speech in which Jesus, praising her, uses a striking suggestive image: "I may not for-ȝetyn þe how þow art wretyn in myn handys & my fete" (30/12-13). A few lines before this, Margery makes use of a suggestive image followed by a photographic one: "sche ymagyned hyr-self þe most soft deth, as hir thowt, for dred of inpacyens, þat was to be bowndyn hyr hed & hir fet to a stokke & hir hed to be smet of wyth a scharp ex for Goddys lofe" (30/3-6).

Parallel to the suggestive "soft deth" of Margery is Julian's "& in this I concyvid a soft drede" (xxxvii/9). Julian, like Margery, also combines suggestive with photographic images but goes beyond her in adding the element of figurative images (metaphors and similes) to the presentation:

he is our clothing that for love wrappith us, halfyth us, & al beclosyth us for tender love (v/4-5)

One tyme mine understondyng was led downe into the se-ground, & there I saw hill & dalis grene, semand as it were mosse begrowne with wrekke & with gravel (x/22-24)

And in this deying was broute to my mynde the words of Criste, "I threst." For I saw in Criste a doble threst, one bodely, another gostly (xvii/1-4)

Synne is the sharpest scorge that any chousyn soule may be smyten with, which scorge al forbetyth man & woman & noyith him in his owne syte (xxxix/1-3)

These last examples are also illustrative of the recurring problem of overlapping. Any simile or metaphor is, or course, a suggestive image, and an examination of this form leads inevitably to the study of figurative imagery. Rickert defines the latter term as "imagery extraneous to the subject, introduced for the purpose of (1) giving clarity and emphasis, (2) intensifying emotional appeal by added associations, and (3) enriching by added pictorial details" (p. 45). Obviously, a number of the illustrations of the methods of presentation and development given earlier do involve "imagery extraneous to the subject", but by "figurative imagery" Rickert specifically means the use of five types of figures: simile and metaphor; metonymy and synecdoche; personification; allegory; symbolism.

Simile and metaphor are found readily in both works being studied, and it is interesting to note the types of comparisons used. Determined by the authors' knowledge and experience, the figures are generally homely, familiar ones rather than "learned" — literary or philosophical — expressions. The resulting naturalness gives the flavor of colloquial usage, simplicity, and artlessness to the work of both writers, especially in their use of similes. Examples of Julian's similes may be loosely classified as follows:

MAN AND DAILY PURSUITS

(1) he will we have knowing here as it were in owr [an, Hudleston] A B C; þat is to seyn that we have a litill knoweing (lxxx/11-13)
(2) I have techyng with me as it wer þe begynyng of an A B C whereby I may have sum vnderstondyng of our Lordis menyng (li/316-318)
(3) as a man that was febil & onwise for the tyme (li/24-25)
(4) the son syttith on the ryte hand, syde be syde as on man sittith be another in this lif (li/378-379)
(5) That is to sey Gods servant, holy church, shal be shakyn in sorowe & anguis & tribulation in this world, as men shakyn a cloth in the wynde (xxviii/6-8)
(6) I saw iiij maner of deyengs: ... the thred, hangyng up in the eyr as men hang a cloth to drye (xvii/41 ff.)
(7) the swete skyne & the tender flesh ... was al rasyd & losyd abov from the bone with the thornys where thowe it were daggyd on many pecys as a cloth that were saggand as it wold hastely have fallen of for hevy & lose while it had kynde moysture (xvii/20ff.)
(8) so wil he that we don as a meke child, seyand thus: "My kind Moder, my Gracious Moder, my derworthy Moder, have mercy on

me. I have made my selfe my [*sic*] foule & onlike to the & I ne may
ne can amenden it but with prive helpe & grace" (lxi/52-56)

(9) That drede that makith us hastily to fleen fro*m* all that is not good
& fallen into our Lords brest, as the child into the Moder barme
(lxxiv/39-41)

(10) I saw our Lord as a Lord in his owne house which hath clepid
al his derworthy servants & frends to a solemne feste (xiv/4-6)

(11) both, to my thynkyng, janglyd at one time, as if they had holden
a parlement with a gret bysynes (lxix/4-6)

RELIGION

(12) if we were as clene & as holy as Angelys be in hevyn (1/16-17)

(13) joy & blis passith as fer reuth & pite as hevyn is aboven erth (li/153-
154)

(14) all that was beside the cross was uggely to me as if it had be mekil
occupyed with the fends (iii/40-41)

(15) And in other manner he [God] shewid him in erth thus as it wer in
pilegrimage: that is to sey he is here with us ledand us, & shal ben
till whan he hath browte us all to his bliss in hevyn (lxxxi/7-10)

NATURE AND THE WORLD

(16) blew as asure (li/143)

(17) it was as round as a balle (v/9-10)

(18) For as the body is cladde in the cloth, & the flesh in the skyne, &
the bonys in the flesh, & the herte in the bouke [*whole* from *bulk*,
Hudleston; but *MED*: *bouk* = "belly", "trunk"], so arn we soule
& body cladde in the goodness of God & inclosyd (vi/43-46)

(19) The skyn*n*e of the flesh that semyd of the face & of the body was
smal rankyllid with a tan*n*yd colour like a dry borde whan it is
skynned (xvii/37-39)

(20) For the beholdyng of other man*n*ys syn*n*es it makith as it were a
thick myst aforne the eye of þe soule (lxxvi/15-17)

(21) all derke about me in the chamber as it had be night (iii/37-38)

(22) I saw the soule so large as it were an endles world & as it were a
blisfull kyngdom. & be the conditions I saw therein I understode
that it is a worshipful syte [*city*, Hudleston]. In the midds of þat
syte sitts our Lord Jesus (lxvii/2-6)

One striking passage by Julian merits quotation in full. A good example of the use of vivid, concrete word choice, it is given here because of the presence of several similes:

And in the slepe at the begynnyng me thowte the Fend set him on my throte, puttand forth a visage ful ner my face like a yong man & it was long & wonder lene — I saw never none such. The color was rede like the tile stone whan it is new brent, with blak spots therein like blak freknes fouler than the tile stone. His here was rede as rust, evisid [*MED*: *evesen* = "cut, trim"] aforn with syde lokks hongyng on the thounys. He grynnid on me with a shrewd semelant, shewing white teeth, & so mekil methowte it the more oggley. Body ne honds had he none shaply, but with his pawes he held me in the throte & wold have stranglid me, but he myte not. This oggley shewing was made slepyng, & so was non other (lxvi/37-50)

Although they sometimes are commonplaces and show familiarity with the Bible, Margery's similes, though much like Julian's in their simplicity, show better development, greater vigor, and more vividness. Most examples can be classified under several recurring centers of comparison.

OBJECTS IN NATURE

(1) On was a maner of sownde as it had ben a peyr of belwys blowyng in hir ere. (90/35-36)

(2) sum scornyd hir and seyd þat sche howlyd as it [had] ben a dogge (105/22-23)

(3) þe Sacrament schok & flekeryd to & fro as a dowe flekeryth wyth hir wengys (47/17-18)

(4) He þat is euyr-mor dowtyng is lyke to þe flood of þe see, þe whech is mevyd & born a-bowte wyth þe wynd (42/31-33)

(5) wex al blew & al blo as it had ben colowr of leed (105/20-21, 69/34-35, 140/23) (cf. Julian "blew as asure" li/143)

(6) þe eyr openyd as brygth as ony levyn [lightning] (8/22-23)

(7) &, as sodeynly as þe leuyn comith from Heuyn, so sodeynly come I in-to thy sowle, & illumyn it wyth þe lyght of grace & of vndir-standyng, & sett it al on fyr wyth lofe, & make þe fyr of lofe to brenn þerin & purgyn it ful clene fro alle erdly filth (182/23-27)

(8) Our merciful Lord as a meke lombe (189/31-32)

(9) as thykke in a maner as motys in þe sunne[18] (88/8-9)

---

[18] Some similarities between Margery and Chaucer's Wife of Bath have already been noted (see Chapter Two, notes 12, 13, and 46). With this simile compare *WB* 868.

(10) þow xalt ben etyn & knawyn of þe pepul of þe world as any raton
knawyth þe stokfysch (17/16-17)

(11) sche ... lech vn-to þe reed-spyr whech boweth wyth euery wynd &
neuyr is stable les þan no wynd bloweth (1/20-22)

(12) every babyl was ful of scharp prekelys as it had ben þe rowelys of
a spor (191/8-9)

(13) þe ... cleuyst as sore on-to me as þe skyn of stokfysche cleuyth
to a mannys handys whan it is sothyn (91/14-16)

(14) faryth wyth ʒow as a smyth wyth a fyle þat makyth þe yron to be
bryte & cler to þe sygth whech be-forn aperyd rusty, dyrke, & euyl
colowryd (44/31-33)

(15) As sekyr as þu art of þe sunne whan þu seest it schynyn bryghtly,
ryth so sekyr art þu of þe lofe of God at al tyme (183/2-4)

HUMAN RELATIONSHIPS

(16) þe mor schame, despite, & reprefe þat þu sufferyst for my lofe, þe
bettyr I lofe þe, for I far liche a man þat louyth wel hys wyfe, þe
mor enuye þat men han to hir þe bettyr he wyl arayn hir in despite
of hir enmys (81/28-32)

(17) al maner of mekenes, lownes, & charite, as any lady in þis werld is
besy to receyue hir husbond whan he comyth hom & hath be long
fro hir (213/30-33)

(18) I far lyke an husbond þat schulde weddyn a wyfe (213/20-21)

(19) for I [Christ] wyl be louyd as a sone schuld be louyd wyth þe
modyr & wil þat þu loue me, dowtyr, as a good wife owyth to loue
hir husbonde. & þerfor þu mayst boldly take me in þe armys of þi
sowle & kyssen my mowth, myn hed, & my fete as swetly as thow
wylt (90/21-26)

(20) trostyng to hir as to hys modyr (97/15)

(21) was as tendyr to hir as sche had ben hys modyr (231/17-18)

(22) þu xal fyndyn me a very modyr to þe to helpyn þe and socowr þe
as a modyr owyth to don hir dowtyr (175/27-28)

(23) sum-tume þe Fadyr of Hevyn dalyd to hir sowle as pleynly and
as veryly as o frend spekyth to a-noþer be bodyly spech (39/16-17)

(24) heryng & vndiestondyng ... in hir sowle as clerly as on frende xulde
spekyn to an-oþer (214/14-16)

(25) The creatur herd as clerly þis answer in þe vndirstondyng of hir
sowle as sche xulde vndirstondyn o man spekyn to anoþer (195/22-
24)

EXCESSES (OF FEELING) CENTERING AROUND DEATH, VIOLENCE, OR INJURY

(26) cryyn ful lowde & wepyn ful sor, as þei sche xulde a deyd (139/24-25, 148/9-10, 191/28-29, 197/36-37)

(27) owr Lady swownyn & fallyn down & lyn stille as sche had ben ded (189/2, 193/18-19)

(28) wept, sobbyd, & criyd as þow sche xulde a deyid for pite & compassyon (191/28-29)

(29) wept, sorwyd, & cryid as sche xulde a deyd for lofe & desir (197/36-37)

(30) wepying & sobbyng as hir hert xuld a brostyn (50/2-3)

(31) wept & cryid ryth lowde as 3yf sche xulde a brostyn for sorwe & peyne (191/12-13)

(32) went waueryng on eche syde as it had ben a dronkyn woman (198/15-16)

(33) sche cryid & gapyd as sche wolde an etyn hem (178/15)

(34) þan þat precyows body aperyd to hir syght as rawe as a thyng þat wer newe flayn owt of þe skyn (192/5-7)

(35) he had leuar ben hewyn as smal as flesch to þe pott (15/27-28, 142/12-13, 204/27-28)

(36) sche ran al a-bowte þe place as it had ben a mad woman, crying & roryng (193/20-21)

(37) sche cryed what tyme sche schulde ben howselyd as 3yf hir sowle & hir body xulde a partyd a-sundyr (138/29-31)

(38) hys wowndys bledyng as fresch as þow he had ben scorgyd be-forn hir (207/18-19)

RELIGIOUS REFERENCES

(39) rygth as þow seyst þe prest take þe chyld at þe funt-ston & dyppe it in þe watyr & wasch it fro oryginal synne, rygth so xal I [Christ] wasch þe in my precyows blod fro alle þi synne (30/21-24)

(40) I [Christ] xuld as wel han excusyd hym 3yf he had fulfyllyd þi wyl as I dede þe chyldren of Israel whan I bad hem borwe þe goodys of þe pepyl of Egypt & gon a-wey þerwyth (35/22-25)

(41) þu art as sekyr of my lofe as God is God (218/23-24)

Two passages from Margery require fuller treatment. One, an extended simile that involves several sentences, would be a good example of symbolism if the symbol were not so precisely explained. Again, as is true of a number of the previous examples, Christ is the speaker:

"I far sum-tyme wyth my grace to þe as I do wyth þe sunne. Sumtyme þow wetyst wel þe sunne schynyth al abrod þat many man may se it, & sum-tyme it is hyd vndyr a clowde þat men may not se it, & ȝet is þe sunne neyyr þe lesse in hys hete ne in hys brytnesse. And rygth so far I be þe & be my chosyn sowlys" (31/14-20)

At the end of Margery's text is a section giving the prayers that she used. In a subordinate clause of an extremely long sentence in this final section occur a number of similes that in themselves offer an example of cataloguing of images and also an excellent example of hyperbole. The alliteration is also notable:

for, þow I had as many hertys & sowlys closyd in my sowle as God knew wythowtyn begynnyng how many xulde dwellyn in Heuyn wythow-tyn ende & as þer arn dropys of watyr, fres and salt, cheselys of grauel, stonys small & grete, gresys growing in al erthe, kyrnellys of corn, fischys, fowelys, bestys & leevys up-on treys whan most plente ben, fedir of fowle er her of best, seed þat growith in erbe, er in wede, in flowyr, in lond, er in watyr whan most growyn, & as many creaturys as in erth han ben & arn er xal ben & myth ben be þi myth, and as þer arn sterrys & awngelys in þi syght er oþer kynnes good þat growth up-on erthe, & eche wer a sowle as holy as euyr was our Lady Seynt Mary þat bar Ihesu owr Sauyowr, and, yf it wer possibyl þat eche cowde thynkyn & spekyn al so gret reuerens & worschep as euyr dede owr Lady Seynt Mary her in erthe & now doth in Heuyn & xal don wythow-tyn ende, I may rith wel thynkyn[19] (252/1-18)

The virtuoso-like control of this passage is impressive. There is no doubt that it could be diagramed, although one may shudder at what the completed version would look like. But Margery certainly seems to have no fear of using similes, and generally her use of them is tellingly superior to Julian's handling of the same device possibly because Margery has a layman's eye instead of the "inward" eye. The freshness and effectiveness of Margery's usages are in direct contrast to the stereotyped comparisons made by Julian in almost an automatic reaction to certain objects. The latter makes little effort, apparently, to think about her descriptions creatively, and is

---

[19]   In a note to this passage Allen discusses this "imagery of multiplicity, so to speak, which appears in the late twelfth century *Liber de Exercitio Cellæ*, written for the pioneer English Carthusians of Witham". Allen also refers to I Cor. xiii. 1 and to the use of the formula by German writers, but says "I know no example in native works" (p. 350).

content to use figures that for the most part lack originality and vigor. At least part of the reason for greater adeptness in seeing likenesses is the previously discussed character and experience of the more worldly, more out-going Margery.

Metaphors, appearing abundantly (some appeared in the examples of methods of presenting and developing images), also show this characteristic distinction between the two writers, with Margery's utterances standing out more vividly. Julian's metaphors generally are briefer, often with only one word providing the figurative image.

(1) shall receive anew [bliss] which plenteously shall be flowing out of God into us & fulfillen us (lxxv/20-22)

(2) we arn his blisse (xxiii/19-20)

(3) & anempt our substance & sensualite it may rytely be clepid our soule, & þat is be the onyng þat it hath in God. The worshipfull cyte that our Lord Jesus sittith in it is our sensualite, in which he is inclosid (lvi/24-27)

(4) He is our clothing that for love wrappith us, halfyth us, & all beclosyth us for tender love (v/4-5)

(5) & for we felyn ryth nowte, for we arn as barren & dry oftentimes after our prayers as wer aforn, & this, in our felyng our foly, is cause of our wekenes, for thus have I felt in my selfe (xli/6-9)

(6) the swete eye of pite & love commyth never of us (xlviii/27-28)

(7) he [God] opynyth the eye of our understondyng (lii/19)

(8) he portraied it with his blissid face, which is the fairhed of heavyn, flowre of erth, & the fruite of the mayden wombe (x/46-48)

(9) it is his wille ... that we holden us with him & festyn us to him homley (lxxvi/28-29)

(10) kind hath ben assayed in the fire of tribulation, & therin founden no lak, no defaut (lxiii/8-9)

(11) And al this browte our Lord sodenly to my mend & shewid these words & said, "I am ground of thi besekyng." (xli/10-12)

(12) we know not truly that our Lord is ground on whom our prayors springith (xlii/19-20)

(13) it is his holy church, he is the ground: he is the substance, he is the techyng, he is the techer, he is þe end, he is the mede, wherfor every kynd soule travellith (xxxiv/18-21)

(14) he [God] is ground on whom our soule stondith (lvi/13-14)

(15) for he is þe hede & we be his members (li/302-303)

(16) Criste whech is our keper (lii/34)

(17) he kydelyth our vnderstondyng (lxi/3)

(18) if God wil shew thee more he shal be thy light (x/12-13)

(19) the cler lyte of our reson (lv/16-17)

(20) Our Lord of his mercy shewith us our syn*n*e & our febilnes be the swete gracious lyte of hymselfe (lxxviii/1-2)

(21) Our feith is a light kindly com*m*and of our endles day þat is our fader God. In which light our Moder Criste & our good Lord the holy Gost ledith us in this passand life. This light is mesurid discretly, nedefully standand to us in the night. The light is cause of our lif; þe night is cause of our peyne & of al our wo, in which we deserven mede & thanks of God. For we with mercy & grace wil fuly knowen & leven our light, goand therin wisely & mytyly. And at the end of wo sodenly our eye shall ben openyd, & in clerite of light our sight shall be full, which light is God our Maker & holy Gost in Christ Ihus our savior. Thus I saw & vnderstode that our feith is our light in our night, which light is God, our endless day. (lxxxiii/14-28)

(22) And thus should every soule thinkyn ineward of his lover [i.e., Christ] (lxv/20)

(23) the Trinite is our everlasting lover, everlasting joy & bliss (iv/12-13)

(24) seand that he [God] is our medecine (lxxii/15-16)

(25) to holy Church, into our Moder brest (lxii/27)

(26) For the foode of mercy that is his dereworthy blood & pretious water is plentious to make us faire & clene. The blissid wound of our savior ben open & enjoyen to helyn us; the swete gracious hands of our Moder be redy & diligently aboute us. For he in al this werkyng usith the office of a kinde nurse & hath not ell [= ellys] to don but to entendyn abouten the salvati*o*n of hir child (lxi/71-78)

(27) Syn*n*e is the sharpest scorge that any chousyn soule may be smyten with, which scorge al forbetyth man & woman & noyith him in his owne syte (xxxix/1-3)

(28) for in that ilk tyme that God knitted him [Christ] to our body in the maydens womb he toke our sensual soule, in which takyng, he us al haveyng onclosid in him, he onyd it to our substance (lvii/49-52)

(29) whan the soule is tempested, troublid, and left to hymself be onreste (xlii/34-35)

(30) For the thrist of God is to have the general man into him, in which thrist he hath drawin[20] his holy that be now in bliss &, gettand his

---

[20] Both Warrack and Hudleston use *drawn* here, and the Paris MS clearly has *drawyn*. Hudleston inserts *ones*: "he hath drawn his Holy [ones]". The Paris MS reads "he hath drawyn his holy soules". Sloane 2499 is difficult to read here, but it could be taken as "in which thrist he hath an win [,] his holy that be now in bliss". This reading, with *wine* and *holy* in apposition (the earliest entry in the *OED* for *holy* as a substantive is 1548), would provide an image of considerable merit. If the word is *drawin*, the *a* in the MS is so light as to be practically invisible, and the top of the *d* is missing. The intervening letter could be either *r* or *n*.

lively members, ever drawith & drinkith & yet he thristith & longith (lxxv/4-8)

(31) Christ is our wey (lv/1)

(32) than is prayer a wittnes þat þe soule will as God will (xlii/3-4)

(33) Than we can do no more but behold hym, enjoying with an hey myty desire to be al onyd into hym, centred to his wonyng [*dwelling*, Hudleston] & enjoy in hys lovyng & deliten in his goodness. (xliii/47-50)

(34) for in us is his homliest home & his endles wonyng (lxvii/13-14)

Although some of the examples (e.g., 21) in the preceding list are extended metaphors, Margery's figures generally are more fully drawn and more widely sustained. Where Julian's metaphors mainly are fleeting, Margery's seem more consciously developed. It is interesting to note, however, considerable evidence of a "common stock": some images similar to those of Julian and some recurring ones.

(1) þu thynkyst þi sowle so large & so wyde þat þu clepist al þe cowrt of Heuyn in-to þi sowle for to wolcomyn me (210/21-23) (cf. Julian's simile 22, above)

(2) my Lady, whech þat is only þe Modyr of God, þe welle of grace, flower & fairest of alle women (252/27-29) (cf. Julian's metaphor 8, above)

(3) þe fyr of loue encresyd in hir (209/8) (cf. Julian's metaphor 10)

(4) þe fyer of lofe kyndelyd so ȝern in hir hert (111/10) (cf. Julian's metaphors 10 and 17)

(5) And þan þis creatur, seyng alle þis aduersytes comyng on euery syde, thowt it weryn þe skowrges of owyr Lord þat wold chastyse hir for hir synne (11/4-7) (cf. Julian's metaphor 27)

(6) Than sche … sekyng socowr vndyr þe wengys of hyr gostly modyr, Holy cherch (2/16-18) (cf. Julian's metaphor 25)

(7) grawnt me a welle of teerys (81/19) (On this common figure, see Miss Allen's note to this passage.)

(8) grawnte me in þis lyfe a welle of teerys spryngyng plenteuowsly (249/1-2)

(9) þi terys arn awngelys drynk & it arn very pyment to hem (161/1-2) (Miss Allen's notes to this and the following passage discuss sources.)

(10) þu hast ȝouyn hem drynkyn ful many tymes wyth teerys of thyn eyne (52/4-5)

(11) sche meltyd al in-to teerys (124/38-39)

(12) a bittyr teer (100/3)

(13) hauyng gret merueyle of hir speche for it was fruteful (120/15-16)

(14) be purchasyng of vertu, whech is frute gostly (121/15-16)

(15) þu receyuyst þer þe frute of euyrlestyng lyfe, þe Sacrament of þe Awter, in ful febyl disposicyon (127/21-23)

(16) Lord Cryst Ihesu ... rauysched hir spyrt (16/31-32)

(17) hir mende was raueschyd in-to beholdyng of owr Lady (198/3-4)

(18) þan was þe mende so raueschyd in-to þe childhod of Crist (200/24-25)

(19) Sche was smet wyth þe dedly wownd of veynglory & felt it not (14/1-2)

(20) creatur, al wowndyd wyth pite & compassyon (167/19-20, 140/13)

(21) I thank þe for as many tymys as þu hast bathyd me in þi sowle at hom in þe chambre as þow I had be þer present in my Manhod (214/1-3)

(22) I have bowt þi lofe ful der (191/2-3)

(23) þei myth thorw hys grace be turnyd to þe feyth of Holy Chirche & ben children of saluacyon (141/3-4)

(24) for I turne þe erthe of her hertys vp-so-down & make hem sore a-feerd (182/30-31)

(25) I am an hyd God in þe (30/26-27) (For a discussion of the source, see Miss Allen's note to this passage. For the same idea in simile form, see 205/4.)

(26) to se þe lombe of jnnocencye so contemptibly be haldyn & drawyn wyth hys owyn pepil (190/4-5)

(27) I have ordeynd þe to be a merowr amongys hem for to han gret sorwe þat þei xulde takyn exampil by þe (186/13-15)

(28) þe nyght fel up-on hyr, & sche was ryth heuy, for sche was a-lone (236/25-26)

(29) lofe, dowtyr, quenchith al synne (49/9-10)

(30) desyryng to be refreschyd wyth sum crumme of gostly vndirstondyng (98/22-23)

(31) þer was a dyner of gret joy & gladnes, meche more gostly þan bodily, for it was sawcyd & sawryd wyth talys of Holy Scriptur (170/21-23)

(32) wher þat he [the devil] fyndyth us most freel þer be owyr Lordys sufferawns he leyth hys snar, whech may no man skape be hys owyn power. And so he leyd be-forn þis creatur þe snar of letchery (14/12-15)

(33) Sum religyows ... seyden, "þis woman hath sowyn meche good seed in Rome sithyn sche cam hydir" (99/9-11)

(34) euery good desyr þat þu hast in þi sowle is þe speche of God (205/1-2)

(35) Dowtyr, 3e sowkyn euyn on Cristys brest, and 3e han an ernest-peny of Heuyn (18/2-3)

(36) þu art my joye, Lord, my blysse, my comfort, & alle þe tresor þat I have in þis world (81/21-23)

(37) hys clothys wer al daggyd & hys langage al uanyte (222/32)

The other groups of figurative images — metonymy, personification, allegory, and symbolism — do not enter very heavily into the work of either mystic and, when they do occur, are generally traditional usages, perhaps recalled from sermons, that lack any freshness, originality, or much conscious effort. Metonymy is the most commonly found form of these remaining groups, but the changed names that this figure provides pertain to very limited subjects. Metonymy[21] is difficult to separate from metaphor in some cases, and in this sense is reminiscent of the kennings of earlier literature. Certain literary techniques tie medieval writings closely to Old English literature. The most obvious linking device — alliteration — will be discussed shortly. But the kennings, some of which were probably traditional long before *Beowulf*, also contributed much to a heritage of figurative language that provided "unlettered" people like Margery and Julian with a stock of — and a feeling for — the metaphors and similes previously mentioned. Metonymy, however, is apparently the device most clearly related to kennings, which Klaeber defines as "those picturesque circumlocutory words and phrases ... which, emphasizing a certain quality of a person or thing, are used in place of the plain, abstract designation".[22] A more recent study of *Beowulf* clearly states the dependence of Old English literature upon metaphor and metonymy and, in so doing, provides both a good definition of the latter and some pertinent comment concerning prose:

Among the simplices for almost any concept we may distinguish purely or primarily poetic words, and those which are as freely used in prose as

---

[21]   Donald Davidson's *American Composition and Rhetoric* (New York, Scribner's, 1959), p. 284, stresses the similarity between metonymy and synecdoche. Since these figures are so closely related, "metonymy" will be used as a general term that includes the figure of synecdoche. Davidson defines both figures as "forms of indirect statement in which a part of an object or some important association connected with the object is used to symbolize the object itself". G. Loane, in *A Short Handbook of Literary Terms* (London, George Allen & Unwin, 1923) pp. 107, 177, similarly includes synecdoche ("a part ... put for a whole", "the material for the thing made of it", "a passion for the object that inspires it") as a form of metonymy ("a change of name").

[22]   *Beowulf and the Fight at Finnsburg*, ed. Fr. Klaeber, 3rd ed. (Boston, Heath, 1950), p. lxiii.

in poetry and belong to the vocabulary of speech. Inevitably the language of poetry must draw more or less heavily upon that of speech. The purely poetic simplices very often — but by no means always — contain (or once contained, before their meaning faded) a metonymy or a metaphor: most frequently they designate the referent in terms of one of its aspects or functions, of its material, or of one of its essential qualities. Thus a ship may be called *flota*, a warrior *freca*, a shield *lind*, a spear *æsc*: the ship is designated in terms of its principal function, the shield and spear in terms of their materials, the warrior in terms of his ferocity in battle.[23]

The prose of Margery and Julian, containing the many examples of metaphor and simile cited a few pages earlier, can thus be described as being part of a tradition of English style — "The continuity of English writing", one might say — with Margery putting that tradition to work with greater effect. At this point it is interesting to note, in addition to the metaphorical and soon-to-be-made alliterative links with older literature, Klaeber's stress on the "trope of litotes", a device already discussed in connection with Margery's and Julian's use of understatement: the figure is "highly characteristic and much fancied by the *Beowulf* poet" (p. lxv). It is, perhaps, anticlimactic then to assert that the two medieval women make little creative use of the important early literary device of metonymy.

Metonymy, thus reduced to formulaic use by the two mystics, applies most often to the Deity and to emotions. God is referred to in terms of principal functions of creator and father: Julian thus says "the beholding & the lovyng of the Maker makith the soule to seeme lest in his owne sight" (vi/70-72) and refers to "our fader God" (lxxxiii/15). Similarly, Margery refers to "hir Makyr" (246/20-21, 71/7-8), "hir Redemptowr" (246/24), and "þe Fadyr of Hevyn" (39/16, 86/10). Some of the metaphors listed earlier could also be included here: Julian refers to the Deity in his function as "light", "lover", "techer", "medecine", "keper"; Margery refers to "þe lombe of jnnocencye" and to "my joye ... my blysse, my comfort, & alle þe tresor þat I have".[24] The use of the word "heart"

---

[23] Arthur G. Brodeur, *The Art of Beowulf* (Berkeley and Los Angeles, University of California Press, 1959), p. 14.

[24] Brodeur, pp. 250-252, discusses the differences among three similar Old

to signify the emotions that supposedly reside there, is also a Scriptural commonplace used by both writers. Particularly in Julian is the formulaic use apparent:

(1) he lighteth our herte (lxi/5)
(2) And he will that our herts ben mytyly reysid (lxvii/41-42)
(3) We ben as homley with him as herte may thinke (lxxvii/55-60)
(4) there are thei made more swete & delectable than herte may thynken or tongue may tellen (xlix/56-57) (for this commonplace, cf. Margery's first example below)
(5) more nere to us than tongue can tellen or herte can thynken (lxxii/30)
(6) in all þe peyne that herte can thyke [*sic*] & tongue may tell (lxxii/53-54)

Margery:

(1) Whech non eye may se, ne eer heryn, ne tunge telle, ne non hert thynkyn (53/4-5)
(2) sche thankyd God wyth al hir hert (67/17-18)
(3) Ser, þis tale smytyth me to þe hert (127/37-38)
(4) assayn ȝyf he myth mekyn hys hert (150/37-38)
(5) … thynk alwey þat I sitte in þin hert (184/12-13)
(6) hir hert was so ful of heuynes (195/5)
(7) hir hert was drawyn a-wey fro þe seying & set mech on meditacyon (216/9-10)
(8) ȝeuyn me al thyn hool hert wyth alle thyn affeccyonis (218/31-32)

Further examples of metonymy occur in other statements where the part represents the whole. Julian gives us "a synfull creture liveing in wretched flesh" (iv/18-20), "treasured & hid in his blissid breast" (xxxii/36), and, straight out of the Book of Job xxv.11, "þe pillers of hevyn shall tremelyn & quakyn" (lxxv/32). Margery provides "sche hungryd ryth sor aftyr Goddys word" (142/15), "sor

---

Norse figures: kennings, *kend heiti*, and *viðkenning*, Briefly the distinctions are these: the kenning "identifies the referent with something which it is not" ("battle-adder" for "arrow" or "javelin"); *kend heiti* "identify the referent as something which it is" ("wave traverser" for "ship"); the *viðkenning* (unlike, and not to be confused with, a kenning) stands for a name of a specific individual ("son of Ecgþēow" for "Beowulf"), and differs from the other two, which stand for concepts or for typical rather than individual features. The *viðkenning*, given the lowest standing in poetic quality, seems to be closest to the type of appellation used by Margery and Julian in the first examples given in the paragraph ("Makyr"); *kend heiti* could be used to describe the next group ("lover", etc.); *kenning*, the third ("lombe", "tresor").

dredyng þe voys of þe pepyl" (21/21), and "As hys name is now, it xal ben throwyn down & þin schal ben reysed up ... þu xalt be in cherch whan he xal be wyth-owtyn'" (156/22-23, God the speaker). Obviously, there is no attempt by either mystic to use metonymy as vigorously and effectively as a good *scop* would use the similar figure of the kenning.

The conscious rhetorical use of allegory, symbolism, and personification likewise is not outstanding in the works of Julian and Margery. Only a few noteworthy examples of allegory — or what comes close to it — occur in their writing. In her fifty-first chapter, the longest section of the entire book, Julian goes into great detail concerning an example that the Lord showed her of a Lord and a Servant. The Servant, sent to do the will of the Lord, is badly hurt and suffers seven great pains but endures them meekly, unable to help himself in any way. Throughout the Servant's difficulty, the Lord is watching him without blaming him. Julian is led to understand that the Servant's woe will be rewarded by great worship and endless bliss. The remainder of the chapter analyzes this example, and Julian takes pains to insure that the essential of allegory — "a second meaning to be read beneath and concurrent with the surface story"[25] — is made clear. The Servant she equates first with Adam (1. 118) and then with Christ's Manhood (1. 250). All details of the Lord-Servant example are then equated with details of the God-Adam-Jesus relationship. The tautness with which the details are tied is striking, even if the overall comparison is not. Even in this one example we do not have "pure" allegory: Julian's careful explanation of the "second meaning" removes the section to the status of mixed allegory.[26]

Close in subject matter to the above example is a shorter passage that belongs to an allegory-symbolism discussion:

he [God] shewid this opyn example. It is the most worshippe that a solemne King or a grete Lord may doe a pore servant if he will be homely with him & namely if he shewith it himselfe of a full trew meneing & with a glad cheere, both prive & partie. Than thinkyth this pore

[25] Joseph T. Shipley, ed., *Dictionary of World Literature* (New York, Philosophical Library, 1943), p. 21.
[26] *Ibid.*

creature thus: "A, what might this nobil Lord doe more worship & joy to me than to shew me that arn so simple this mervelous homlyhede? Sothly it is more joy & likeing to me than he gave me grete gifts & were himselfe strange in maner." (vii/34-44)

Julian provides another instance of the carefully explained allegory:

And in this tyme I saw a body lyand in the erth, which body shewid hevy & oggley without shappe & forme as it were a bolned quave of styngand myre, & sodenly out of this body sprang a ful faire creature, a little childe, full shapen & formid, swifie & lively, whiter than lilly, which sharpely glode up on to hevyn. And the bolnehede of the body betoken-ith gret wretchidnes of our dedly flesh, & the littlehede of the child betokenith þe clenes of purity in þe soule (lxiv/31-39)

Similarly, Margery tells a story to the Archbishop of York and then goes on to explain it:

"Sir, wyth ȝowr reuerens, I spak but of o preste be þe maner of exampyl, þe whech as I haue lernyd went wil in a wode thorw þe sufferawns of God for þe profite of hys sowle tyl þe nyght cam upon hym. He, destytute of hys herborwe, fond a fayr erber in þe whech he restyd þat nyght, hauyng a fayr pertre in þe myddys al floreschyd wyth flowerys & belschyd, and blomys ful delectabil to hys syght, wher cam a bere, gret & boistows, hogely to beheldyn, schakyng þe pertre & fellyng down þe flowerys. Gredily þis greuows best ete & deuowryd þo fayr flowerys. &, whan he had etyn hem, turnyng hys tayl-ende in þe prestys presens, voydyd hem owt ageyn at þe hymyr [Meech: "probably a miswriting of hyndyr"] party. Þe preste, hauyng gret abhominacyon of þat lothly syght, conceyuyng gret heuynes for dowte what it myth mene, on þe next day he wandrid forth in hys wey al heuy & pensife, whom it fortunyd to metyn wyth a semly agydd man lych to a palmyr er a pilgrime, þe whiche enqwiryd of þe preste þe cawse of hys heuynes. The preste, rehersyng þe mater be-forn-wretyn, seyd he conceyuyd gret drede & heuynes whan he beheld þat lothly best defowlyn & deuowryn so fayr flowerys & blomys & aftirward so horrybely to deuoydyn hem be-for hym at hys tayl-ende, & he not vndirstondyng what þis myth mene. Than þe palmyr, schewyng hym-selfe þe massanger of God, þus aresond hym, 'Preste, þu þi-self art þe pertre, sumdel florischyng & floweryng thorw þi Seruyse seyyng & þe Sacramentys ministryng, thow þu do vndeuowtly, for þu takyst ful lytyl heede how þu seyst þi Mateynes & þi Seruyse, so it be blaberyd to an ende. Þan gost þu to þi Messe wyth-owtyn deuocyon, & for þi synne hast þu ful lityl contricyon. Þu rece-yuyst þer þe frute of euyrlestyng lyfe, þe Sacrament of þe Awter, in ful febyl disposicyon. Sithyn al þe day aftyr þu myssespendist þi tyme, þu

ʒeuist þe to bying & sellyng, choppyng & chongyng, as it wer a man of
þe werld. Þu sittyst at þe ale, ʒeuyng þe to glotonye & excesse, to lust
of thy body, thorw letchery & vnclennesse. Þu brekyst þe comawndmentys of God thorw sweryng, lying, detraccyon, & bakbytyng, &
swech oþer synnes vsyng. Thus be thy mysgouernawns, lych on-to þe
lothly ber, þu deuowryst & destroist þe flowerys & blomys of vertuows
leuyng to thyn endles dampnacyon & many mannys hyndryng lesse þan
þu haue grace of repentawns & amendyng.'" Þan þe Erchebisschop
likyd wel þe tale & comendyd it, seying it was a good tale (126/24-127/35)

Any allegory of course includes a type of symbolism[27]: one element
stands for, or symbolizes, something else. Thus the Servant in
Julian's fifty-first chapter symbolizes Adam-Christ's manhood relationship to the Lord (God). The A=B equation basic to allegory
also appears in briefer symbolic form. Margery, in Capitulum 86,
tells of a conversation with Christ in which He tells her that in her
soul she thinks as though she had cushions of cloth of gold, red
velvet, and white silk. The gold cushion is for the Father and
represents might and power. Jesus, the Second Person, sits on the
red cushion, symbolic of the red blood He shed. The Holy Ghost
sits upon the white silk cushion, which represents love and clean-
ness, the giving of all holy thoughts and chastity. Margery's
desire for "þe mantyl & þe ryng & clothyn me al in whygth clothys"

[27] In his *The Allegory of Love* (New York, Oxford-Galaxy, 1936, 1958), C. S.
Lewis carefully distinguishes between allegory and symbolism: allegory is the
inventing of *visibilia* to express immaterial facts; symbolism is the use of the
material, "real" world to see the "invisible world" that it copies (pp. 44-45).
A similar distinction is made by S. Barnet, M. Berman, W. Burto, in *A Dictionary of Literary Terms* (Boston, Little, Brown & Co., 1960), pp. 84-85: while
an allegory makes use of an invented world in order to talk about the real
world, "the symbolist commonly presents the phenomena of what we usually
call the real world ... to reveal a 'higher' eternal world of which the symbol is
a part". A proper symbol, accordingly, must be *"part of something else* and
is itself too", in addition to standing for something else. The editors admit,
however, a growing tendency to blur the distinction between allegory and
symbolism. Lewis (p. 45) states that the two are "closely intertwined", but
further distinguishes symbolism as "a mode of thought" and allegory as "a mode
of expression" (p. 48). According to Lewis, then, much of Julian's analytical
mode of thought concerning her revelations could be called "symbolic" in the
sense that she constantly interprets her experiences as symbols of God and
His goodness. Within the scope of my study, however, I am applying the terms
to prose style, to "mode of expression", in which the author invents a figure to
convey meaning more effectively, and not to "mode of thought", which, in
Julian's case, is really an expression of belief in her (non-invented) experiences.

(34/10-12) involves symbolic objects common in the religious life
of the times. Similarly, God speaks to Margery of a symbolic
action: "'And, dowtyr, þu hast an hayr vp-on þi bakke. I wyl þu
do it a-way, & I schal ʒive þe an hayr in þin hert þat schal lyke me
mych bettyr þan alle þe hayres in þe world'" (17/6-9).

Julian's use of symbolism may be illustrated by several passages.[28]
"I saw God in a Point" (xi/1), already mentioned in the discussion
of understatement, is clearly a symbolic statement, and, at the
same time, a paradox with the tininess of a created object standing
for the incomprehensible force that created it. Also symbolic is
Julian's statement concerning the Passion: "For I saw in Criste a
doble threst — one bodely, another gostly" (xvii/3-4). In a longer
passage, Christ's wound is described symbolically:

Than with a glad chere our Lord loked into his syde & beheld, enjoyand,
& with his swete lokyng he led forth the understondyng of his creture
be the same wound into his syde withinne. And than he shewid a faire
delectabil place & large enow for al mankynd that shal be save to resten
in pece & in love (xxiv/1-6)

Similar to the expression of "God in a Point" is a longer passage
which again symbolically illustrates the idea of littleness representing greatness:

Also in this he showed a littil thing, the quantity of an hesil nutt in the
palme of my hand & it was as round as a balle. I lokid thereupon with
eye of my understandyng & thoute, "What may this be?" And it was
generally answered thus: "It is all that is made." I mervellid how it
might lesten, for me thoute it might suddenly have fallen to nowte for
littil. And I was answered in my understondyng, "It lasteth & ever shall
for God loveth it." And so all thing hath the being be the love of God.
   In this litil thing I saw iij properties. The first is that God made it;
þe second is that God loveth it; the iij þat God kepith it (v/8-19)

As in the case of allegory, the explanation of what is being represented is stressed by both Margery and Julian in most of their
uses of symbols. Although today, perhaps largely because of the
influence of modern poetry and art, such bald explication might be
decried as the ruination of symbolism, the medieval mystics, in a

---

[28]   It is interesting to note how well Julian's symbols fit the idea of symbolism
as "part of something else".

time of general illiteracy, would naturally explain their symbols. Jesus spoke in parables, and if today on television ministers must explain the meaning behind these parables to a literate audience that supposedly could study sources for themselves, so much more the medieval writer, particularly one of Julian's analytical character, would be inclined to clarify, to explain all meanings for the edification of the uninitiated reader — or, more important, *listener* — who had not himself experienced the effects of mystic communion with God.

Personification — the attribution of human characteristics to inanimate objects, non-human organisms, or abstract ideas — is the least used of all the figurative devices, and even some of the uses suggested here are questionable. What of the soul for example? If the soul is generally considered as different from the physical body, then such statements as Margery's "My sowle is euyr a-lych hungry"[29] (142/20-21) and Julian's "the eye of the soule" (lxxvi/17) may be called personifications. More definite are Margery's "had þe myghty hand of owr Lordys mercy not withstande hys [the Devil's] gret malyce" (201/21-22) and "þan was pompe & pryde cast down & leyd on syde" (2/12-13). Julian invests abstract ideas with human characteristics in "Treuth seith God & wisedam beholdyth God" (xliv/8) and "Love & drede are brethren" (lxxiv/22); she also combines metonymy with personification: "whan the herte is drey & felyth not or ell be temptation of our enemy, than it is dreven by reason & be grace to crye upon our Lord with voyce, rehersyng his blissid passion & his gret goodness" (xli/69-72).

What appears to govern both Margery Kempe and Julian of Norwich in their word choice and in their use of figurative imagery is, first, their own characters. Both supposedly illiterate, they would be expected to use words that would be in general use during their times, especially those heard in church, and generally they do so. Figures of speech, also expectedly, are generally trite, or superficial and lacking in vigor; they are mostly non-contrived, belonging rather to natural expression. But experience, a second factor governing their writing, causes the more worldly Margery in

---

[29] As always, the omnipresence of Scriptural influence must be remembered. Cf. Psalm cvii. 9, Proverbs xxvii.7.

particular to produce some vivid and striking images, especially those concerned with nature. Julian, with her contemplative character and experience, is noteworthy for detailed treatment in both word choice and imagery. Finally, the audience of their day being generally illiterate, there is a striving for clarity and detail, particularly in both mystics' treatment of images with double meanings.

Images generally are taken to apply to the senses of sight, touch, taste, smell, and sound. The sense of sound is used in the works of both mystics beyond its involvement in figurative imagery. Elements of sound are important in their own right, both historically and qualitatively. Of great importance historically is one of the most obvious devices of both Margery and Julian — alliteration. But before a lengthy discussion of alliteration, and its cousins assonance and consonance, another device of sound merits attention. Examples of rhyme appear in both works, and, although almost any one example could be said to be accidental ,the number of examples involved is striking. Since, in another chapter, we shall see that rhythm and balance are two of the important elements in the syntax of both writers, the use of an occasional rhyme might be considered to add further to a type of poetic prose. Although rhyme does not appear frequently enough to give any sustained feeling that the authors are using it to be poetic, it does seem to appear at critical moments for emphasis or for special effect. Like alliteration, similes, metaphors, and metonymy some rhymed phrases give evidence of the survival of Old English literary traditions.[30] Julian's "wide & syde" (li/142, 360-361; Hudleston substitutes "loose and long"), where "syde" is a survival of the OE adjective meaning "large" or "broad", is an example of the stereotyped half-line frequent in *Genesis*, *Exodus*, *Andreas*, and other poems. Similarly, Margery's "sum crumme" (98/22) is much like the consecutive rhyme seen in OE "wordhord" (*Beowulf* 259, *Widsith* 1) "mōde frōd" (*Beowulf* 1844) and "foldbold" (*Beowulf*

---

[30] "Rime Before the Norman Conquest", an unpublished study sheet by Professor Roland M. Smith, shows that "rime is found as early as *Beowulf* and is far from rare in the later OE period". The study sheet provides the basis for the following specific examples in my text.

773). In some of the following examples, to heighten the rhyming effect, I have taken the liberty of breaking lines to achieve end-rhyme.

Julian:

(1) as ye shall se (vi/69)
(2) teaching & preching (x/57) (Inverted xxiv/14-15, xxxiv/17-18)
(3) prechyth & teachyth (xxvi/10-11)
(4) prechith the & techith the (lx/41)
(5) with might & ryght (xiii/22)
(6) shal be browte to nought[31] (xv/46-47)
(7) may we sey (xxx/11)
(8) plese hym & ese our selfe (xxx/20)
(9) owen to knowen (li/168)
(10) wide & syde (li/142, 360-361)
(11) gronyng & monyng (li/346, 357)
(12) nedefull & spedefull (liii/27)
(13) And this drede we taken sumtime for a mekenes, but this is a foule blyndhed & a waykenes (lxxiii/46-47)

Margery:

(1) þan was pomp & pryde[32]
    cast down & leyd on syde (2/12-13)
(2) "þan xalt þu blysse the tyme þat þu wer wrowte
    & þe body þat þe hath bowte" (52/7-8) (The Lord is the speaker.)
(3) gold ... whech may spede
    in euery nede,[33]
    & þat is rewth
    þat mede
    xuld spede
    er þan trewth (59/15-16)

(4) "þerfor, Lord, now wyl I lyn stille
    & be buxom to þi wille;[34]
    I pray þe, Lord, speke in me

---

[31] Chaucer frequently rhymes *bro(u)ght[e* with *no(u)ght[e* (e.g., *Monk T* 3614, *Sum T* 2022, *Fkl T* 1273, *SNT* 393). Pronunciation, not unstandardized spelling, is what matters.
[32] Common alliteration, as in *Religious Lyrics of the Fourteenth Century*, ed. Carleton Brown (Oxford, Clarendon Press, 1924), p. 194, l. 18.
[33] Compare Julian's "nedefull & spedefull" (liii/27). R. M. Wilson, "Three English Mystics", *Essays and Studies 1956*, n.s. 9, p. 108, lists this passage as a proverb.
[34] Note the reappearance of this frequent expression in Margery's example 6.

what þat is most plesawns to þe"
(146/31-34) (Margery is the speaker.)

(5) "'Lord, for alle þi wowndys smert,
drawe al þe lofe of myn hert into thyn hert'"[35]
(161/18-20, 217/6-7) (The Lord is telling Margery what she might
have cried to him.)

(6) "I xal make þe buxom to my wil
þat þu xalt cryin whan I wil,
& wher I wil,
bothyn lowde & stylle,
for I teld þe, dowtyr,
þu art myn
& I am thyn,
& so xalt þu be wyth-owtyn ende" (182/8-11)
(The Lord is the speaker of this noticeably rhythmic passage.)

(7) "Der Modyr, my peyne is al a-goo,
& now xal I leuyn for euyr-mo" (196/31-32)
(The Lord is speaking to Mary on the third day after burial.)[36]

A number of examples of rhyme involve the same words: "me",
"þe", "be".

(1) "Dowtyr, why hast þow forsakyn me,
and I forsoke neuyr þe?" (8/20-21)
(The Lord is the speaker).

---

[35] In a note on this passage, Miss Allen calls attention to the same couplet at
217/6 and 249/30 and mentions parallels to the figure in other works, but both
she and Professor Meech appear to have missed the closest source. The
couplet appears in a work by Richard Castyr [or Caister], who is mentioned
frequently in the *Book* and is discussed in Meech's note on 38/12. In this note,
Professor Meech refers to the wide currency of Castryr's "lovely English hymn
'Ihesu lord þat madist me'". In the third stanza of this hymn appears "Iesu for
þi woundes smerte / Of feet, & side, of hondes two / Thou make me meek and
low of herte". My quotation is from W. W. Skeat's normalized version of the
text, which appears in Rev. Dundas Harford's "Richard of Caister, and his
Metrical Prayer", *Norfolk and Norwich Archæological Soc.*, xvii (1910), 224-225.
I am grateful to Professor Roland M. Smith for the use of his copy of this
article. A version of the hymn also appears in Carleton Brown's *Religious
Lyrics of the Fifteenth Century* (Oxford, Clarendon Press, 1939), pp. 98-100,
with the couplet in the second stanza.

[36] In a note to the passage of which this entry is a part, Miss Allen mentions
that both Margery and Nicholas Love, whose work on the Passion Margery
probably knew (note to 187/19 *sq.*, although Allen notes "no coincidences in
vocabulary or otherwise"), contradict Mark xvi. 9 by having Jesus appear first
to the Virgin rather than to Mary Magdalene. The couplet does not appear in
the passage from Mark.

(2) "takyn þe a-wey fro me" (77/10-11) (The speaker is Richard, Margery's escort to Rome.)

(3) "far fayr wyth me,
  & I xal far fayr wyth the,
  for þu xalt etyn wyth me
  þis day" (109/30-31)
  (The Bishop of Worcester is speaking to Margery.)

(4) "ne to sweryn be me
  but ȝyf it be
  a gret peyne to þe" (160/20-21)
  (The Lord is the speaker.)

(5) "Take a-wey
  þis peyn from me,
  for I may
  not beryn it.
  þi Passyon wil sle
  me" (164/26-27)
  (Margery prays to the Lord).

(6) "in al þis werld was neuyr so gret an enmye to me
  as I have ben to þe" (183/35-184/1)
  (Margery speaks to the Lord.)

(7) "Lord Ihesu, blissyd mote þu be,
  for þis deseruyd I neuyr of þe" (214/20-21)
  (Margery is the speaker.)

(8) "for to dredyn þe in me
  & for to louyn þe in me" (249/31-32)
  (From Margery's Prayers.)

In some cases rhyme words occur too close to each other to be broken into lines: "sum crumme" (98/22); "ij hundryd ȝer befor & mor" (60/15); "neuyr ete mete tyl I wete" (38/27). Margery, like Julian, also has rhyming pairs of words joined directly by a conjunction: "smytyn & bityn" (178/3); "al helth & al welth" (251/33); "prechyng & techyng" (48/18-19; 53/15); "preche þe & teche þe" (98/26); "to knowyn & to trowyn" (249/19); "al-to-raggyd & al-to daggyd" (109/11).

Inexact or questionable rhyme appears in Margery's work in examples such as "God to louyn a-boue" (249/27); "I schal not sesyn whan I may wepyn" (142/4); and "þe frer wyth gret preyer was leyd in a berne" (240/40, where assonance, at least, is involved). She, like Julian with "fulhede ... fairhede ... goodhede" (lxii/21-22), also makes use of identical unstressed suffixes, as in "sobbyn ryth boistowsly & wepyn ful plentyowsly" (233/34-5), but one suffix in particular is used repeatedly:

(1) in deuocyon of holy medytacyon of hy contemplacyon (2/31)
(2) hey medytacyon and very [= true] contemplacyon (17/30-31)
(3) put in hir sowle of compunccyon, contricyon, swetnesse & devocyon, compassyon wyth holy meditacyon & hy contemplacyon (42/10-12)
(4) terys of contrisyon, deuosyon, er compassyon (42/37)
(5) hir meditacyon & hir contemplacyon (209/10-11)
(6) gret deuocyon & ful hy contemplacyon. Sche had plentivows teerys of compunccyon & of compassyon (245/34-36)

One example is particularly interesting in its blend of "pure" rhyme, "suffix" rhyme, alliteration, and balance of post-noun adjectives:

> he was an amyabyl persone,
> fayr feturyd, wel faueryd
> in cher & in cuntenawns,
> sad in hys langage and dalyawns,
> prestly in hys gestur
> & vestur (56/5-8)

In general, rhyme appears more strikingly in Margery's work than it does in Julian's. Noticeable especially in Margery's "pure" examples is the common occurrence of these rhymes in passages involving speeches to or by God. That the majority of these examples appear at moments of religious exaltation or stress seems to be more than coincidence: an attempt at a heightened style may be the answer.

IV

STYLE: ALLITERATION

Of all the devices used by the two mystics, alliteration is the most obvious. Little research has been conducted on alliteration in prose; when one begins to explore such a topic, the words of R. W. Chambers become newly meaningful: "we realize how much still remains to be done in the history of English prose and of English thought".[1] In this study, Chambers traces some of the elements of alliteration that indicate at least partially the reasons for widespread use in the times of Julian and Margery. In 1066 "there was still good command of the old technique of alliterative verse" (p. lxvi). Although alliterative poetry declined until the fourteenth century, when a strong revival occurred, alliteration must have been strong in the spoken language or "it could never have emerged in this way" (p. lxvii). This oral tradition could have had great influence on the supposedly illiterate female mystics and their works. Chambers stresses (pp. lxvii-lxviii) the importance of this tradition to the continuity of English literature:

There can be few stranger things in the history of literature than this sudden disappearance and reappearance of a school of poetry. It was kept alive by oral tradition through nine generations, appearing in writing very rarely, and then usually in a corrupt form, till it suddenly came forth, correct, vigorous, and bearing with it a whole tide of national feeling. Two of our three greatest Middle English poets are alliterative poets. And though alliterative verse died out after a century and a half, with the poem on the battle of Flodden, it had nevertheless endured into the Tudor age, and had formed a link between Old England and Modern England.

[1] R. W. Chambers, *On the Continuity of English Prose*, EETS 191A (London, Oxford University Press, 1957), p. c.

All of which shows how little the absence of documents for some particular type of literature at some particular date justifies us in denying its existence, and asserting a break in continuity. We are therefore not justified in asserting such a break in the continuity of English poetry, and in then extending to prose also, by analogy, this alleged break. On the contrary, the history of alliterative verse shows that continuity is demonstrable, despite the paucity of documents for the generations immediately before and after the Norman Conquest.

Later, Chambers asserts that the purpose of his essay is to maintain that the English prose of the fourteenth century is *not* a new thing, "but that the old prose of Alfred and AElfric, despite evil days, had nevertheless lived on, to find a new future opening before it in the Fifteenth Century" (p. xc). This continuity of English prose, he maintains, is to be found in every kind of devotional writing.

The writings of Margery and Julian admirably meet Chambers' criteria for prose that acted as a link between eras. Their prose is devotional; it is part of a tradition of woman-centered writing in English, for female recluses (p. xciii) and *by* anchoresses (p. ci); they wrote in Norfolk, which "seems to have led the way in the civic revival of English" (note, p. cxi). That both mystics make considerable use of alliteration would seem to be another point in their favor as links in prose continuity, for as we have seen, Chambers stresses the importance of alliteration in the oral tradition. At first glance, then, it might be surprising to realize that Chambers subordinates the role of alliteration in later prose. He gives only grudging approval to it as well as to another characteristic of both mystics: "More, like Ascham after him, does not eschew alliteration or the duplication of words. But these things are not allowed to become literary mannerisms. They are not used unless 'the matters do rise' in such a way as to permit of them" (p. cxx).[2] It might appear that Chambers is overlooking a ready-made device to stress continuity in English writing. But his purpose is twofold: he wants to show the continuity, but he also wants to stress the high quality of early prose. The best early prose had been characterized by simple lucidity and strength (p. cxv); excessive embel-

---

[2] Chambers is referring to More's "school" here and does not imply that works such as *Euphues* are free of "literary mannerisms".

lishment, too much "rhetoric", would be inefficient, affected, contrary to the early ideals. Chambers of course realizes the dichotomy: "pompous tautology", "an English ... trying to assert its dignity by 'augmenting itself'", as opposed to "an English which, while not despising ornament or eschewing the coupling together of synonyms, never makes that excessive use of tricks which marks those who seek to enrich the English language" (p. cxxii). Yet in Chambers' culminating example, there is praise for devices which are dominant elements in both Margery's and Julian's works: "It is from this homiletic tradition that [Thomas] More sometimes borrows the tricks of balanced sentences, many of which can be scanned as rough alliterative lines" (p. cxxiv). The point that Chambers makes is proper: excess most certainly does weaken writing. The problem, of course, is to determine exactly when a device becomes overused. But the use of alliteration in prose clearly has historical importance and sanction; and whether or not it is excessive in the work of Julian and Margery is significant in an examination of their styles.

Alliteration generally has been studied in its relationship to poetry. The alliterative revival referred to by Chambers has drawn the lion's share of scholarly attention to poetry rather than prose — with some justification. When one thinks of Old English literature, it is the alliterative *Beowulf* that immediately comes to mind. Admittedly, in Middle English writings, poems of the alliterative revival are generally more enjoyable, more popular, more valued as literature than the primarily religious, frequently didactic, prose of the period. Continuity of poetry also is more readily apparent, and such scholars as Oakden[3] and Schipper[4] have explored the poetic tradition in terms of alliteration and metrics. Prose, however, does not lend itself to statistical analysis as does poetry with its divisions into lines, beats, feet, or measures. A recent work[5] has studied intensively the alliteration in Middle English lyrics and

[3] J. P. Oakden, *Alliterative Poetry in Middle English*, I, II (Manchester, University Press, 1935).
[4] Jakob Schipper, *A History of English Versification* (Oxford, Clarendon Press, 1910).
[5] Merle Fifield, "Alliteration in the Middle English Lyrics", unpub. dissertation (University of Illinois, 1960).

makes use of the ready-made division inherent in poetry to com-
pile frequency charts according to lines. Prose, lacking such carefully
measured units, is another thing entirely. Probably some exact
measurement could be made in prose as in poetry, perhaps in terms
of lines, or sentences, or even phrases. But prose also lacks the
restrictive traditions of such alliteration as is found in Old English
poetry with its four-beat line in which at least two, and usually
three, of the four accented syllables alliterate. In prose, then,
alliteration is bound to be erratic; according to Chambers, anything
more regular would be a flaw, a defect in the style. I have made no
attempt to formulate frequency charts for alliteration in the prose
of Margery and Julian; to do so might actually be misleading,
for very frequently alliteration will occur heavily in one or two
lines of prose (perhaps involving two or more alliterating sounds)
and then disappear for a half page or more. Most readers will, I
feel, nevertheless be struck by an alliterative "flavor" in the mystics'
writing, especially in that of Margery.

Alliteration may be considered as falling into three classifications.
In its commonest sense, it is usually defined as repeated initial consonants of *stressed* syllables. It is this type that is basic to Old
English alliterative verse: "Bēowulf was brēme — blǣd wīde
sprang" (*Beowulf*, 1. 18). However, in this poetry initial vowel
sounds, when stressed, also were considered alliterative although
involving different vowels: "īsig ond ūtfūs, æþelinges faer" (*Beowulf*,
1. 33). By the time of Julian and Margery these stressed initial
vowel sounds occur in some passages along with similar *non-
stressed* or non-initial vowel sounds as in Margery's "onyment þat
þei myth a-noyntyn" (196/18); perhaps "assonance-alliteration"
or "eye-alliteration" would be useful terms here to describe such
mixed constructions. Similarly a number of unstressed syllables,
especially prefixes, will involve initial consonants that match
those of *stressed* syllables as in Margery's "comfort of any confessowr" (44/10-11) or "beholdyn þi blisful body" (249/29).[6] Although
there is some breakdown of the older tradition in both this "con-

---

[6]   As an illustration of similar use, this last example may be compared to
Margery's "þi blisse and þe beholdyng" (249/11-12) and Julian's "beholding
the body plentiously bleding" (xii/1) and "begynning myn beholding" (li/108).

sonance-alliteration" and the "assonance-alliteration", such elements justify inclusion under alliteration on the basis of both sight
and sound.[7] Probably Margery and Julian are here the recipients
of an oral tradition: they were not necessarily the ones who were
"consciously" repeating sounds. But the problem of where personal
creativity begins and where older tradition leaves off (and, it must
be added, where amanuenses inject *their* influence) is extremely
difficult. Certainly the possibility of conscious effort, especially
by Margery, exists.

In Appendix C, an extensive alphabetical listing illustrates the
wide use of alliteration in the works of Margery and Julian. In
addition to alphabetical listing, however, examples of alliteration
fall into structural classifications that have drawn little comment.
In attempting to find some order in the sea of alliterative examples
provided by medieval authors, I found that most passages involving
only a few alliterating words were of three types. In the following
discussion of these types I wish to make it clear that the examples
given do not provide a complete listing. Using only Margery as
a source, because of her ready availability, a non-intensive investi-
gation reveals the numerous examples given here. The fact that
such a number can be found from an overall, sweeping-type of
reading is significant. Study of the following lists will indicate
general lack of originality on Margery's part: many of the entries
are commonplaces, often traceable to Scriptural influence.

The first type involves paired words. The use of both alliterative
and non-alliterative pairs is common in Middle English writings,
and more will be said later about non-alliterative tautological pairs.
The history of such terms goes back farther than the Middle English
period, of course. In a discussion of stereotyped elements in *Beowulf*, Klaeber (lxvi) gives examples of "copulative alliterative
phrases", such as *ord ond ecg, mēaras ond mādmas, word ond weorc*.
In Margery's work, too, a number of alliterating pairs appear to be
used as formulas, making Chambers' idea of continuity in English
writing even more striking. Although representing a non-exhaustive
study, and alphabetized to prevent undue repetition, the following

---

[7]   Appendix A gives examples of what may be called "pure" consonance and
assonance.

examples may provide the reader with an idea of the total alliterative impression built up by Margery's *Book*.

a-for-noon & aftyr-noon (27/21-22)
bareyn & bare (2/12)
bar-foot & bar-legge (179/8-9)
begotyn & born (103/9-10)
betyng hym & bofetyng hym in þe heuyd & bobyng hym beforn hys
    swete mowth, criyng ful cruelly (190/8-9) (*h* and *c* alliteration also)
þi blisse & þe beholdyng (249/11-12)
bowndyn & beholdyn (231/28-29)
brokyn & bresyd (179/11)
buxom & bonyr (87/20)
cam & comfortyd (77/29)
cawse ne occasyon (181/22)
charite & chastite (121/7-8, 207/13-14)
hys cher & hys charyte (22/5)
cheryd & cherisched (93/32)
in chirche & in hir chawmbre (88/12)
clepyd & kallyd (11/3)
clothys & kerchys (19/14)
come & kyssyn (190/1)
comyn a-geyn & comfortyn (196/8-9)
conselyd & curyd (12/25)
continent & clene (114/14-15)
her craft & her cunnyng (229/21)
dampnyd or departyd (91/28)
ne drynke ne dalyawns (199/27)
þe felyng of grace & þe feruowr of deuocyon (205/19)
feynt & feble (38/11)
folwyn þeraftyr & fulfyllyn (24/33)
gret grace & gladnesse (19/1)
grace & goodnes (25/3, 48/13, 156/25, 159/4, 208/18)
gresly & grevows (70/15, 101/25)
of þe haburion or of þe hayr (89/20-21)
neiþer herrowr ne heresy (134/23)
hir hevyd & hir hodys (9/14)
heyl & hoyl (104/37)
hurte hym ne harmyn hym (233/25)
so hy & so holy (50/13, 72/3, 230/21) (inverted 201/34)
neuyr kyd ne knowyn (244/10)
ful grete languryng & ful gret longyng (185/36)
lofe ne lakkyng (173/21)
lofe & leue (57/11, 225/27-28, 240/6)

her lust & her likyng (179/33)
thorw hys mercy & be what menys (224/11)
mercy & gremercy (41/12)
for meryte & for mede (72/32-33) (Inverted, 48/32-33, 72/34-35)
merueyl & myracle (234/17-18)
mynde & meditacyon (203/13-14)
myrthe & melodye (51/32)
of on & of oþer (45/2)
pety & compassyon (1/18, 48/14, 153/8)
pur pyte & compassyon (70/22)
peyn(es) & passyon(s) (75/26, 138/20-21, 245/36-37)
peyn & ponyschyng (54/35)
compleynt & compassyon (222/33)
pomp & pryde (2/12-13)
of compunccyon & of compassyon (245/35)
redily & resonabely (113/9-10)
so sadly & streitly (192/1)
no sauowr ne swetnesse (199/34)
schakyd & schoderyd (192/37)
schrewdly & shortly (9/19-20)
scorne & slawndrys (107/22)
vn-sekyr & vncerteyn (55/9)
slawndyr & speche (51/15)
slory & slugge (184/22)
smale & softe (183/6)
sobbyngys & syhyngys (11/21-22)
softly & stilly (139/31)
sorwe & sadnes (94/14)
sothfast & sekyr (60/16-17)
mor sotyl & mor softe (209/13)
special & synguler (168/33)
speryd & spyid (242/2-3)
spred & sprong (148/30)
stabyl & stedfast (42/29)
stabely & stedfastly (215/3)
hir staffe & hir scryppe (118/13)
was stille & suffyrd (244/25)
swet & acceptabil (186/25)
swownyd & lay stille (191/23)
sor syhyng & sorwyng (167/7-8)
a syngular & a specyal (99/22)
trespasyd & takyn (222/33)
walwyd & wrestyd (68/13-14)
in wel ne in wo (17/21, 87/22)

what wyth wel & wyth woo (234/39)
þe wille & þe werkyng (229/8)
worthy & worschepful (3/21, 164/33)
wynde & wederyng (102/5-6)
wynde & wedyr (229/12-13)
ʒet but ʒong (87/12)

The second type of structural alliteration involves consecutive
words: alliterative words are not paired but rather follow one
another without any other word except an occasional article intervening. As was obvious in the preceding list also, this type of
alliteration occurs with words of various grammatical functions
within the sentence, and occasionally the alliterative sound extends
beyond the adjacent words. The examples of this type, many of
them trite commonplaces, are listed in Appendix B.

"Grammatical alliteration" is a fitting term for the third type of
structural alliteration. Not as obvious, perhaps, as either consecutive or paired-word alliteration, both of which depend upon position, the grammatical type involves a number of structural varieties,[8] the only link being grammatical function, and is actually more
numerous than the other types. Words that work together often
alliterate. In the list of examples here occurs alliteration between
groups like verb and noun, participle and noun, noun and verb,
noun and object of preposition modifying that noun. Objects, both
direct objects and objects of prepositions, are particularly noticeable
elements in this type and seem to point to a pattern of expression
that could easily become habitual and, eventually, stereotyped.
Present-day trite expressions offer a number of similar examples:
bolt from the blue, green as grass, busy as a bee, method in his
madness. A number of such formations seem to be stock expressions in Margery's time: "forsake hys synne" (23/5-6. Cf. Chaucer,
Phys 286), "sorwe in þe synne" (48/8-9, 208/15. Cf. Psalm xxxviii.
18), "Day of Dom" (51/12, 114/16-17), "saue hir sowle" (54/1,
158/33), "makyn ful mery" (54/24-25), "condemnyd to þe deth"
(71/2), "born of hir body" (101/4), "heuynes of her hertys" (130/37.

---

[8]   Phyllis Hodgson, in her edition of *Deonise Hid Diuinite*, EETS 231 (London,
Oxford University Press, 1955), p. li, lists nineteen grammatical combinations
of alliteration in *The Cloud of Unknowing* and other treatises. The number of
varieties indicates one of the difficulties in analyzing prose alliteration.

Cf. Psalm lxix. 20, Prov. xii. 25), "hom in-to Heuyn" (131/23, 158/3). Some other examples may be hackneyed specialized terms like the legal "put in ple" (59/9) or the common mystical expressions "flawme of fyer" (88/28, 163/20, 197/15, 200/35, 219/3) and "brennyng in hir brest" (88/31, 88/33-34, 219/3-4). The following listing has been sub-classified according to the parts of speech involved, the most frequent types coming first.

VERB (INCLUDING PARTICIPLES WHEN PART OF VERB PHRASE AND INFINITIVES) ... NOUN

browt forth a boke (126/16)
cam to þe creatur (5/14)
chongyd hir cher (78/35)
clad in white clothys (76/8)
clepist al þe cowrt (210/22)
excludyn al occasyon (168/17)
compleyned to þe creatur (5/23, 110/6)
comyn in hys contre (56/2-3)
comyn of worthy kenred (9/20)
cowde kepyn hir fro crying (70/20)
encresyd hir cryes (138/23)
inquired of þis creatur (22/13)
don in dede (204/7)
don hys diligence (53/14-15)
dowt it neuyr a deel (204/34)
dred no devylle (13/35)
drede þe not, dowtyr (22/37, 51/30, 62/33, 75/31, etc.)
dreuyn to deuelys (154/22)
durst for dred (32/29)
faylyd of hys fotyng & fel (179/9)
fel down at hys feet (197/20)
fulfilt in effect (80/8)
fled fro hys frendys (56/2)
fond no defawt (37/1, 131/33, 165/36, 222/15)
fond hir felyngys (75/32, 170/16)
informyd hir in hir feyth (39/21)
get I grace (193/37)
grawntyn hir grace (242/18)
haddyn gret help (59/13)
hast an hayr (17/6)

herd þe gret behestys (214/17)
howsyld hir wyth hys owyn handys (40/22)
languren in lofe (20/10)
leue þe lady (38/2-3)
louen ower Lord (3/17)
mad hys Mawnde (72/14-15, 115/15)
met wyth a monke (237/31-32)
metyn wyth þe at morwyn (77/22)
ministryd to hir mynde (208/19)
passyd many perellys (233/15)
supportyd be ȝowr preyers (41/18)
prechyn þin owyn persone (149/23)
preuyn hyr paciens (123/19)
preyed þe preste (57/6)
preyid þe pilgrimys þat weryn in þe wayne (239/39-40)
prophecyed in euery poynt (44/16-17)
purchasyn hir mor pardon (75/21-22)
put hym in perel (4/29)
putte hym in preson (118/14, 133/38)
sattelyn in her sowlys (149/25)
saw in hir sowle (174/13)
sent fro be-ȝonden þe see (4/33-34)
sesyn of her synne (141/30, 183/16-17)
cesyth of ȝowr sorweng (188/13)
settyn hys stody (221/29)
sey þe synne (48/6-7)
seyd a sermown (149/1, 166/26-27, 185/14, 219/20)
seyde vn-to hir spyrite (53/13)
sobbyn for his owyn synne (172/21)
sowyn meche good seed (99/11)
asoyld þe of þi synnes (72/38-73/1)
spak on-to hir sowle (50/4)
stodyn vp-on stolys (114/35)
vndyrstond in my sowle (59/36-37)
suffyr þis sorwe (187/30)
toke to hys teme (167/18)
toke hys toos (208/23)
turnyd be þe teerys (212/28-29)
was in wyl (1/16)
wept for þe world (13/25)
werkyn my wil (210/4)
wetyn hir wille (243/1)
wex ful of whelys (222/11)
wrytyn it betyr wyth good wylle (4/20)

Some forms of this type involve cognate accusatives, in which the noun nearly repeats the idea of the governing verb (or, in one case, verbal):

byddyng of many bedys (17/26, 89/28-29, 90/3) (Cf. 205/30, bedys
    byddyng)
drawe no drawt (10/19)
telde hem good talys (102/23)
thynkyn no good thowt (15/10)

NOUN + PREPOSITION ... NOUN

vndyr þe bed on þe bordys (79/4-5)
benefys of hys blyssyng (100/26)
body wyth hys precyows blood (192/2, 249/9)
þe cawse of þe crying (68/29, 150/9)
cloke ful of clowtys (77/9)
comfort of any confessowr (44/10-11)
cownsel of hys clerkys (35/32-33)
creatur in-to þe contre (33/8)
request of þis creatur & compellyng of hys owyn consciens (6/19, 45/18)
credens to þe cownsel (144/23-24)
dreed sche had of dampnacyon (7/19)
affecyon to hir gostly fadyr (45/13-14)
swech grace as þe Holy Gost of hys goodnesse (3/13-14)
grownd fro þe gresys (179/10)
an hayr in þin hert (17/7-8)
hom in-to hys owyn hows (112/23-24, 133/3, 241/28-29)
a lettyr to þe worshepful Lady (133/39)
leue of ower Lord (18/6-7)
to hir mend in þis maner (35/19-20, 53/12)
mende of thy many-fold mercy (230/1)
moryng of my meryte (251/38)
at hys nede in my name (180/33)
ornamentys of þe awter (153/19-20)
compassyon of hir preying (112/13)
peny owt of my purse (141/29)
pouerte a-mong þe pepyl (94/22-23)
prees of þe pepil (122/4-5)
prestys in þe same place (147/36-37)
repreuys of þe pepil (158/25)
prouysyon of þe Priowr (169/8)
pynte of wyn in a potte & toke hir a pece (131/7)

secretys of hir sowle (33/34)
sobbyngys for hir synnes (13/16-17)
sorwe in þe synne (48/8-9)
gret sorwe for þi gostly fadyrs synnys in special (212/22-23)
in þe cite of hir sowle[9] (68/16)
sowle be-for þe sone (87/14)
sowle be þe sufferawns (230/24)
sowle in þe sygth (44/35)
in specyal of þat synne (12/24)
sylens in hir sowle (86/19)
wawe on þe watyr (232/35-36)
worshepys of þe world (13/4-5, 138/7)

PARTICIPLE ... NOUN

beryng a botel wyth bere (23/11)
beyng in hir bed (95/38-96/1, 109/6)
clad in a cloth of canvas (243/11-12)
dwellyng in Dewchlond (4/4-5)
fellyng down þe flowerys (126/32-33)
floreschyd wyth flowerys (126/30)
forȝetyng þe frute (223/5)
hauyng gret heuynes (65/4-5)
heldyng up hys handys (41/11)
meuyd in þis mater (245/4)
compleynyng to þe preste of pouerte (55/24-25)
prechyng þe pepil (151/31)
preseruyng þe pepyl (96/18)
forsakyng hys seruawnt (8/13)
seylyng ouyr þe see (221/18)
seyng hys stabylnes (15/29-30)
staryng to mennys sygth (9/17)

[9] The *MED*, under *cite* 4. *Fig.*, indicates that figurative uses for this word were common: "cite of God (heven)"; "neue cite of Jerusalem", the community of the saved or chosen. Although no entry listed prior to Margery's makes use of this interesting figure of the "city of the soul", immediately following hers is an entry for *The Abbey of the Holy Ghost*, dated c1440 (?1375): "Goddis cete, þat es, mannes soule, þat es Goddes cete." Another testimony to common tradition rather than to originality on Margery's part occurs in Julian's work: "I saw the soule so large as it were an endless world & as it were a blisfull kyngdom. & be the conditions I saw therein I understode that it is a worshipful syte [*city*, Hudleston; *cytte*, Paris MS]. In the midds of þat syte sitts our Lord Jesus" (lxvii/2-6).

syttyng ful of sorwe & sadnes (94/14)
wyst of þe werld (40/19)

VERB ... VERB (INCLUDING INFINITIVES)

bad hem borwe (35/23-24)
badde hir beleuyn (144/20)
dede hir drynkyn (164/33-34)
dedyn hir don (62/16)
desyryd to a drawyn (221/19)
don þis hors drawyn (10/21)
be-gan to grutchyn (165/7)
let me to lofe (49/8-9)
makyn it mete wyth þe hole (192/20-21)
it semyth hym to sittyn (211/9)
suffred hir to sey (37/11)
went to þe man to wetyn (15/25)

NOUN ... VERB (INCLUDING SOME PARTICIPIAL AND INFINITIVE FORMS)

frendys han forsakyn (44/14)
key to kepyn (112/25-26)
Lady ȝaf leue (193/37)
mech mone was mad (54/10)
meny wer gretly merveylyng (34/34)
modyr to metyn (221/26)
prest was euyl plesyd (56/27-28)
spyrit xal speke (17/34)
strength wold seruyn (8/37)
summe to be sauyd (54/33-34)
tretys schal tretyn (1/12-13)
world xal wondryn (73/9)

NOUN + PREPOSITION + NOUN

doctowrs of dyuynyte (3/11-12, 164/28)
dowt of deth (104/30-31)
dred of defilyng (237/1)
mater in mende (171/33)

in party of penawnce (28/10, 85/34-35)
pylgrimys in preson (114/8)
skyn of stokfysche (91/15)
swetnesse of spech (50/3)
plentyuows teerys of contricyon (2/21-22)
tym of temptacyon (1/20)

NOUN ... NOUN

clerkys askyd þis creatur many hard qwestyons (35/2-3)
creatur had greet cownsel (6/7-8)
enmy had envye (5/24)
hys heuyd was in holying (179/12-13)
meny was at mete (133/9)
modyr, hauyng gret merueyl (223/34)
at myddenyght to heryn her Mateyns (200/32-33)
peyne to haue any preysyng (173/17)
Sone owr Sauyowr (198/4)

ADVERB ... NOUN

forth wyth hir felaschip (110/24)
forth wyth þe frerys (77/24)
to-gedyr in gret gladnes (25/18)
owte fer fro hir ostel (96/1)
perauentur of mor profyte (54/29)
pleynly to hys owyn persone (116/1)
sor in hir sowle (98/33)
sor for hir synne (107/18, 108/12)

ADJECTIVE ... NOUN

forseyd creaturys felyng (58/23)
homly wyth hir husbond (90/11)
mekar to hys modyr (195/16)
mor is ʒowr meryte (43/16)
how prone þe pepil was (180/7-8)
soget to syn (41/29)
sotyl in vndirstondyng (209/7)

VERB ... ADJECTIVE

beth not a-baschyd (149/11)
drede me to be deed (100/35)
fyndyth us most freel (14/12-13)
herd so hedows (39/6)
made hem mythy (167/34)
sche sey a semly man (86/31-32)
I wolde I wer as worthy (176/17)

VERB ... ADVERB

ferd so fowle (190/14)
grawntyd it goodlych (24/21)
lofe me þe lesse (91/22)
satt al stille (97/26)
sattelyn as sor (212/30)
syhyd ful sor (192/16)

ADJECTIVE + VERB

best to beryn (163/11)
good to gon (134/30)
hogely to beheldyn (126/32)
redy to recordyn (117/29-30)
strong for to suffyr (119/36)

ADVERB ... VERB

a-non it was answeryd (223/21)
cotidianly to kepyn (234/37)
long ben labowrd (8/9)

NOUN ... VERB ... NOUN

creatur was clad in blak clothyng (38/20-21)
dowtyr, do þu þi deuer (186/18)

A number of grammatical types are represented only by single examples: *Noun ... Adjective*, "cloþis wer al for-clowtyd" (76/25); *Noun ... Adverb*, "Frer proferyd hir to wryten frely" (6/9); *Participle ... Adverb*, "criyng ful cruelly" (190/9); *Participle ... Verb*, "purposyng to passyn (223/25); *Conjunction ... Verb*, "lych as sche had leryd" (66/5-6).

A number of combinations of these grammatical types also appear, sometimes involving only one alliterating sound, sometimes more than one:

SINGLE SOUNDS

prechyn mech of hys Passyon so compassyfly (167/4-5)

whan þu art in silens & sufferyst me to speke in thy sowle (89/24-25)

sithyn sche spak so sadly a-geyn syn & her mysgouernawns þat þei wer in sylens (109/18-20)

swettest of alle sauowrys softly sowndyng in hir sowle (98/25-26)

went wil[10] in a wode (126/25-26)

went to þe worschepful woman, wenyng (240/7)

DIFFERENT SOUNDS

heuynes ocupying hir hert cawsyd hir to compleyn (98/20-21)

ȝyf þu wilt be hey in Heuyn wyth me, kepe me al-wey in þi mende as meche as þu mayst & forȝete me not at þi mete (184/9-11)

receyuyn me to þe saluacyon of thy sowle wyth al maner of mekenes (213/30-31)

wrytyn þis booke & neuyr to be-wreyn it as long as sche leued, grawntyng hym a grett summe of good (4/35-37)

One passage provides an example of all three main alliterative types — grammatical, paired, consecutive — used in succession: "perfeccyon of prechyng spred & sprong wondyr wyde" (148/29-30).

One of the most interesting aspects of Margery's alliteration in

---

[10] "wil" = "erring, wayward" from ON *villr*, "bewildered, astray" (*OED*: *wild*). Cf. *OED*: *wil*, "misery, ill", obs. rare (?ON *vil*).

respect to older tradition is found in some lines which approximate poetic alliterative form.[11] Stress on particular syllables
provides lines that conform well to common poetic patterns. The
normal Old English pattern was *aa Ax*, in which *A* indicates the
first stressed syllable of the second half-line which commands the
alliteration of the whole line, *a* (or *b*) indicates other stressed alliterative syllables, and *x* indicates a stressed non-alliterating syllable.
In Middle English verse, a number of differences and alterations
occur in the poetry of the Alliterative Revival (1340-1450). Some
of these patterns are duplicated in Margery's prose.

Normal *aa Ax* of old English poetry:

> /   /   /   x
> maner of musyk, melody, & joy (188/29)

Sometimes the second strong stress in the second half-line carries
the alliteration (*aa xA*):

> /   /   x   /
> confessowr feryd þat sche xuld a fallyn (55/2-3)
>
> /   /   x   /
> he þat was hir husbond is now in good hele (53/26-27)
>
> /   /   x   /
> happyd hir to be herberwyd in a good mannys hows   (78/22-
> 23)
>
> /   /   x   /
> no personys beyng þer present þan þe tweyn preistys (200/19-
> 20)

Alliteration in the *Book of Margery Kempe* seems to be under-
estimated generally. In her note to 98/20-35 (p. 305), Hope Emily
Allen, the most thorough examiner of Margery to date, implies an
infrequency of alliterative passages:

The frequent rhythm and alliteration in this passage should be compared
with that which is perceptible in 100/20-30. No other similar passages
have been noted, and no clue is given as to the element in Margery's
reminiscences (probably a special emotion connected with her mysticism
in some way) which has made her break out into these patches of poetical
style. In each example she is describing a contact with "Duchemen".

[11] The following discussion is based upon Fernand Mossé, "Note on Middle
English Alliterative Verse", *A Handbook of Middle English*, transl. James A.
Walker (Baltimore, Johns Hopkins, 1952), pp. 381-383.

R. M. Wilson follows Miss Allen here in referring to 100/20-30: "very rarely we find a pale reflection of the rhythmical alliterative prose of Rolle".[12] Certainly the two passages cited are striking examples of alliteration, as we can see:

sodeyn sorwe & heuynes ocupying hir hert cawsyd hir to compleyn wyth mornyng cher for lak of vndirstondyng, desyryng to be refreschyd wyth sum crumme of gostly vndirstondyng vn-to hir most trustyd & entyrlyest belouyd souereyn, Crist Ihesu, whos melydious voys swettest of alle sauowrys softly sowndyng in hir sowle, seyd, "I xal preche þe & teche þe my-selfe, for þi wyl & thy desyr is acceptabyl vn-to me." Þan was hir sowle so delectabely fed wyth þe swet dalyawns of owr Lorde & so ful-filled of hys lofe þat as a drunkyn man sche turnyd hir fyrst on þe o syde & sithyn on þe oþer wyth gret wepyng & gret sobbyng; vn-mythy to kepyn hir-selfe in stabilnes for þe vnqwenchabyl fyer of lofe whech brent ful sor in hir sowle (98/20-33)

toke hir leue of hir frendys in Rome, & most specyaly of hir gostly fadyr, whech, for owr Lordys lofe, had supportyd hir & socowrd hir ful tendirly a-geyn þe wykked wyndys of hir invyows enmyis, whos departyng was ful lamentabyl as wytnessyd wel þe pur watyrdropys rennyng down be her chekys. Sche, fallyng on hyr knes, receyued þe benefys of hys blyssyng, & so departyd a-sundyr whom charite ioyned bothyn in oon, thorw þe whech þei trostyd to metyn a-geyn, whan owr Lord wolde, in her kendly cuntre whan þei wer passyd þis wretchyd wordelys exile (100/20-30)

But the long lists of alliterating words provided both in this chapter and in Appendices B and C (and I again wish to stress the non-exhaustive nature of my examination) indicate that alliteration is much more basic to Margery — and to Julian, whose alliteration, says Wilson, "is confined to the use of alliterating ... doublets" (p. 99) — than these critics are willing to admit. In addition, a number of examples may be cited here from both mystics to illus-trate a wide-spread use of alliteration, especially in various com-binations of sounds, that may challenge the Allen-Wilson position.

In Margery:

He, destytute of hys herborwe, fond a fayr erber in þe whech he restyd þat nyght, hauyng a fayr pertre in þe myddys al floreshyd wyth flowerys & belschyd, and blomys ful delectabil to hys syght, wher cam a bere, gret & boistows, hogely to beheldyn, schakyng þe pertre & fellyng down

---

[12] Wilson, p. 106.

þe flowerys. Gredily þis greuows best ete & deuowryd þo fayr flowerys. &, whan he had etyn hem, turnyng hys tayle-ende in þe prestys presens, voydyd hem owt ageyn at þe hymyr party (126/27-127/2)

a man in gret age passyng thre scor ȝer, as he wolde a comyn down of hys chambyr, bar-foot & bar-legge, he slederyd er ellys faylyd of hys fotyng & fel down to þe grownd fro þe gresys, & hys heuyd vndyr hym greuowsly brokyn & bresyd, in so meche þat he had in hys heuyd v teyntys many days whil hys heuyd was in holyng (179/7-13)

of owr Lordys Passyon & swech oþer gracys & goodnes as owr Lord ministryd to hir mynde, & sodeynly, sche wist not how sone, sche was in a maner of slep, & a-non in þe syght of hir sowle sche sey owr Lord standyng ryght up ouyr hir so ner þat hir thowt sche toke hys toos in hir hand & felt hem, & to hir felyng it weryn as it had ben very flesch & bon (208/18-24)

as þer arn dropys of watyr, fres and salt, cheselys of grauel, stonys smale & grete, gresys growing in al erthe, kyrnellys of corn, fischys, fowelys, bestys & leevys up-on treys whan most plente ben, fedir of fowle (252/4-7)

And þerfor, syster, I cownsel ȝow þat ȝe dyspose ȝow to receyuyn þe ȝyftys of God as lowly & mekely as ȝe kan & put non obstakyl ne obiec-cyon a-ȝen þe goodnes of þe Holy Gost, for he may ȝevyn hys ȝyftys wher he wyl, & of vnworthy he makyth worthy, of synful he makyth rygtful. Hys mercy is euyr redy vn-to vs, les þan þe fawt be in owyrself, for he dwellyth not in a body soget to syn. He fleth al fals feynyng & falshede; he askyth of us a lowe, a meke & a contryte hert wyth a good wyl. Owyr Lord seyth hym-self, "My spyrit schal restyn vp-on a meke man, a contryte man, & dredyng my wordys". (41/22-33)

A good man whech was a gret frend to þis creatur & an helply to þe powyr pepyl was strongly seke many wekys togedyr. & mech mone was mad for hym (54/7-10)

In Julian:

the iijd is þe plentyous bledyng of þe body in semys of the scorgyng; the iiijth is þe depe deyng. These iiij are aforseyd for the peynys of the passion (xxiii/11-14)

I have matter of mekeness that savith me from presumption. And in the blissid shewing of love I have matter of tru comfort & of joy þat savith me fro dispeir. All this homley shewing of our curtes Lord it is a lovely lesson (lxxix/22-26)

for mekehede of joye mervelyng at the greatness of God the Maker &

of the litilhede of all that is made. For the beholdyng of this makith the creature mervelous meke & mylde (lxxv/35-38)

þu wisely know thi penance & shalt then sothly seene that al thi living is penance profitable. This place is prison & this lif is penance, & in the remedy he will we enjoyen (lxxvii/41-44)

we werkyn his will & his worship (where say *we* menith man that shall be savid), for sothly I saw þat we arn that he lovith, & don that he lekyth, lestingly withoute ony styntyng; & of the gret riches & of the hey noble virtues be mesur come to our soule what time it is knitt to our body, in which knitting we arn made sensual. & thus in our substance we arn ful, & in our sensualite we faylen, which faylyng God will restore & fulfill be werkyng mercy & grace plentiously flowand into us (lvii/2-11)

& that is spoken of in the xvj shewing, wher it seith he sittith in our soule. For it is his likeyng to reygn in our vnderstondyng blisfully & sitten in our soule restfully & to wonen in our soule endlesly, us al werkeng into hym, in which werkyng he will we ben his helpers, gevyng to hym al our entendyng, lerand his loris, keped [*sic*] his lawes, desirand that al be done he doeth, truely trosting in hym, for sothly I saw þat our substance is in God (lvii/62-71)

In which shewing I saw & understode ful sekirly that in every soule that shal be save [*sic*] is a Godly wille that never assent to synne (liii/11-13)

For I saw full sekirly that our substance is in God. And also I saw that in our sensualite God is; for the selfe poynte that our soule is mad sensual, in the selfe poynt is the cite of God ordeynid (lv/28-31)

saw the Lord sitten solemnly and the servant stondand reverently (li/189-90)

Also God shewid that synne shal be no shame but worship to man. For ryth as to every synne is answeryng a peyne be trewth, ryth so for every synne to the same soule is geven a bliss by love (xxxviii/1-4)

sterid be foly to seyn or to thinken, if this be soth then were it good to synne (xl/30-31)

ryght so he was most strong & myghty to suffir. And ffor every mannys synne that shall be savid he suffrid, & every manys sorow & desolation he sawe & sorowid for kyndenes & love. For in as mekyl as our lady sorowid for his peynes, as mekyl he suffrid sorrow for her sorow, & more, in as mekyl as the swete manhode of hym was worthier in kynd. For as long as he was passible he suffryd for us & sorowyd for us, & now he is up rysyn & no more passibyl, yet he suffryt with us. And I beholdyng al this he his grace saw þat þe love of hym was so strong whych he hath to our soule, that wilfully he ches it with gret desyr, & myldly he suffrid it with wel payeyng (xx/17-30)

In the case of Margery, Miss Allen and Mr. Wilson at least indicate that alliterative passages do occur; their opinions are stated subjectively. Disagreement with them is relative, for Margery Kempe's prose is obviously not as alliterative as that of Richard Rolle. But two points need emphasis here. First, although not excessive, alliteration abounds in Margery's prose — in distinct opposition to the Allen-Wilson implications. Second, on the basis of the examples above and in Appendix C, it is clearly misleading to state flatly, as Wilson does, that Julian's use of alliteration is "confined" to doublets of the "wele and wo" variety.

V

SYNTAX: MERITS AND MONOTONY

It is basically in terms of sentence structure that R. M. Wilson gives Julian of Norwich the laurel as one of the greatest of the Middle English mystic writers.[1] His greatest praise is for her straightforward style (p. 99), in which rhetorical devices are subordinate and used as they "should be" to emphasize thought rather than to obscure it through overabundance. He lists eight devices, with examples, used by Julian: six forms of repetition plus parallelism and antithesis. Inversion is "not uncommon" but is generally used skilfully to emphasize thought.

The prose of Margery Kempe he finds "very different" (p. 105) — meaning in part "worse" — again primarily in terms of structure and syntax. Margery is criticized for her lack of construction: many digressions, repetitions, difficult order. Syntactically, her sentences are short and occasionally monotonous because of a lack of variety in conjunctions, although they do occasionally lengthen and become more complex. He mentions Margery's fondness for tautological pairs but deplores her carrying the device further: "a general piling up of words for the sake of emphasis" (p. 106). Inversion he finds comparatively rare, without the gain of any special effect.

It seems to me that much more remains to be said about the ways in which words go together to form sentences in the works of both mystics. Most certainly a basic element in both styles is repetition, both of words and of sentence structure. The former *does* provide much of the weakness of Margery; the latter gives Julian much of her strength. However, the merits and defects in-

[1] Wilson, p. 111.

volved are definitely not limited to one or the other mystic; it is
this point — not made by Wilson — that I wish to stress, along
with the idea that the two women may not be as "different" as
Wilson indicates. In sentence structure Julian may be superior to
Margery, but both make use of similar devices effectively.

Repetition is obviously a weakness in Margery. One does not
have to look far to encounter the monotony caused by unvaried
conjunctions. On page 6, for example, even before the reader is
in the first chapter, the following passage occurs:

not-wythstondyng þis creatur had greet cownsel for to don wryten hir
tribulacyons & hir felingys, and, a Whyte Frer proferyd hir to wryten
frely yf sche wold. And sche was warnyd in hir spyrit þat sche xuld not
wryte so sone. And many ȝerys aftyr sche was bodyn in hyr spyrit for
to wryten. And þan ȝet it was wretyn fyrst be a man whech cowd
neiþer wel wryten Englysch ne Duch (6/7-14)

Of the next fourteen sentences on pages 6-7 that follow this excerpt,
no less than eleven begin with the conjunction *and*. Adding to
this use the frequent occurrence of *and* within the sentences, one
can agree easily with Wilson's criticism. He does not say, however,
that Julian can be criticized for the same fault. From early in her
work comes an example that illustrates this point, apparently un-
noticed by Wilson:

And when I was thirty years old and half, God sent me a bodely seke-
ness in which I lay iii dayes and iii nights, and on the fourth night I tooke
all my rites of holy Church and I wened not a levyd till day, and after
this I langorid forth ii dayes and ii nights, and on the iii night I wened
often-times to have passyd and so wened they that were with me, and in
youngith yet I thought great sweeme to dye (iii/1-9)

Several points need to be made about the use of "and". Its overuse
was apparently widespread: George Saintsbury, in his still valuable
study, describes Mandeville's prose:

arranged for the most part in very short sentences, introduced (exactly
like those of a child telling stories) by "And". I open a page of Halliwell's
edition absolutely at random: the sentences are not quite as short as they
are sometimes, but there are eleven of them in thirty-three lines of large
and widely spaced print; ten of which begin with "and", and the eleventh
with "also".[2]

---

[2]   *A History of English Prose Rhythm*, 2nd ed. (London, Macmillan, 1922)
p. 64.

Saintsbury also provides a source for this habit:

The chief resemblance to early French prose ... is the already-mentioned evidence of short sentences beginning with "And" — "Et", a habit most undoubtedly derived from the similar one in the *laisses* or tirades of the *chansons de geste*.[3]

Margery and Julian both are thus simply doing what other (and highly praised) authors were doing at the time — with some literary precedent. Dictation and the use of amanuenses also may have played a part here: "like those of a child telling stories". And still another point should be considered. Although a reader frequently is annoyed by Margery's repetition of conjunctions, they surprisingly are not as annoying as the foregoing comments might indicate. Despite the number of repeated uses in Margery's *Book*, the effect is softened by sentence length, a point contradicting Wilson's indictment of "short" sentences. The excerpt given above, although illustrating the use of *and*, is not as typical of Margery's sentences as are the fourteen subsequent ones, omitted because of their length. Although there is excessive coordination, Margery's sentences do not give the impression of being short, whatever that term might mean. Wilson himself seems to contradict this idea with his objection to Margery's "general piling up of words". Is it likely that words would pile up in short sentences? It is this very wordiness of Margery that helps to counterbalance the damaging monotony of repeated conjunctions.

Is Margery then merely ameliorating one weakness with another one? Certainly wordiness is a flaw in much of her work, but not entirely so. Margery's type of repetition adds a flavor that is missing in the work of Julian: it helps provide an air of informal chattiness and spontaneity that is one of the merits of the book. As Saintsbury says of Mandeville:

the real secret of his extraordinary success is his positive mastery of the fact that for certain purposes, and among them pure narration and description, a simple "writing down" of simple conversational style is the best device possible.[4]

---

[3] Saintsbury, p. 109.
[4] Saintsbury, p. 64.

Wilson finds much to praise in Margery, and much of it is traceable
to this element of her work: she has "talent for description", "eye
for character", "power of communicating feelings"; she knows" the
value of detail", uses homely illustrations and proverbs, is an
effective story teller and has a "gift for reporting dialogue". Saintsbury, in his praise for another writer, makes some comments that
are similarly applicable to Margery:

There are plenty of sentences in Malory beginning with "and"; but
it is not the constant go-between and usher-of-all-work that it is in
Mandeville. The abundance of conversation gets him out of the difficulty at once; and he seems to have an instinctive knowledge — hardly
shown before him, never reached after him till the time of the great
novelists — of weaving conversation and narrative together.[5]

Had Saintsbury known Margery's work, he might have qualified
even more his judgment of "hardly shown before [Malory]". She
possesses the traits of many a gossipy old woman who, despite —
or perhaps because of — irrelevancies and repetitions, can tell a
story well and hold an audience in sometimes unwilling but fascin-
ated attention. We all know the "So I said to him ... so he said to
me" type. The modern reader's interest in Margery rather than
Julian has been stressed earlier: the character and varied subject
matter of the one, I think, would appeal much more to a general
reader than would the unrelieved stress on religion of the other.
And the gossipy, spontaneous character, the humanness, of Margery Kempe emerges in great part through the very "weakness"
of conversational wordiness.

There are, of course, various forms of repetition and wordiness.
Some are definite rhetorical ornaments which may or may not be
used for special effect: repetition of word or phrase at the beginning
of successive sentences or clauses (*anaphora*), at the end of successive sentences or clauses (*epistrophe* or *antistrophe*), at both the
beginning and the end (*symploce* or *exoche*). Others are apparently
needless or awkward repetitions of words; still others are repetitions
of thought — redundancies. Various forms of repetition occur in
the works of both authors; Wilson stresses the rhetorical types
found in Julian's writing and the tautological pairs of Margery. He

[5] Saintsbury, p. 88.

does not, however, mention Margery's use of rhetorical types or Julian's tautological pairs — although he euphemistically includes the latter in his reference to alliterative or rhyming "doublets". The point, again, is that both writers are using the same techniques. Julian's work generally does give a feeling of more balance, more use of rhetorical repetition than does Margery's, but the "very different" work of Margery seems upon reflection very similar. Most of the rhetorical types found in Julian's work by Wilson can be found in Margery's. If they are more difficult to find, the praise for a style in which rhetorical devices are subordinated belongs perhaps to both writers rather than to one.

Wilson found the most obvious and freely used device of Julian to be anaphora, the repetition of a word or words at the beginning of successive phrases, clauses, or sentences. Certainly the same statement could be made for Margery. Examples abound in both works,[6] but even the few given here (Wilson gives one example, which is not used here) may indicate that, despite the perhaps more artful emphatic use by Julian, Margery was not far behind.

Julian:

the wound of very contrition, the wound of kinde compassion, and the wound of willfull longyng to God (ii/39-41)

Our Lord Jesus often tymes seyd: "I it am, I it am, I it am þat is heyest; I it am that tho lovist; I it am þat þu lykyst; I it am that þu servist; I it am that thou longyst; I it am that thou desyrist; I it am þat þu menyst; I it am þat is al; I it am þat holy Church prechyth & teachyth the; I am [sic] þat shewed me here to thee."[7] (xxvi/5-11)

---

[6]   A number of examples of the rhetorical types of repetition can also be found in the examples of balanced sentences and parallelism found later in this chapter.

[7]   This passage also offers examples of other types of repetition: *climax* or *gradatio* — the same kind of repetition continued through three or more clauses; *epanados* or *traductio* — speedy iteration at frequent intervals; *diacope* and *epizeuxis* — repetition of word with no, one, or few words between. The "I it am" is also found in Margery (189/39). Miss Allen in a note to the passage says that Margery followed the gospels quite closely in telling of Christ's capture. It is interesting to note, however, that the phrasing of both mystics follows more an Anglo-Saxon colloquial version of the Gospel of St. John found in Joseph Bosworth and George Waring, *Gothic, Anglo-Saxon, Wycliffe and Tyndale Gospels* (London, Gibbings, 1907), "Ic hit eom" than it does the Wycliffe version of John xvii.5 "I am", Luke xxii.47, Mark xiv.44 ff., Matthew xxvi.47 ff., or even the Latin "Ego sum" quoted by Margery five lines earlier.

As veryly as God is our Fader, as verily God is our Moder, & that shewid he in all, & namely in these swete words where he seith: "I it am." That is to seyn: "I it am, þe myte & the goodnes of the faderhed; I it am, þe wisdom of the Moderhede; I it am, the lyte & the grace þat is al blissid love. I it am, the trinite; I it am, the Unite; I am þe sovereyne goodness of all maner of thyngs. I am that makyth the to loven; I am that makyth the to longen; I it am, the endles fulfilling of al trew desires. (lix/12-21)

For kindly the Child disperith not of the Moder love; kindly the Child presumith not of the selfe; kindly the Child lovith the Moder & ilke on of the other (lxiii/43-46)

It longith to the Lordshippe & to the faderhede to be dred, as it longith to the goodnes to be lovid; & it longith to us þat arn his servants & his children to dreden him for Lordshippe & faderhede as it longith to us to loven him for Goodhede (lxxiv/26-30)

our Lord is Almyty & may punish me mytyly, & he is al wisdom & can punish me skilfully, & he is all goodnes & lovith me full tendirly (lxxvii/18-21) ("Almyty ... mytyly" is another type of repetition: *polyptoton* — words from the same root but with different endings or forms.)

"... if it had ben thus than it had bene full wele"; but we shall seyn al without voice [Hudleston: "with one voice"]: "Lord, blissid mot thou ben. For it is thus, it is well ..." (lxxv/15-17)

Margery:

hys eyn myssyd so þat he mygth not se to make hys lettyr ne mygth not se to mend hys penne (5/19-21)

Sum-tyme he led hym be þe heed, sum-tyme he beet hym, & sum-tyme he chershyd hym, and alle avayled not, for he wold raþer gon bakward þan forward (10/22-24)

rygth as I spak to Seynt Bryde ryte so I speke to þe (47/32-33)

Whan þu plesyst God, þow plesyst hys Modyr & al þe seyntys in Heuyn (49/30-31)

sum seyd sche was a good woman, & sum seyd nay (124/32)

for þei þat louyd hir for God er sche went owte þei wolde louyn hir for God whan sche come hom (247/17-18)

Similarly, the other forms of rhetorical repetition cited for Julian can be matched by examples from Margery. In addition, however, we may note some types not mentioned by Wilson. In the following listings, a term is italicized until it is defined under its heading.

(a) *epistrophe* (called *antistrophe* by Wilson[8]) — repetition of words
   at the end of successive constructions

Julian:

it was the most likyng word þat he might have gove me of hir with þe
gostly shewyng that he gave me of hir (xxv/40-41)

but al shal be wel, & al shal be wel, & al manner of thyng shal be wele
(xxvii/13-15)

Margery:

let me to lofe whom I wele & as mech as I wyl (49/8-9)

onys louyd & euyrmor lovyd (49/27)

Whom þat God louyth þei louyn (49/29-30) (Could be considered an
example of *polyptoton* — repetition of words from the same root but
with different endings or forms)

þu hast be despysed for my lofe, & þerfor þu xalt be worshepyd for my
lofe (52/20-22)

þei obeyd not ne lyked not (60/9)

sche sey wyth hir bodily eye lych as sche had beforn wyth hir gostly
eye (78/5-6)

þu vndirstondyst my wyl & I vndirstond þi wyl (210/7-8) (also an example of *antimetabole* — logical conversion)

(b) *symploce* (or *exoche*) — a combination of anaphora and epistrophe

Julian:

I saw him & sowte him, & I had him & I wantid hym (x/19-20)

I sey not that ony evil is worshipful, but I sey the sufferance of our Lord
God is worshipfull (xxxv/25-27)

it seith God, it beholdyth God, & it lovyth God (xliv/16)

---

[8] My source for the names of these types, some of which differ from those
used by Wilson, is Sister Miriam Joseph, *Shakespeare's Use of the Arts of
Language* (New York, Columbia University Press, 1947), pp. 305-307. Wilson's
technical terms are from Margery M. Morgan, "*A Talkyng of the Love of God*
and the Continuity of Stylistic Tradition in Middle English Prose Meditations",
RES, N.S. 3 (1952), 97-116. As in the case of anaphora, Wilson gives only one
example of each type, and that example is not included in these listings except
as another type (e.g., Julian's example of epanalepsis li/312-313 is cited by
Wilson as anadiplosis).

Margery:

sum-tyme rampyng at hyr, sum-tume thretyng her [*sic*], sum-tym pullyng hyr & halyng hir (7/25-27)

For þei þat worshep þe þei worshep me; þei þat despysyn þe þei despysen me, & I schal chastysen hem þerfor. I am in þe, and þow in me (23/14) (Also observable here are *antimetabole* and rhyme.)

I take none hede what a man hath ben, but I take hede what he wyl ben (49/20-21)

and for þei wold han al þei lost al (60/12-13)

(c) *epanalepsis* — repetition at the end of a construction of the word or phrase which begins it

Julian:

Jesus is al þat shal be savid, & al þat shal be savid is Jesus (li/312-313) (Also an example of *anadiplosis* and *antimetabole*)

our soule with our body & our body with our soule (lv/39-40) (Also *anadiplosis* and *antimetabole*)

Margery:

þat þer schal neuyr deuyl in Helle parte þe fro me, ne awngel in Heuyn, ne man in erthe, for deuelys in Helle mow not, ne awngelys in Heuyn wyl not, ne man in erthe schal not (17/22-25) (also an example of epistrophe)

& of unworthy he makyth worthy (41/26-27)

Thy sowle is mor sekyr of þe lofe of God þan of þin owyn body, for þi sowle xal partyn fro thy body but God xal neuyr partyn fro þi sowle (89/11-14) (The first two clauses also provide an example of symploce.)

make my wil þi wyl & þi wil my wil (249/35) (also *anadiplosis* and *antimetabole*)

(d) *anadiplosis* — repetition of the last word or words of one construction at the beginning of the next.

Julian:

this was on mervel. Another mervel was that ... (li/220)

he toke gret sore: the sore þat he toke was our flesh (li/329-330)

Margery:

and teld it mech pepyl, & mych pepyl magnyfied mech God in þis creature (21/21-22)

"Lord, what betokenyth þis?" "It betokenyth veniawnce." "A, good Lord, what veniawnce?" (47/28-29) (also an example of epistrophe)

þow þe state of maydenhode be mor parfyte & mor holy þan þe state of wedewhode, & þe state of wedewhode mor parfyte þan þe state of wedlake (49/4-7)

þer is no ȝyft so holy as is þe ȝyft of lofe, ne no þing to be so mech desyred as lofe, for lofe may purchasyn what it can desyren (49/11-13)

Owyr Lord seyd þan to hys blysful Modyr, "Blyssd Modyr, ..." (49/35)

þu wost wel wher-þat-euyr þe Holy Gost is þer is þe Fadir, & wher þe Fadyr is þer is þe Sone (89/3-5)

(e) *polyptoton* — the repetition of words from the same root but with different endings or forms[9]

Julian:

Lord, thou wotist what I would if it be thy will that I have it; and if it be not thy will, good Lord, be not displeased for I will naught but as thou wilt (ii/33-36)

in the makyng vnyd to the Maker (lv/48-49)

that shall be on the last day fulfillid ever to lesten (lxxv/16-17)

fro withouten begynning, in which on beginne love (lxxxv/9)

Margery:

maner of dalyawns þat owyr Lord dalyid (36/34-35)

don as þow dost (48/12)

þu art a synguler louer, & perfor þu xalt have a synguler loue in Heuyn (52/24-25)

preyng hir to prey (53/8-9) (similarly 127/10-11)

as þis creatur lay ... in hir preyers, a prest cam to hir & preyde hir to prey for a woman (53/29-30)

owyr blyssed Lord aperyd to hys blysful Modyr (75/4-5)

he seyd to þe seyd creatur (108/17-18)

knelyng on hir knes (124/16)

---

[9] It is interesting to note that although Wilson says that Julian makes no use of "plays on words", his source for the technical names (Margery Morgan) includes polyptoton under such a heading. Wilson does show Julian making use of polyptoton.

(f) *paronomasia* — the repetition of words nearly but not precisely alike. Wilson claims that Julian made no use of plays on words and mentions this figure in particular. The following example, however, is a possibility:

The body was in the grave till Estern Morow, & from þat tyme he lay never more (li/354-5)

Margery gives a more definite example:

þat was gret merueyl to hir þat Mary [Magdalene] enioyid, for, ȝyf owr Lord had seyd to hir as he dede to Mary, hir thowt sche cowde neuyr a ben mery (197/30-32)

In passing, we may take note of some figures not mentioned by Wilson.

(g) *antimetabole* — logical conversion, the repetition of words in converse order (some have been noted in other examples)

Margery:

I have ronnyn a-wey fro þe, & þow hast ronnyn aftyr me (50/27-28)

he had leue to spekyn to hir & sche to hym (170/17)

Whan sche herd þe wordys & þe compassyon þat þe Modyr had of þe sone & þe sone of hys Modyr, þan sche wept, sobbyd & cryid (191/26-28)

(h) *traductio* (*epanados* or *ploce*) — the speedy iteration of one word at frequent intervals

Margery:

benyngne Lady, meke Lady, chariteful Lady (252/32-33)

(i) *diacope* — the vehement repetition of word or words with one or few between.

Julian:

Ya, good Lord, gramercy; ya, good Lord, if it be thy wille (xxv/26-27)

(j) *climax* (*gradatio*) — the same kind of repetition continued through three or more constructions

Julian:

the first is that God made it, þe second is that God loveth it, the iii þat God kepith it (v/17-19)

Margery:

a fals strumpet, a fals loller, & a fals deceyuer of þe pepyl (112/11-12)

sche suffryd mech despite, meche reprefe, many a scorne, many a slawndyr, many a bannyng, & many a cursyng (137/3-5)

He xal neiþyr welyn good, ne do good, ne desiryn good (186/32-33)

(k) *oxymoron* — contradictory terms joined so as to give point to the statement

Julian:

This shewing was quick & lively & hidouse & dredfull, swete & lovely (vii/29-30)

I saw him & sowte him, & I had him & I wantid hym (x/19-20)

soft drede (xi/4, xxxvii/9)

pretious plenty (xii/23, 26, 28)

Margery:

helth in-to sekenesse, prosperyte in-to aduersyte, worshep in-to repref, & love in-to hatered (1/24-26) (cf. Chaucer, *Book of the Duchess*, 599-615)

Finally, three examples of climax in Margery also show a combination of other types and serve to indicate that Margery was capable of control not far behind that of Julian, if not equal to it. As is true of most of the examples of rhetorical repetition from Margery, the three excerpts are all from passages spoken by Christ to Margery . The frequency with which "rhetorical" writing appears in such passages may have several significances. First, they may support some in the contention that Margery's experiences were authentically divinely inspired. Second, they may indicate some efforts by the amanuensis to improve important passages. On the other hand, they may be considered more definitely Margery's own words than are other parts of the book: an amanuensis, even a priestly one, might be less inclined to revise, develop, or embellish what a mystic claimed to be the words of God. Finally, such passages as the following indicate that Margery's work — like Julian's — makes effective use of rhetorical devices by adapting style to speaker — truly, as Wilson says of Julian, to emphasize the sense and to be used as ornament "should be".

climax, epistrophe, polyptoton, epanalepsis, anaphora:

þerfor þow has gret cawse to louyn me ryth wel, & зet þu xalt han grettar cawse þan euyr þu haddyst to louyn me, for þu xalt heryn þat þu neuyr herdist, & þu xalt se þat þu neuyr sey, & þu xalt felyn þat þu neuyr feltist. For, dowtyr, þu art as sekyr of þe lofe of God as God is God. (89/6-11)

climax, anaphora, epistrophe, antimetabole:

for wher-so God is Heuyn is, & wher þat God is þer be many awngelys, & God is in þe & þu art in hym (88/18-20)

climax, anaphora, epistrophe or epanalepsis:

eche knowyth þat oþer knowyth, & eche may þat oþer may, & eche will þat oþer wil (211/23-24)

In an effort to show the merits of a writer there is always the danger of being partisan, of seeing only the merits. It is necessary to keep in mind always that Margery and Julian have flaws in their writing and that, as they are not the first contributors to, so they are not the most recent beneficiaries of, a long history of English prose style.[10] There are other forms of repetition used by both writers that bring the idolater back to earth in a hurry. One such is the simple, overused repetition of a single word. We have already seen examples of overused conjunctions in Margery and Julian. But both mystics can make other individual words burdensome:

[10] For discussions going beyond Chambers to indicate the classical background of prose continuity, see J. A. K. Thomson, *Classical Influences on English Prose* (London, George Allen & Unwin, 1956); George Williamson, *The Senecan Amble* (London, Faber and Faber, 1951). For mention of anadiplosis and polyptoton some two centuries before Margery, see M. W. Thompson, *þe Wohunge of Ure Lauerd*, EETS 241 (London, Oxford University Press, 1958), p. xxviii. Thompson goes on to say: "Rhetoric they [the 'Wooing Group'] have; as has all impassioned utterance. Their style is the style of a school, of their day, and of their ancestry. It was already old in its devices, which had probably long since become largely an unconscious element in literary technique" (p. xxix).

Julian:

as if a man love a creature syngularly above al creatures, he wil make al creature to loven & to lyken þat creature þat he lovith so mekyl (xxv/36-38)

Margery:

on of her felawshep cam to hir preyng hir to gon to hys felaschep & asayn ȝyf þei wolden receyuen hir a-geyn in-to her felawshep. & so sche dede. "ȝyf ȝe wyl gon in owyr felawshep ..." (65/29-32)

Margery especially has the tendency to be redundant but, as distinct from the preceding example, often manages to achieve emphasis:[11]

sche was pour & had no mony (105/2-3)
knelyng on hir knes (124/16)
Whan sche was alone be hir self (151/30-31)
a fals feynyd ypocrite (156/4)
stondyn on hir feet (198/18)
by hym-self a-lone (246/5)

The most dominant type of repetition in Margery, however, is, as Wilson indicates, tautologically paired words. This device, it should be stressed, is part of a well established writing tradition.[12] In Old English, stereotyped alliterating copulative phrases are found in *Beowulf*; and other writings, such as the Old English translation of Bede's *Ecclesiastical History*, also testify to doubling. Later, in such works as the *Ancrene Riwle* (c. 1225) and *Genesis and Exodus* (c. 1250), a French word is often used side by side with an English synonym, perhaps in order to explain the former. By the time of Chaucer, paired words, found in the works of most writers, are used not as an explanation of a foreign term but more definitely

[11]   Gaining emphasis through such repetition has considerable historical precedent, e.g. "knelyng on his knes": cf. I Kings viii.54, II Chron. vi.13, Daniel vi.10.
[12]   For the historical survey of tautological pairs, I am indebted to an unpublished study sheet on the topic prepared by Professor Roland M. Smith. For continuity in classical features, see note 10, above. Thompson, *Wohunge*, mentions doublets as "familiar to all readers of the literature of this period" (p. xxix) and speaks of the "highly conventional" literary medium from which is derived the diction of the "Wooing Group": alliterating tags, doublets, and catch-phrases.

as a stylistic device to strengthen an effect ("faire and fetisly", "in angwissh and in wo", "drugge and drawe", "wexe and multiply"), a use found also in the later Book of Common Prayer (1549) in such phrases as "dissemble nor cloak", "requisite and necessary", "bless and sanctify", and "rule and govern". Extensive use of paired words for stylistic emphasis, then, could be expected in the time of Margery and Julian, another sign of the continuity of English prose.

In his listing of this device for Margery, however, Wilson considers it one of the elements that make Margery's prose "very different" from Julian's, including it with such habits as the previously mentioned "short" sentences, lack of varied conjunctions, and lack of inversion for the purpose of gaining special effect. After this list, Wilson states that "despite frequent monotony, there is much to show that Margery had considerable skill as a prose writer, if only it had been allowed to appear more frequently" and goes on to praise her storytelling techniques. Paired words clearly seem to be condemned here as part of Margery's style. But Wilson fails to criticize the same habit in Julian, whose "doublets" receive no disapproval. It hardly seems fair to condemn something as part of the weakness of one writer and to ignore the same element in the work of a praised author. That both writers do make use of tautological pairs should be evident from the following listings. The use of this device by Julian is particularly noteworthy in her long and poetic fifty-first chapter. Some of her examples here may also lead to a questioning of Wilson's statement (p. 99) that there is "not much use" of concord of sound between unstressed final syllables (homoeoteleuton) in Julian's work. The examples from Margery outnumber those of Julian in these listings and indicate the obvious quantitative difference. Only non-alliterating pairs are included here: many alliterating types have already been listed, and others may be found in the alphabetical lists of Appendix C. Some similarities to Julian's work, probably indicative of widespread Middle English usage rather than borrowing, are noted among Margery's examples. Certain entries are more hackneyed than others ("joye & gladness"), and some couplets also come closer than others to being exact synonyms.

Julian:

doeth & werkith (i/14)
behold & see (i/43, xxvi/41)
joy & blisse (i/56; xlv/50; li/153, 305; lv/60)
saveand & keepeand (i/60)
the cheife & principal mene (vi/26)
treuly & sothly (vii/51)
we willen & trowen, joyen & liken, comfortyn us & solacyn us (vii/53-54)
faith & beleve (vii/63)
openyd & declarid (vii/66)
mekil & large, faire & gode (viii/10-11)
be happe ne be aventure (xi/6-7)
wo & tribulation (xii/51-52)
no comfort nor none ease (xv/9)
in sorrow & mornyng (xv/36, xxxii/14)
myrth & joy (xxv/1)
I answerid & seyd (xxv/26)
ruth & pity (xxi/49; xlviii/14; li/46, 152; lii/87, 107; lxi/59; lxxi/20)
threst & longyng (xxxi/50)
ruth & compassion (xxxi/61)
to litil & to smale (xxxii/6)
to wetyn & to knowen (xxxiv/12-13, lv/46, lxxv/40)
so plenteiously & so fully (xxxv/1-2)
many & fele, heygh & mervelous, worshipful & grete (xxxvi/65-67)
sorrow & shame (xxxix/16)
barren & dry (xli/7) (see also li/169 below)
in dryhede & in barrenhede, in sickness & in feeblehede (xli/49-50)
syte & beholdyng (xliii/27)
sweteness & delite (xliii/29)
nede & cause (xliii/32-33)
supple & buxum (xliii/35-36)
wenyn & thynken (xliii/46-47)
shal sen & endlesly beholden (xliii/62-63)
hoole & save (xlv/2)
good & esye (xlv/9)
herd & grevous (xlv/10, li/36)
accordid & onyd (xlv/17-18)
swete & delectabil (xlv/23)
blame & wreth (xlv/29)
can or may tell (xlv/30-31)
sen & known (xlv/48)
groundid & rotid (xlix/5, lvii/24, lviii/50)
westith & destroyith (xlix/11)
debates & strives (xlix/24)

in rest & in peace (li/11, 116, 132, 321-322, 335, 377, 385)
lovely & swetely (li/13)
gronith & monith & waylith & writhith (li/18) (see also li/346 below)
will & shall (li/50; li/186-187)
harme & disese (li/54-55)
his afray & his drede, his hurt & his maim (li/57)
his fallyng & his wo (li/68)
hey & overpassing worship (li/69-70)
in syte & in shewing (li/72-73)
no manner or way (li/79)
cannot ner may (li/94)
levyn & trostyn (li/96)
mysty & indifferent to thy syte (li/104)
witt & understondyng (li/107)
his nobleth & his godeness (li/112)
commenden & approven (li/125-126)
blamith & punishith (li/137)
comfortith & sorowith (li/137-138)
wide & syde (li/142, 360-361) (see also li/360-361 below)
most faire & semely shewand (li/145-146)
knowen & levyn (li/168)
barreyn & desert (li/169)
sorow & peyne (li/172, lxxv/18)
stirt & ran (li/208, 294)
lovesome & plesant (li/217-218)
gretest labor & herdest travel (li/224)
wisdam & goodnes (li/265)
the vertu & the goodnes (li/270)
the febilnes & the blindnes (li/271)
may ne will (li/274)
swete incarnation & blisful passion (li/301)
wo & sorow (li/304)
longyng & desire (li/308)
langor & desire (li/311)
the sweppys & the scorgis, the thornys & þe naylys, þe drawyng & the
      draggyng (li/340-342)
wallowyng & wrythyng, gronyng & monyng (li/346)
slain & ded (li/349, 356-357)
white & bryte (li/360)
wyde & syde, fairer & richer (li/360-361)
mercies & forgevenes (lii/107)
pite & love (lv/21)
incresyd & fulfillid (lv/24)
waxen & growne (lv/39)

swete & mervelous to beholden, pesible & restful, sekir and delectabil (lv/49-51)

seene & felt (lv/62, lxv/13, lxxv/31)

fulfillid of feling & mynd of Cristes passion (lv/63-64)

verily & trewly (lvi/33)

rayhid him & dyte him (lx/14)

to morne & to wepen (lxi/58-59)

faire & clene (lxi/73)

redy & diligently aboute us (lxi/75)

our frelte & our fallyngs, our brekyngs & our nowtyngs, our dispits & our outcastings (lxii/1-3)

swifie & lively (lxiv/35)

likyng & joy (lxv/7)

reverens & mekenes (lxv/8)

swete & delectable (xlv/17)

lyghtings & tuchyngs (lxv/43)

faire & sekirly (lxv/47)

his homliest home & his endles wonyng (lxvii/13-14)

thristith & longith (lxxv/8)

convenient & spedefull (lxxv/13)

so deep & so hey (lxxv/29)

for wonder & marvell (lxxv/29-30)

tremelyn & quakyn (lxxv/32, 50, 51)

tremeland & quakand (lxxv/35)

this syte & this working (lxxv/41)

swemefully & monyngly [morynfly?] (lxxix/43)

rulith us & governith us (lxxx/19)

thankeing & prayseing (lxxxii/18) (see lxxxv/7 below)

wisely & truely (lxxxv/4)

praysand & thankand (lxxxv/7)

light & solace (lxxxvi/12)

sorow & merkness (lxxxvi/13-14)

(It is also interesting to note that in his brief addition at the end of Julian's MS the scribe uses "comfort & solace" and "shewings & revelations.")

Margery:

solas & comfort (1/2-3, 2/27, 29/28, 142/25-26, 219/27) (cf. scribe's addition above and Julian vii/53-54 above)

worschepd & magnyfyed (1/5)

hys nobeley & hys goodnesse (1/7) (cf. Julian li/112 above)

exampyl & instruccyon (1/8)

meued & stered (1/15, 47/22)

in wyl & in purpose (1/16-17, 137/6-7, 247/6)

drawyn & steryd (2/1-2)

plentyuows & abundawnt (2/11) (cf. Julian xxv/1-2 above)

lost reson & her wyttes (2/8)

slawndred & repreued (2/24, 12/29)

spak & dalyid (2/33; 178/26-27)

secret & preuy (2/37)

wepyn & sobbyn (3/1) (This idea is frequently doubled in other terms
    also: "wepyng & crying", "crying & roring", "wept, sobbyd, &
    cryed", "sobbyng & crying", etc. 12/7; 50/2; 61/6-7; 71/4-5; 71/33;
    74/26; 78/7; 83/33; 84/11; 86/35; 98/15; 107/29-30; 148/9-10;
    178/1,18; etc.)

illusyons & deceytys (3/8-9, 54/38, 63/12, 219/35)

hyr meuynggys & hyr steringgys (3/19)

voyded & deferryd (4/24-25)

diuers contres & places (6/2)

obloquie & slawndyr (6/15)

vexid & labowryd (7/22)

hastyli & qwykly, but fayr & esly (8/24)

weel & freschly (10/29)

pride & vanyte (11/3)

sotyllych & preuylich (12/32)

hir synnes & hir trespas (16/30)

bydde þe & comawnd þe (17/4)

etyn & knawyn (17/16, 154/23)

helpyn þe & kepyn þe (17/22)

my preuyteys & my cownselys (17/32, 86/17-18)

as mekely & as deuowtly (18/5)

seruyse & plesawns (19/8)

hol & sownd (22/5) (cf. Julian xlv/2 above)

opteyn & getyn (24/39, 59/30)

despysed hir & set hir at nowt (25/32)

tremelyng & whakyng (28/34, 124/24) (cf. Julian lxxv/32 and 35 above)

chedyn & fletyn (29/29)

a very spowse & a wyfe (31/32-33)

supportyn hir & helpyn hir (33/3)

preysyng & worshepyng (34/32, 179/3)

preuyd & knowyn (35/15)

benyngly & mekely (37/11, 236/2, 246/17)

prowde & veyne (38/34)

cher & contenawns (40/3-4, 56/6, 70/24, 78/35, 114/19, 195/4; etc.)

rumowr & grutchyng (40/9) (cf. 152/24 below)

chargyd & comawndyd (41/1, 63/17)

myschevys & dysesys (41/19-20)

lowly & mekely (41/24, 45/1-2, 103/15)

spechys & dalyawns (42/13; 73/20; 74/32; 113/26-27; 144/27, 32-33; etc.)
mevyd & born a-bowte (42/32)
mornynggys & wepyngys (43/3) (cf. Julian lxi/58 above)
tryfelys & japys (44/11)
ȝowr norych & ȝowr comfort (45/1)
schok & flekeryd (47/17)
prechyng & techyng, pestylens & bataylys, hungyr and famynyng
     (48/18-19) (see also 53/15 below)
gret peyn & gret dysese (48/31) (cf. Julian lxv/31 above)
tawt þis creatur & informyd hir (50/11)
speke it or telle it (50/12-13)
dredys & turmentrijs (51/17)
swet smellys & good odowrys (51/32-33)
joye & gladnes (53/1, 170/21-22)
hys cure & hys benefyce (53/14)
my lawys & my comawndments (53/16-17)
prechyng & techyng (53/15)
levyn & faryn (54/7, 14; 147/10)
helth & prosperite (54/15)
many tymes & dyuers tymes (55/7)
qwestyons & demawndys (55/8)
wer loth & not wylly (55/11)
langage & dalyawns (56/17)
relevyng & comfort (56/9, 93/14)
holpyn & relevyd (56/20)
gret ple & gret heuynes (59/1-2)
þe grettar & þe fayrare (59/6)
rest & pes (59/25, 213/25) (see also 122/19 below; cf. Julian li/11 above)
angyr & tene (62/4)
gret dissese & gret turbyl (62/12-13)
mech shame & mech reprefe (62/13-14, 74/24)
help & socowr (62/32, 124/22-23, 124/37, 102/36, etc.)
wroth & in gret angyr (64/12)
hevy cher & rewful (65/4)
mych dyspyte & mech reprefe (68/26-27, 81/28-29, 209/4)
synned & trespasyd (71/7)
mornyd & sorwyd (71/8)
detractyn hem & hyndryn hem (71/14)
thowtys & medytacyons & holy contemplacyons (71/35, 107/29, 209/10-
     11)
conueyd hir & leddyn hir abowtyn (75/15-16)
in gret heuynes & gret diswer (76/10, 231/34, 240/17)
swet deuocyon & swet meditacyons (77/37)
wondirfully & mythtyly (78/7-8)

joy & blysse (82/8, 214/12, 246/27) (cf. Julian i/56 above)
symulacyon & ypocrisy (83/20-21)
al hir lofe & al hir affeccyon (86/21-22)
sowndys & melodijs (87/36, 185/34)
sotyl & comfortabyl (88/9)
in hir brest & at hir hert (88/31)
ly to-gedir & rest to-gedir in joy & pes (90/13-14) (cf. 238/37 below)
welth & prosperyte (95/3)
slawndir & euyl wordys (95/8-9)
homly & goodly (95/21)
speryng & inqwyryng (96/21-22)
humbely & mekely (96/31)
dalyawns & communycacyon (96/35-36, 97/23)
sorwe & heuynes (98/20, 113/36, 123/18, 152/22)
pacyently & mekely (99/20, 120/1, 121/7)
deed & slayn (100/35) (cf. Julian li/349, 356-357 above)
glad & mery (102/24, 120/5, 123/25)
meche despyte & meche schame (104/24-25)
mad redy & arayd (108/24-25) (cf. Julian lx/14 above)
glosyng er flateryng (108/35)
gret noye & hynderawns (109/25)
euyl & horybyl (112/5)
ryth feyth & ryth belue (114/17-18) (cf. Julian vii/63 above)
recordyn & witnessyn (117/30)
inqwir & se (117/37)
heuy & abaschyd (119/30)
mythy & strong (119/36, 215/1)
in peys & qwyet & in reste (122/19)
wel & trewly (122/27-28, 125/9)
techyn ne chalengyn (125/38)
comownycacyon & good wordys (126/19-20)
ete & deuowryd (126/33)
heuy & pensife (127/5)
drede & heuynes (127/9-10)
flowerys & blomys (127/11, 31)
bying & sellyng (127/24)
glotonye & excesse (127/26)
letchery & vnclennesse (127/27)
repentawns & amendyng (127/33-34)
velani or blame (128/30)
wysly & discretly (135/24)
fayr & goodly (136/39)
so holy thowtys & so holy mendys (147/30-31, 149/28)
fleschly er erdly (147/34)

hy & goodly (148/2)
many tymes & ofte (152/3)
ful holily & ful deuowtly (152/16, 165/4-5)
murmowr & grutchyng (152/16, 165/4-5)
thankyngs & preysyngys (160/2) (cf. Julian lxxxii/18 above)
febyl & weyke (162/25)
trustyng & beleuyng (163/8)
brygth & cler (164/6)
clowdys & derkys (164/7)
sweme & heuynes (168/21)
trewe & not deceyuabyl (170/16)
smytyn & bityn (178/3)
hir witte & hir mende (178/34)
to rewlyn ne to gouernyn (179/2) (cf. Julian lxxx/19 above)
hys hy mercy & hys goodnes (179/4)
swetnes & deuocyon (184/33)
preying & desyryng (187/17)
so fowle & so venymowslych (190/14)
sorwe & peyne (191/13)
petows & rewful (192/7)
tendyrnes & compassyon (194/31-32)
as gret mede & as gret reward (203/11-12)
answeryd & seyd (207/1) (cf. Julian xxv/26 above)
trewe & stedfast (207/5)
visyons & felyngys (208/30)
set & purposyd (208/31)
chast & clene (208/35-36)
lofe & desir (209/6)
joye & comfort (209/25, 32)
grace & reward (210/1)
so large & so wyde (210/21-22)
myght & power (210/36)
worschep & reverens (211/38)
grace & mercy (212/35)
feer & drede (213/27)
hir dred & hir heuynes (220/3)
whelys & bloberys (222/11)
his aray & hys condicyonis (223/31)
glad & mery (226/2)
stormys & tempestys (229/16)
greuows & hedows (229/18)
a fayr man & a semly (233/26-27) (cf. Julian li/145 above)
fryke & lusty (234/20)
betyn & stongyn (237/26)

lyn & restyn (238/37)
to agyd & to weyke (239/10)
ran & lept (239/11)
ravischyd er defilyd (241/9-10)
so wery & so ouyrcomyn (241/17-18)
goodly & honestly (241/21)
plesyd & content (241/24)
voydyng & castyng ful boistowsly & vnclenly (242/22)
vn-sperd & vn-botenyd (242/36)
merueyl & wondyr (246/2, 250/30) (cf. Julian lxxv/29 above)
kan & may (246/13) (cf. Julian xlv/30-31 above)
synne & wikkydnes (248/14)
peyne & sorwe (249/10-11)
to knowyn & to trowyn (249/19)
qwyk & gredy (253/21)
qwik & ded & crucifijd (253/24)
feithyn & trustyn (253/34)

Similar to the use of paired words, but not as frequently tautological, are series: triplets, "foursomes" or more equal elements
grouped together in parallel fashion. Again, numerous examples
occur in both works, but let us notice only a sampling of some
characteristic passages (some of them are also types of rhetorical
repetition):

Julian:

almighty, al wise, all gode (v/29)
nakidly, & pleynly, & homely (v/37-38)
the hey, mervelous, singular love (xxv/8-9)
so hey, so noble, & so worthy (xxv/17-18)
hir truth, her wisdam, hir charite (xxv/23)
hey & noble & glorious & plesyng to hym (xxv/31-32)
The first was as sche grewd [*grevid*? Hudleston has *was with child*],
     þe iid was as she was in hir sorows under the Cross, the iii is as she
     is now in likyng [*pleasing*, Hudleston], worshippe, & joye (xxv/43-46)
this blissid parte is hopyn & clere & faire & lite & plentious (xxx/2-3)
the same blissid myte, wisdam, & love (xxxv/16-17)
his hey myte, his hey wisdom, his hey goodness (xxxv/33-34)
he is endles soverain trueth, endles sovereyn wisdom, endles sovereyn
     love (xliv/12-13)
he seith his God, his Lord, His Maker, so hey, so gret, & so good
     (xliv/19-20)
Our fayling is dredful, our falling is shameful, & our deyng is sorowfull
     (xlviii/25-27)

obediens, mekeness, & patience (li/314)

the fadirs joye, the sonys worshippe, the holy gost lekyng (li/373-374)

joye to the fader & bliss to the son & likyng to the holy Gost (lv/7-8)

in kind, in mercy, & in grace (lv/25-26)

for ther the soule is heyest, noblist, & worthyist when it is lowest, mekest, & myldhest (lix/22-23)

peyne, wo, & disese (lxv/31)

pite & ruth & compassion (lxxi/12-13)

love, longing, pite (lxxv/2)

for it ledith us in ryte wey, & kepith us in true life, & onyth us to God (lxxv/41-42)

Margery:

how mercyfully, how benyngly, & how charytefully (1/14-15)

pouerte, sekenes, schamis, & gret repreuys (6/1)

hir pride, hir coueytse, & desyr (11/7-8)

In prayng, in thynkyng, in wepyng, in pylgrimage goyng, in fastyng, er in any good word spekyng (20/34-35)

so swet, so holy, & so devowt (40/1)

a lowe, a meke, & a contryte hert (41/30-31)

compunccyon, contricyon, swetnesse, & deuocyon, compassyon wyth holy meditacyon & hy contemplacyon (42/10-12)

mercy, pite, & compassyon (48/14) (cf. Julian lxxi/12-13 above)

sche wept, sche sobbyd, sche cryed so lowde (71/33)

mete, drynke, & herborwe (77/26)

to purchasyn grace, mercy, & forȝeuenes for hir-self, for alle hir frendys, for alle hir enmys, & for alle þe sowlys in Purgatory (79/26-28)

þu art my joye, Lord, my blysse, my comfort, & alle þe tresor þat I haue in þis world (81/21-23)

wondir hoot & delectabyl & ryth comfortabyl (88/28-29)

cuntreys, cyteys, & townys (104/25-26)

þer had sche gret cher, bothyn bodily & gostly, hy deuocyon, & many gret cryes (110/29-30)

slawndryd hir, scornyd hir, & despysed hir (120/16-17)

to glotonye & excesse, to lust of thy body, thorw letchery & vnclennesse (127/26-27)

sweryng, lying, detraccyon, & bakbytyng, & swech oþer synnes vsyng (127/28-29)

muche despite, meche reprefe, many a scorne, many a slawndyr, many a bannyng, & many a cursyng (137/3-5)

for thyn owyn synnes, for þe gret compassyon ... for þe sorwys ... for þe angwischys ... for þe teerys ... for þe holy martyres in Heuyn ... for þe gret sorwe þat þu hast for al þis world ... & forþermor for þe sorwys þat þu hast for þe sowlys in Purgatory (159/28-160/7)

a man knelyng at hir bak, wryngyng hys handys & shewyng tokenys of
   gret heuynes (177/30-32)
mor sotyl & mor softe & mor esy to hir spiryt (209/13)
my blissyd Modyr, Mary Mawdelyn, alle apostelys, martirys, con-
   fessowrys, Kateryne, Margaret, & alle holy virginys (210/28-30)
Al myghty & al witty & al grace & goodnes (211/15-16) (cf. Julian's
   series v/29 above)
for euery good thowt, for euery good word, & for euery good dede, &
   for euery day of contemplacyon, & for alle good desyrys (213/
   7-9)
as my derworthy derlyng, as my blissyd spowse, & as myn holy wife
   (213/10-11)
bannyd me, curseyd me, & warijd me (229/29-30)
non so fayr & so semly ne so good (233/29)
qwik & ded & crucifijd (253/24)

Like the forms of repetition and paired words, series contribute
much to balance and rhythm in prose. Many of the examples
listed in the preceding pages are notable for just such characteristics;
and, indeed, balanced rhythmical constructions are a dominant
part of both Margery's and Julian's styles. In some of the series
noted above, rhythm is noticeably affected by the use (polysynde-
ton) or omission (asyndeton and brachylogia) of conjunctions,
achieving slowness and deliberateness on the one hand, and celerity
and vehemence on the other. In summing up the use of pairs and
series at the end of the fifteenth century, Saintsbury comments:

The doublets, triplets, and "foursomes" are often superfluous and
sometimes absurd as they occur. But they present, in themselves,
an infinite possibility of rhythmical adjustment and ornament, not
least because of the tendency to group Romance with Teutonic equivalents, and so to get the advantage of the different rhythmical values
and colors.[13]

Phyllis Hodgson, discussing *The Cloud of Unknowing* and related
treatises, makes much the same point: "The rhythm within these
basic designs of balanced sentences is constantly quickened by the
use of paired words, with another characteristic means of variation
being 'triple movement', or the use of series."[14]

   Parallelism, the joining of equal grammatical units, is obvious

---

[13] Saintsbury, p. 100.
[14] *Deonise Hid Diuinite*, pp. xlviii-xlix.

in the construction of paired words and items in series, but there is more to rhythm and balance than this. A difficulty occurs in the definitions of the terms themselves. To separate "rhythm" and "balance" would be difficult, and indeed there seems to be no reason to do so. According to Saintsbury, one equals the other: "that undulating movement, balanced but varied, parallel but not stichic, which constitutes the rhythm of prose" (p. 50). Although definitions and ideas of early scholars like Saintsbury and Oliver Elton often conflicted ,[15] there is no reason to oppose Saintsbury's ideas here. Herbert Read, in a recent edition of his well-known work on style,[16] says, "The scientific study of English prose rhythm, despite the very complete and provocative history devoted to it by Professor Saintsbury, is still very much in its infancy" (p. 58). Read also cites various definitions of rhythm (p. 59) that are certainly no more satisfying than Saintsbury's: "'an instinct for the difference between what sounds right and what sounds wrong' (Fowler: *Modern English Usage*)"; "'prose rhythm is a matter of emphasis; it is putting the important words where they sound important. It is a matter of coherence; it is putting the right idea in the right place'" (W. K. Wimsatt, *The Prose Style of Samuel Johnson*). For general purposes here, then, "rhythm" and "balance" may be used interchangeably with the tacit consent, at least, of some authorities.

Another difficulty occurs in the classifying of examples. Methods of classifying rhythmical patterns may be extremely complex,[17] requiring more apparatus than is really needed here; yet other forms of parallelism besides that of individual words are involved. The rhetorical types of repetition, as has been said, also provide balance and rhythm: one needs only to think of Julian's "our Lord is Almytye & may punish me mytyly, & he is al wisdam & can punish me skilfully, & he is all goodnes & lovith me full tendirly" (lxxvii/18-21) and Margery's "for þei þat louyd hir for God er sche went owte þei wolde louyn hir for God whan sche come hom"

[15] A survey of early scholarly work on rhythm appears in Norton R. Tempest, *The Rhythm of English Prose* (Cambridge, University Press, 1952).
[16] *English Prose Style* (Boston, Beacon Press, 1952).
[17] For example, John H. Scott and Zilpha E. Chandler, *Phrasal Patterns in English Prose* (New York, Ronald Press, 1932).

(247/17-18). In addition, there is the parallelism of expression often found in antithesis, in which opposed ideas are usually emphasized by the balance of opposite words. Balanced words, phrases, and sentences; antithesis, pairs and series — all mingle freely in various combinations to achieve rhythmic balance with enough variation to relieve monotony. Read (p. 59) cites Saintsbury's refusal to classify rhythms. Because a massive work devoted entirely to prose rhythm can eliminate scientific classification of examples, because definitions and systems vary and are extremely complex, I have made no attempt to classify prose rhythm technically in this brief analysis.

Briefness, however, should not be taken as a measure of importance. Carried to excess in the Euphuism of later prose, balanced and rhythmical construction is perhaps the strongest stylistic device of both Margery and Julian, for by its use thought is given an emphasis and stateliness. With her organization, analytical and single-minded approach, careful treatment of every small detail of thought, yet stress on interpretation of the abstract and the theoretical, Julian shows more thought than does Margery. Similarly, her submerging of self-interest, self-praise, and self-importance in devotion to a chosen single goal of benefit to many gives Julian a more sincere air than Margery achieves.[18] The possession of these two qualities obviously has much to do with a writer's style. Some comments by Herbert Read concerning the relationship between rhythm, sincerity, and thought are especially pertinent here:

Rhythm is not an *a priori* construction. It is not an ideal form to which we fit our words. Above all it is not a musical notation to which our words submit.

Rhythm is more profound than this. It is born not with the words, but with the thought, and with whatever confluence of instincts and emotions the thought is accompanied. As the thought takes shape in the mind, it takes *a* shape. It has always been recognized that clear thinking precedes good writing.[19]

It seems that only in writers who forget self but retain sensation, and

---

[18] This is not to say that Margery does not have a sincerity of her own. Her particular type of fidelity is consistent, and her candor is remarkable.
[19] Read, p. 61.

whose thought is an inspired contemplation (which is to say, only in true mystics) do we get this rare quality of soft rhythmical emphasis.[20]

But *rhythm* is the accent of expression and its accompaniment. It is created in the act of expression. To justify an elaborate rhythm, therefore, there must be an underlying mental activity of corresponding complexity. To invent the rhythm and fill it up with syllabic sounds is to reverse the natural process, confusing sense and sound, literature and music. Thus all prose whose rhythm is, as it were, *a priori*, is false and artificial, and though like all artificialities it may be justified as a pastime, it is not be confused with art, which is nothing if not sincere.[21]

Because both the thought and the sincerity of Julian are deeper, her extensive use of balanced structure achieves a more striking and powerful effect throughout her work: manner and matter are interwoven to produce a strong but pliable prose. Despite the deficiencies in sincerity and, more definitely, in thought, however, Margery can again make frequent artful use of the same device. Nevertheless, Julian's constructions are usually more complex, involving a number of different balancing forces and frequently achieving their greater emphasis by means of series rather than pairs, by means of reaching a climax rather than stating equivalents.

The following examples of balance are classified roughly by the chief elements involved — words, phrases, or clauses — and generally in order of increasing complexity within these groups. In many cases other balanced elements are noted, as are the frequent use of antithesis and the less common device of isocolon (parallel sentence structure with elements nearly equal in length), all indicating the complexity of construction. Some examples of rhythm in Margery are listed separately after balanced entries: although having some regularity of accent, they lack the parallelism or antithesis found in most balanced sentences.

BALANCED WORDS

Julian:

for ne nere hey ne low (li/34) (adjectives)

[20]   Read, p. 153.
[21]   Read, p. 154.

For he þat is heyest & worthyest was fullyest nowtyd & utterlyest dispitid (xx/9-10) (adjectives, adverbs, also antithesis)

But hereof am I not lerid to longen to seen hir bodyly presence while I am here, but the vertues of hir blissid soule (xxv/21-22) (nouns and antithesis)

for all that God sufferith him [the Fiend] to doe turnith us to joye & him to shame & wo (xiii/14-15) (complements, nouns, phrases, antithesis)

And if I shuld do wysely after this techyng, I shuld not only be glad for nothyng in special, ne gretly disesid for no manner of thyng (xxxv/13-15) (auxiliary verbs, predicate adjectives, prepositional phrases)

al those that lyke in hym should lyken in hir & in the likyng that he hath in hir & she in him (xxv/33-35) (verbs, prepositional phrases)

gave me ageyne the comfort & the rest in soul, in likyng & sekirnes so blisful & so myti þat no drede, no sorow, ne peyne bodily that might be suffrid should have desesid me (xv/11-14) (nouns, adjectives)

he was blinded in his reason & stonyed in his mend (li/30-31) (adjectives and prepositional phrases)

wer worshipfull to God & ryte way to me (xlv/39) (predicate complements and prepositional phrases)

& thus I saw him & sowte him, & I had him & I wantid hym; & this is & should be our comon werkeyng (x/19-21) (predicates and clauses, also antithesis and paradox)

Margery:

þe whech xal helpyn þe at al thy nede, gon wyth þe, & supportyn þe in euery place (76/17-19) (predicates)

þei wyl not deny it but be ryt glad to haue it (60/4) (predicates and pronouns)

sworyn many gret oþis & spokyn many rekles wordys (36/6-7) (predicates and adjectives)

Her werdly goodys, whech wer plentyuows & abundant at þat day, in lytyl whyle after wer ful bareyn & bare (2/10-12) (copulative verb constructions, internal paired adjectives as predicate complements, antithesis)

"þu xalt go forth wyth þes too men & woman, & I xal metyn wyth þe at morwyn & at euyn, for I must gon on my purchase & beggyn my leuyng. ["omitted in text] & so sche dede aftyr hys cownsel & went forth wyth þe frerys & þe woman (77/21-24) (nouns, prepositional phrases, predicates)

Good Lorde, make it wel & sende down sum reyn er sum wedyr þat may thorw þi mercy qwenchyn þis fyer & esyn myn hert (163/24-26) (predicates and nouns)

nowt wastyng but euyr incresyng (88/29) (participles, antithesis)

most plesawns to God & profyte to hir owyn sowle (124/10-11) (alliterative nouns, prepositional phrases)

þat whech is worshep to God & profyte to thy sowle (76/20-21) (nouns and prepositional phrases)

he ros fro þe tabyl & leyd hym on a bed (225/11-12) (predicates, phrases)

have mynde of þi wykkydnes & thynk on my goodnes (207/30-31) (predicates and phrases)

Ne hyr-self cowd neuyr telle þe grace þat sche felt, it was so heuenly, so hy a-bouen hyr reson & hyr bodyly wyttys, and her body so febyl in tym of þe presens of grace þat sche myth neuyr expressyn it wyth her word lych as sche felt it in her sowle (3/3-8) (adjectives, nouns, clauses)

sche schuld forsake hir Crystendam hir feyth, and denyin hir God, hys Modyr, & alle þe seyntys in Heuyn, hyr goode werkys & alle good vertues, hir fadyr, hir modyr, & alle hire frendys. And so sche dede. Sche slawndred hir husbond, hir frendys, and her owyn self; sche spak many a repreuows worde and many a schrewyd worde; sche knew no vertu ne goodnesse; sche desyryd all wykkydnesse; lych as þe spyrytys temptyd hir to sey & do so sche seyd & dede (7/29-37) (series of nouns, series of clauses with internal series and pairs)

þat þer shal neuyr deuyl in Helle parte þe fro me, ne awngel in Heuyn, ne man in erthe, for deuelys in Helle mow not, ne awngelys in Heuyn wyl not, ne man in erthe schal not (17/22-25) (nouns, phrases, clauses)

BALANCED PHRASES

Julian:

somtime to be in comfort & somtyme to faile & to be left to hemselfe (xv/23-24) (antithesis)

that thou myte joy with me in the love that I have in her & she in me (xxv/12-13)

these I had in truthe but litil in feling (xv/10) (antithesis)

us al havand in him that shal be saved be him (lx/3-4)

the fadir in the son & the holy Gost in the fadir & in the son (li/386-387)

at his outward havyng & at his inward goodnes (li/114-15) (paired phrases with balanced adjectives and nouns, antithesis)

but for nothing that was in earth that me lekid to leven for; ne for no

peyne that I was aferd of; ffor I trusted in God of his mercy (iii/9-11)
(phrases modified by clauses)

It needyth us to have knoweing of the littlehede of creatures & to nowtyn
all thing that is made, for to love & have God that is unmade (v/24-26)
(infinitive phrases, adjective clauses, antithesis)

fro the peyne that we felen into the bliss that we trosten (lxxxi/32)
(phrases modified by clauses, antithesis, isocolon)

Margery:

þat is thorw here charite & not thorw my merytys (251/24-25) (antithesis)

He xal joyen in þe & þu in hym (52/8-9)

many mo þan be wretyn, boþe of leuyng & of deyng, of summe to be
sauyd, of summe to be dammyd, weryn to þis creatur gret peyn & ponyschyng (54/32-35) (antithesis, isocolon, alliterative noun pair)

to wythstonde her intent & to slakyn her bost (60/7-8)

Sche sey hem many dyuers tymes & in many dyuers placys, boþe in
chirche & in hir chawmbre, at hir mete & in hir praerys, in felde & in
towne, bothyn goyng & syttyng (88/11-14)

owte of Inglond in-to Rome (96/20-21)

in party to comfort hym & in party er ellys meche mor to preuyn þe werk
of God (97/32-33) (prepositional and infinitive phrases)

sche was takyn wyth swet deuocyon & swet meditacyons þat sche wept
wyth gret sobbyng & lowde crying (77/36—78/1) (phrases and
nouns)

Sche was so vsyd to be slawndred & repreued, to be cheden & rebuked
of þe world for grace & vertu wyth whech sche was indued thorw þe
strength of þe Holy Gost þat it was to her in a maner of solas & comfort
whan sche sufferyd any dysese for þe lofe of God & for þe grace þat God
wrowht in hyr (2/24-28) (infinitive and prepositional phrases, nouns)

For þes & for alle oþer good thowtys & good dedys þat þu hast thowt in
my name & wrowt for my lofe þu xalt haue wyth me & wyth my Modyr,
wyth myn holy awngels, wyth myn apostelys, wyth myn martirys, con-
fessouris & virginys, & wyth alle myn holy seyntys al maner joye &
blysse lestyng wyth-owtyn ende (214/7-13) (phrases in both pairs and
series, nouns, predicates)

sche myth han grace to obeyn hym, louyn & dredyn hym, worschepyn &
preysyn hym, & no-thyng to louyn but þat he louyth, ne no-thyng to
welyn but þat he wolde (199/4-7) (verbal phrases, subordinate
clauses)

BALANCED CLAUSES

Julian:

for he will be sene & he wil be sowte; he wil be obedyn & he wil be trosted (x/32-33) (antithesis, isocolon)

herein were seene ii properties: that one is rightfull prayer; that other is sekir truste (i/49-50) (isocolon)

weneing that I should dye and that all creatures might suppose the same that seyen me (ii/22-23)

In this litil thing I saw iii properties: the first is that God made it, þe second is that God loveth it; the iii þat God kepith it (v/17-19) (series of clauses, both independent and subordinate clauses balanced)

I wend a sen hir in bodily presens, but I saw hir not so (xxv/28-29) (antithesis)

to the same end our good Lord ledyth it continually, & thereto hymself shal bryng it, & whan it is tyme we shal sen it (xxxv/17-19)

the servant not only he goeth, but suddenly he stirteth (li/15)

the vertu & the goodnes that we have is of Jesus Criste; the febilnes & the blindnes that we have is of Adam (li/270-271) (paired nouns, antithesis)

for the lyter we taken hem [dis-eases] & þe less price we setten at hem for love, þe less peyne shall we have in þe feling of hem, & the more thanks & mede shal we have for hem (lxiv/68-71) (nouns, adjectives, antithesis)

And as good as God is, as gret he is, & as mekil as it longith to his Godhede to be lovid, so mekill it longyth to his grethede to be dredid (lxxv/43-45) (isocolon)

For the bodily syte I have seid as I saw as trewly as I can; and for the words I have seid them ryth as our Lord shewid hem to me; & for þe gostly syghts I have seyd sum dele but I may neve[r] full tellen it; & therefore of this syght I am sterrid to sey more as God will give me grace (lxxii/3-8) (independent and dependent clauses, phrases)

For in the syte of God al man is on man & on man is all man (li/121-122) (nouns and adjectives)

al that our Lord doeth is rythful, & that he suffrith is worshipful, & in these ii is comprehendid good & ille, for all þat is good our Lord doith, & þat is evil our Lord suffrith; I sey not that ony evil is worshipful, but I sey the sufferance of our Lord God is worshipfull (xxxv/22-27) (independent and dependent clauses, nouns, antithesis, isocolon)

And ryth as he ordeyned onto to the best, ryth so he werkyth continualy & ledyth it to the same end (xxxv/34-35) (predicates)

sumtyme it is good & esye, & sumtyme it [is] hard & grevous (xlv/9-10) (paired adjectives within balanced clauses)

wilfully he ches it with gret desyr & myldly he suffrid it with wel payeyng [= "pleasing", but *paining*, Hudleston] (xx/28-30) (phrases)

For aboven the feith is no goodnes kept in this life as to my sight, & beneath the faith is no helpe of soule, but in the feith there will þe Lord þat we kepe us (lxx/40-42) (series of clauses, balanced introductory phrases)

By contritio*n* we arn made clene, be compassio*n* we arn made redy, & be trew longyng to God we arn made worthy (xxxix/28-30) (series of clauses, balanced introductory phrases)

And by his suffrance we fallyn, & in his blisful love with his myte & his wisdom we are kept, and be mercy & grace we arn reysid to manyfold more joyes (xxxv/47-49) (series of clauses with introductory phrases, paired nouns internally)

Desir we of our Lord God to dredin him reverently & to love him mekely & to trosten in him mytyly; for whan we drede him revrently & loven him mekely our troste is never in vaine. For the more that we trosten & the mytlier, the more we plesyn & worshippe our Lord that we trosten in (lxxiv/55-59) (two sets of paired clauses; series of verbal phrases; paired predicates, adjectives, and verbs)

He is with us in hevyn, very man in his owne person, us updrawand; & that was shewid in the gostly thrist. And he is with us in erth, us ledand; & that was shewid in that thrid [shewing] wher I saw God in a poynte. And he is with us in our soule, endlesly, wonand, us reuland & gemand [Hudleston and Warrack both have *keeping*]; and þat was shewed in the xvith [shewing] as I shal sey (lii/39-45) (Series of three sentences with same pattern of parallel main clause, parallel inverted participial phrase, and parallel second main clause; paired participles)

Margery:

grace ... is ower profyth yf lak of charyte be not ower hynderawnce (1/9-10) (antithesis)

Sadly he trad it & dewly he went it be-forn (2/4)

þei þat be-forn had worshepd her sythen ful scharply repreuyd her; her kynred & þei that had ben frendys wer now hyr most enmys (2/13-16) (predicates)

And lech as hys felaw dede so dede he (10/30-31)

fro when it comyth er whedyr it goth (40/19-20)

þe mor envy thei han to þe for my grace, þe bettyr xal I lofe þe (48/1-2) (antithesis)

Have mende of þi wykydnesse & thynk on my goodnes (49/17) (antithesis)

ȝyf þei do neuyr þe bettyr, hys mede xal neuyr be þe lesse (53/18-19)

sche myth a leuyd þerby ȝyf they wolde a lestyd (87/34-35)

þe brygtare þat þe sunne schyned, þe bettyr sche myth se hem (88/9-10)

mad an alyon to vndirstondyn hir whan hir owyn cuntre-men had forsakyn hir (98/6-8) (antithesis)

I am as redy, ser, to gon to preson for Goddys lofe as ȝe arn redy to gon to chirche (112/3-4)

for, ȝyf hir sorwe wer gret beforn þis gostly syght, ȝet it was wel grettar aftyr þan it was be-forn (207/21-22)

þu thynkyst þu maist not worschepyn þe Fadyr but þu worschep þe Sone, ne þu may not worschep þe Sone but þu worschep þe Holy Gost (211/11-14)

þe mor sche wept, þe yrkar was hir man of hir cumpany (233/35-36)

þe mor þat hir loue encresyd þe mor was hir sorwe for synne of þe pepil (208/14-16) (antithesis)

of vnworthy I make worthy, & of synful I make rytful (49/25-26; 41/26-27) (phrases, antithesis)

techyng hyr how sche schuld be despysed for hys lofe, how sche schuld han pacyens, settyng all hyr trost, alle hyr lofe, and alle hyr affeccyon in hym only (2/33-36) (series of nouns with same modifier repeated)

For euyr þe mor slawnder & repref þat sche sufferyd, þe mor sche incresyd in grace & in devocyon (2/29-31)

and, as þu dreue a-wey alle hir enmyis fro hir & sche stod a-lone by þe, so verily mot þu dryuyn a-wey alle myn enmijs fro me, boþin bodily and gostly, þat I may stondyn a-lone by þe (253/17-20) (predicates, phrases, paired nouns)

Gra-mercy, Lord, for alle þo synnys þu hast kept me fro whech I have not do, and gra-mercy, Lord, for al þe sorwe þat þu hast ȝouyn me for þo þat I have do, for þes gracys & for alle oþer gracys whech arn nedful to me & to alle þe creaturys in erth (253/29-33) (imperative constructions, direct address, balanced phrases, subordinate clauses, paired phrases)

RHYTHM (SOME REGULARITY WITH LACK OF PARALLELISM
OR ANTITHESIS)

Margery:

I swer to þe be my mageste þat I schal neuyr forsakyn þe (17/20-21)
(rhyme also)

þan hir husbond & sche went forth to ȝorke & to other dyuers placys
(23/7-8)

And so þer was a man of Newe Castel — hys name was Thomas Mar-
chale — whech ofte-tymes bad þis creatur (108/3-5)

went wil in a wode thorw þe sufferawns of God for þe profite of hys
sowle tyle þe nygth cam up-on hym (126/25-27)

And, ȝyf ȝe wil be contrite & schreuyn of ȝowr synne, wilfully don
penawnce & leuyn it whil ȝe may, in wil no mor to turne aȝen þerto,
I dar wel say ȝe schal be sauyd (136/6-9)

Whan hir crying was cesyd, sche seyd to þe preste (148/12-13)

I kan þe mor thank to etyn þi mete for my lofe þan to fastyn, þat þu
mayst enduryn thy perfeccyon of wepyng (162/26-28)

He seyd it stod ryth hard wyth hym, for hys wyfe was newly delyueryd
of a childe & sche was owt hir mende. "&, dame", he seyth, "sche
knowyth not me ne non of hir neyborwys" (177/33-178/1)

I prey ȝow, Lady, cesyth of ȝowr sorwyng, for ȝowr Sone is ded & owt
of peyne (193/23-24)

Of course, all stylistic devices — not merely balance and rhythm —
have effectiveness as their common purpose: keeping the reader's
interest while providing meaning, and achieving emphasis where it
is desired. Certainly one element to avoid in effective writing is
monotony, a sin of which Margery Kempe has already been accused
and partially exonerated. A further defense against this accusation
exists in her use of some positive ways of achieving variety. Subject
matter, of course, is one such element. As has been said before, the
concentrated analysis by Julian becomes monotonous for most
modern readers. But shifting the movement of Margery's chronicle
— from conversations with Christ to arguments with fellow tra-
velers, from piety and mysticism to vulgar elements of everyday
life — does much to avoid one type of monotony, as does the
reader's interest in Margery's unfolding personality and character.

In terms of style itself, Margery shows some techniques of varied expression that are also found in Julian's work, but in addition uses some devices that are more individualistic.

Inversion is one of the most obvious ways to achieve variety, and both mystics make use of it, although Wilson believes that there is a considerable difference: Margery's use is "comparatively rare" and "not apparently to gain any special effect", while Julian's is "not uncommon" but "as a rule is used skilfully to emphasize sense".[22] I believe the following examples of inverted syntax indicate both a fairly frequent use by Margery and a similarity to the effectiveness of Julian's use.

One of the commonest types of inversion, as might be expected, involves the basic sentence elements: subject, verb, and object. Of the five relative positions these elements might occupy in addition to normal SVO order,[23] Julian uses at least four:

(OVS) other sight ner shewing of God desired I never none (ii/15-16)

(OSV) hir he shewid iii tymys (xxv/43)

(SOV) I it am (lx/41)

(VSO) sett we it at nowt (lxv/34)

Margery does not show Julian's variety here, but does have a number of examples like Julian's "than was I answerid in my reson" (xxxv/6), in which subject-verb inversion occurs after an adverb.[24]

Margery:

Than had þis creatur mech drede (3/8)

þan went sche (3/9) (but, "þan sche gan", 120/24)

Than had þe creatur no wryter (4/2)

for in schort tyme aftyr on Corpus Cristi Evyn fel þis merueyl (10/14-15)
Sodeynly fel down fro þe heyest party of þe cherch-vowte fro vndyr þe fote of þe sparre on hir hed & on hir bakke a ston whech weyd iij pownd & a schort ende of a tre weyng vj pownd þat hir thowt hir bakke brakke a-syndyr (21/25-29) (Inversion clearly seems to be used "to gain a special effect" here.)

[22] Wilson, pp. 100, 106.
[23] Mossé, p. 122.
[24] Mossé, p. 127 (item 5), indicates that such inversion occurs "frequently" in Middle English.

Than askyd sche þe man (178/4)

so had sche now horybyl syghtys & abhominabyl (145/7-8)

The last example shows another frequent type of inversion — the use of post-noun adjectives, sometimes matching an adjective in normal pre-noun position.

Julian:

there be dedes evyl done in our syte (xxxii/11-12)

the erth barreyn & desert (li/169)

kirtle, sengil, old, & al defaced (li/195)

Margery:

on Estern Day at Morwyn fyrst of alle oþer (75/5-6)

þis good preste, newly come to Rome (97/12)

many gret othys & horryble[25] (110/37)

enmyis, gostly & bodily (124/23-24)

He, destytute of hys herborwe (126/27-28)

a bere, gret & boistows, hogely to beheldyn (126/31-32)

a hydows fyer & greuows (162/31)

Participles frequently seem out of normal position to modern readers, often being preceded by their objects:

Julian:

Crist is our wey, us sekirly ledand in his lawes (lv/1)

he is our Moder in mercy in our sensualite takyng. And thus our Moder is to us dyvers manner werkyng in whom our parties are kepid ondepartid (lviii/50-53)

him praysand & thankand (lxxxv/6-7)

Margery:

hem þat slen hym euery day be gret othys sweryng[26] (37/8-9)

þe seyd creatur at þe bordys ende syttyng & no word spekyng (63/29-30)

þu schalt non oþer-wyse ben slayn þan be schrewyd wordys sufferyng (85/31-32)

---

[25] For Chaucer's earlier use of much the same expression, see *PardT*, 629, 659.
[26] For earlier use of this same idea in Chaucer's Parson's Tale and elsewhere, see John M. Manly, ed., *Canterbury Tales* (New York, Holt, 1947), p. 617, note on 474 ff.

amende ȝow of ȝowr othys sweryng (124/5)

swech oþer synnes vsyng (127/29)

swetnesse þat sche had in þe word of God heryng, of þe wondirful compassyon þat sche had in hys Passyon thynkyng (153/2-4)

Her is þi name at þe Trinyte foot wretyn (207/1-2)

thorw þe vertu of hys Passyon sufferyng & hys precyows blod schedyng sche was redemyd (246/25-26)

Some other inversions also break up normal sentence flow to achieve variety:

Julian:

dygte thus nobly it (li/241-242)

Margery:

wyth hym þat wrot fyrst þe booke (4/31)

Meche was þe grace owyr Lord schewyd to þis creatur whyl sche iij wekys was in Jerusalem (72/4-5) (Subject-verb are also inverted)

so it was teld þe sayd creatur of hys sekenes (169/20-21)

In one case, Margery's syntax quite unintentionally achieves variety from the humor of a misrelated modifier:

And, whan þis creatur saw Ierusalem, rydyng on an asse (67/16-17)

Many of the positive elements of a modern, varied style are also found in both women's works, but some are surprisingly more common in Margery's. Subordination of ideas, one of the chief means of gaining emphasis, is visible in a number of forms. Participial modifiers have been noted above in inverted forms, but they appear very frequently in both works in their modern function as shortcuts to replace clauses ("The boy was tired; he went to sleep" becomes "The tired boy went to sleep.") For example in one chapter from Julian — the impressive and frequently quoted fifty-first — occur a number of present participles: "stondand", "flemand", "thynkand" and "thynkyng", "abydand", "haveing", "passand", and "clyngand". Margery also provides a number of examples showing good command of a technique that modern college teachers of composition often recommend to beginning writers — many times without success:

sche put a grote in hys hand, makyng to hym a token for to bryng hir on-to þe Mownt (74/15-16)

Frerys ... mad hir gret cher and ȝouyn hir ... relykys, desiryng þat sche schuld a dwellyd stille a-mongs hem (75/12-14)

þis creatur, beyng in gret heuynes (76/10)

he, purposyng to se þis creatur (96/27)

he clepyd hir modyr, preying hir (96/31-32)

sche, discuryng þe preuyte of hert (96/36-37)

many ..., despisyng hir, callyng hir "loller" (123/37-124/1)

The subordinating function of nominative absolutes, again making use of participles, also may be exemplified from Margery:

þe creatur beyng in hir preyers hauyng mende of þis mater, Crist seyde ... (53/12-13)

þe seyd creatur beyng present (97/22)

meche pepil beyng present (124/34)

the Erchebischop seying ful boystowsly vn-to hir (125/4)

Appositives are still another method of subordination used by both writers; but Margery makes an easier, more modern, and less wordy use of the device.

Julian:

our fader, God, as he is (li/165)

double understondyng, on withouten, another within (li/191)

The Lord is the fadir, God; the servant is the son, Christ Jesus; the holy Gost even love which is in them both (li/253-255)

his owen son, derworthy Criste (li/275)

þe son, very God & man (li/384)

our pretious Moder, Jesus, he may fedyn us with himself (lx/35-36)

our very moder, Jesus, he, al love, beareth us (lx/22-23)

Margery:

Wyllyam Sowthfeld, a good man and an holy leuar (41/3-4)

Qwen of Mercy, Goddys Modyr (50/5)

a Saraȝyn, a welfaring man (74/14)

a preste, a good man (96/20)

her owyn langage, Englysch (97/24)

þe Duche preste, a worthy clerke ..., confessowr to ... (97/24-25)

þe frute of euyrlestyng lyfe, þe Sacrament of þe Awter (127/21-22)

a worthy clerk, a good prechar (128/2)

Maystyr Robert, hir confessowr, ... Maistyr Aleyn, a doctowr of dyuinite (136/15-16)

I, synful Petyr (195/26-27)

Sentences often display varied combinations of these elements that effectively break up what could have been a monotonous listing. Julian, for example, varies a list of adjectives by alternating single words and phrases: "The place that our Lord sat on was symple, on the earth, barren & desert, alone in wildernes" (li/140-141). Similarly, Margery can control adjectives well; note in the following example how a series of superlatives is modified by a subordinate clause and then the adjectives are renewed in a different form — verbals — but with the internal variety of both past and present participles:

most semly, most bewtyuows, & most amyable þat euyr mygth be seen wyth mannys eye, clad in a mantyl of purpyl sylke, syttyng up-on hir beddys syde, lokyng vp-on hir (8/15-18)

Margery can also artfully blend a series of appositives with post-noun adjectives:

Sithyn a worshepful doctowr of divinite, a White Frer, a solem clerk & elde doctowr, & a wel a-preuyd ... toke wyth hym a worthy man, a bachelor of lawe, a wel growndyd man in scriptur & long exercisyd (150/23-28)

In another passage subordination is used effectively to pack a sentence with parallel participial constructions in a quite sophisticated manner: the subject is modified by two participial constructions (one a metaphor including an appositive) before the compound verb appears, then another participial phrase, and finally a third predicate:

Than sche, consyderyng þis wondyrful chawngyng, sekyng socowr vndyr þe wengys of hyr gostly modyr, Holy Cherch, went & obeyd hyr to hyr gostly fadyr, accusyng hyr-self of her mysdedys, & sythen ded gret bodyly penawns (2/16-20)

The use of four subordinate clauses in one sentence also indicates a control of syntax worth noting: in the following passage there is a balance between the first two and third subordinate clauses, but they are broken up by a main clause, and the fourth subordinate clause quite effectively creates a pause between the second main clause and an emphatic modifier.

ȝyf þu be þe spiryt of God þat spekyst in my sowle & I may preuyn þe for a trew spiryt wyth cownsel of þe chirche, I xal obey þi wille, and, ȝyf þu bryng me to Rome in safte, I xal weryn white clothys, þow alle þe world schuld wondyr on me, for þi lofe (76/11-16)

But differing modes of statement are a source in Margery of much variety that is lacking in Julian. The biggest single reason for this difference is Margery's excellent use of dialogue. Other types of statements — aphorisms, interpolations, an occasional proverb — are provided by Margery's looser organization and more varied subject matter; her storytelling approach makes possible narrative techniques such as the refusal to narrate[27] (133/32) and foreshortening (18/26 ff.); but, more distinctively, questions, exclamations, and direct address come about frequently in the give-and-take of conversation provided by Margery. Julian occasionally may give a quotation, but it is a statement to be analyzed or a key term of explanation or an example of thought or expression:

I cryed inwardly ... thus, "A, Lord Jesus, King of bliss, how shall I ben esyd? Ho that shall techyn me & tellyn me that me needeth to wit, if I may not at this time sen it in thee?" (1/40-44)

Julian simply does not give dialogue as such. But quite different is the work of Margery with its abundance of reported conversation. Many passages of rapid-fire dialogue occur with the accompanying questions, answers, nouns of direct address, exclamations, and revelations of character in real speech. Stichomythy is present: each speaker gives one line of dialogue, sometimes disputatious, sometimes involving antithesis or repetition of the opponent's words. To show Margery's gift for dialogue most effectively, the

---

[27] This technique is found in the *Revelations* also, but it generally involves the inability to express the mystical experience. Margery uses it in recounting human affairs.

following examples are presented not in the solid, single-paragraph form of the MS, but in modern line division for each new speaker. The first two examples are notable for the omission of dialogue tags (he said, she said).

Whan Messe was endyd, þe creatur seyd to our Lord Cryst Ihesu, "Blyssed Lord, what answer schal I ȝeue to þis man?"

"My derworthy dowtyr, sey in þe name of Ihesu þat he hath synned in letthery, in dyspeyr, & in worldly goodys kepyng."

"A, gracyows Lord, þis is hard for me to sey. He schal do me mech schame ȝyf I telle hym any lesyng."

"Drede þe not but speke boldly in my name in þe name of Ihesu for þei arn no leesyngys."

And þan sche seyd a-ȝen to owyr Lord Ihesu Crist, "Good Lord, schal he be savyd?"

"ȝa", seyd owyr Lord Ihesu, "ȝyf he wyl forsakyn hys synne & don aftyr þi cownsel. Charge hym þat he forsake hys synne & be schreue þerof & also hys offyce þat he hath wyth-owtyn-forth."

Than cam þe monk a-ȝen, "Margery, telle me my synnes."

Sche seyd, "I pray ȝow, ser, askyth not þeraftyr, for I vndyrtake for ȝowr sowle ȝe schal ben savyd, ȝyf ȝe wyl do aftyr my cownsel."

"Forsoþe I wyl not leuyn ȝow but ȝyf ȝe telle me my synne."

"Syr, I vndyrstond þat ȝe han synned in letchery, in dyspeyr, & in kepyng of wordly good."

þan stod þe monke stylle sumdel a-baschyd, & sythen he seyd, "Wheþyr haue I synned wyth wyfes er wyth sengyl women?"

"Ser, wyth wyfes."

þan seyd he "Schal I be sauyd?"

"ȝa, syr, yf ȝe wyl do aftyr my cownsel." (26/16-27/5)

þan seyd owyr Lord Ihesu Crist to þe creatur, "þow xalt no mor sen it in þis maner, þerfor thank God þat þow hast seyn. My dowtyr, Bryde, say me neuyr in þis wyse."

þan seyd þis creatur in hir thowt, "Lord, what betokenyth þis?"

"It betokenyth veniawnce."

"A, good Lord, what veniawnce?"

þan seyd owyr Lord a-ȝen to hir, "þer xal be an erdene, tel it whom þow wylt in þe name of Ihesu. For I telle þe ..." (47/24 ff.)

Sche, lyftyng vp hir hande, blissid hir. & þan þei seyd to hir, "What deuyl eyleth þe?"

Sche seyd a-ȝen, "Whos men be ȝe?"

þei answeryd a-ȝen, "þe Bischopys men."

And þan sche seyd, "Nay, forsoþe, ȝe arn lykar þe Deuelys men." (109/12-16) þan seyd þe worschepful doctowr to hir, "Woman, what doest þu her in this cuntre?"

"Syr, I come on pilgrimage to offyr her at Seynt William."

þan seyd he a-ȝen, "Hast þu an husbond?"

Sche seyd, "ȝa."

"Hast þu any lettyr of recorde?"

"Sir", sche seyd, "myn husbond ȝaf me leue wyth hys owyn mowthe. Why fare ȝe þus wyth me mor þan ȝe don wyth oþer pilgrimys þat ben her, whech han no lettyr no mor þan I have? Syr, hem ȝe latyn gon in peys & qwyet & in reste, & I may no rest have a-mongys ȝow. And, syr, ..." (122/10 ff.)

Whan sche sey hym sche cryed, "Patryk, sone, wher ha ȝe ben so long fro me?"

"ȝa, ȝa, modyr", seyd he, "I haue ben in gret peril for ȝow. I was in poynt to a ben put in preson for ȝow, & þe Meyr hath gretly turmentyd me for ȝow, & he hath takyn a-wey ȝowr scrippe fro me."

"A, good Patryk", seyd sche, "be not displesyd, for I xal prey for ȝow, & God xal rewardyn ȝowr labowr ryth wel; it is al for þe best." (118/19-26)

(The following passage is directly preceded by twelve other lines of dialogue and also follows a number of other conversations from the beginning of Capitulum 52.)

Than þe Erchebischop [of York] seyd vn-to hir, "I am euyl enformyd of þe; I her seyn þu art a ryth wikked woman."

And sche seyd a-geyn, "Sir, so I her seyn þat ȝe arn a wikkyd man. And, ȝyf ȝe ben as wikkyd as men seyn, ȝe xal neuyr come in Heuyn les þan ȝe amende ȝow whil ȝe ben her."

Than seyd he ful boistowsly, "Why, þow, what sey men of me [?]"

Sche answeryd, "Oþer men, syr, can telle ȝow wel a-now."

þan seyd a gret clerke wyth a furryd hood, "Pes, þu speke of þi-selfe & late hym ben."

Sithyn seyd þe Erchebischop to hir, "Ley þin hand on þe boke her be-forn me & swer þat þu xalt gon owt of my diocyse as sone as þu may."

"Nay, syr", sche sayd, "I praye ȝow, ȝeue me leue to gon ageyn in-to ȝorke to take my leue of my frendys."

Þan he ȝaf hir leue for on day er too. Sche thowt it was to schort a tyme, wherfor sche seyd aȝen, "Sir, I may not gon owt of þis diocyse so hastily, for I must teryin & spekyn wyth good men er I go, & I must, ser, wyth ȝowr leue, gon to Brydlyngton & spekyn wyth my confessor, a good man, þe whech was þe good Priowrys confessor þat is now canonysed."

Þan seyd þe Erchebischop to hir, "þow schalt sweryn þat þu ne xalt techyn ne chalengyn þe pepil in my diocyse."

"Nay, syr, I xal not sweryn", sche seyde, "for I xal spekyn of God & vndirnemyn hem þat sweryn gret othys wher-so-euyr I go ..." (125/16-126/3)

(Conversation continues, including Margery's heavily alliterative tale of a "lothly bere", to 128/31.)

Such passages obviously do much to enliven Margery's book, and they occur frequently: to the above examples can be added sections beginning at 32/9, 76/26, 116/1, 123/23, 135/26, 136/9, 147/34, 206/33, and 234/9, to name only a few. Margery's outspokenness, her attitude towards "sone Patryk", the Archbishop's concern about what people are saying about him are only some of the flashes of character typically revealed in her conversations. Such bonuses are difficult to find in Julian, but are a basic device of later and modern narrative technique.

Using conciseness to achieve emphasis is another highly praised modern technique. Although Margery has been criticized for her wordiness, the ease with which the conciseness of a modern writer like Hemingway can be parodied indicates the danger of carrying even this literary method to excess. But Margery frequently does have a sharp, brief statement to break up her long constructions. She can be terse and understated in "And sythen he deyd" (4/11-12), summary and economical in "Alle oþer thyng he mygth se wel a-now" (5/21) and "And so sche dede" (7/32-33). A periodic sentence, in itself a device for emphasis, can appear in brief form: "þerfor þe prest leued fully þer schuld neuyr man redyn it, but it wer special grace" (4/17-18). Another concise construction that gains considerable vigor is the contact clause: an adjoining, frequently short, parallel construction closely related to its preceding clause in thought and usually having the same subject. Strength and emphasis are apparent in the following examples:

þe man þat went wyth hir wolde not abedyn hir, he wolde a gon fro hir (234/28-29)

þan sche gan to spekyn for Goddys cawse; sche was not a-ferd (120/24-25)

I preche not, ser, I come in in no pulpytt (126/18-19)

Of course, all of the elements that have been mentioned in this section contribute to effective emphasis of ideas. All of the methods of variety lead to vigor, for without them would be vigor's opposite, monotony. Concerning the eighteenth century, it has been said that Dryden has greater vigor in poetry than does Pope because of the varied pauses in, and at the ends of, Dryden's lines, as against the monotonous regularity of the pauses in Pope's; that, in prose, both Addison and Johnson have the defect of excessive uniformity, of depressingly regular pace: "nothing is more fatal than monotony, whether it be the regularity of a saunter [Addison] or the regularity of a strut [Johnson]".[28] Some three centuries earlier many of the devices which would prevent such regularity and thus achieve a gain in vigor had already been developed and were present in English prose, especially in the narrative technique of Margery Kempe.

[28] Henry Betts, *Some Secrets of Style* (London, George Allen & Unwin, 1932), pp. 168-171.

VI

CONCLUSION

There is always the danger that intensive analysis of a literary work may lead to a deadening of that work's esthetic effect. Although the foregoing study of the "trees" may have cost some vision of the "forest", detailed examination of small parts will always be a necessary element of literary study. Here it has shown that there are many merits in the works of Julian of Norwich and Margery Kempe, although they are often obscured by some glaring weaknesses: poor organization, repetition, excessive coordination, lack of variety, and overuse of devices such as tautological pairs and stereotyped phrases. We have noted these weaknesses, but the general purpose has been a positive one: to point out the values. Where variety in subject matter and refinements in syntax are needed, we should remember that vividness, homely style, effective use of alliteration, balance, and structure are already present.

As suggested in the Introduction, it is hoped that analysis of individual works will help lead to a needed overall picture of medieval prose and the continuity of English prose style. From the two works examined here, certain facts have been observed. Alliteration continues to be abundant although critics have not considered this prose alliterative. Sentence structure is a very important element, making more use of repetition, rhythm, and balance than we feel proper today, but being a source of emphasis in its joining of appropriate form to match the thought. Diction, although not modern, frequently has the merit of vividness and vigor. Variety and the means to achieve it are visible more than they have been admitted by some scholars. Narrative technique and dialogue are used in a surprisingly effective fashion. The monotony of unvaried conjunctions, repetition, and awkwardness of diction are the main weaknesses indicating the road that prose still has to travel.

More particularly, Margery Kempe shows many features similar to those of Julian of Norwich, considered one of the best Middle English prose writers. The stress on Margery in this study should not be taken to mean that she is a better writer than Julian; both have their merits and their flaws. Julian is more thoughtful and better organized. In her deeper thought she possesses one of the most important elements of writing:

> The greatest English prose writers Swift, Milton, Taylor, Hooker, Berkely, Shelley, are great not only by virtue of their prose style, but also by virtue of the profundity of their outlook on the world. And these are not separable and distinct virtues, but two aspects of one reality. The thought seems to mould and accentuate the style, and the style reacts to mould and accentuate the thought. It is one process of creation, one art, one aim.[1]

Expectedly, then, Julian surpasses Margery in sentence structure and the effective use of balance and rhythm to match the thought. In addition, she has the "true eloquence" determined, according to Read, by the dominance of some idea in the writer's mind ordering the rhetoric to the single purpose of that idea.[2] Margery may have the eloquence of emotion, but Julian's is of a higher, controlled type: eloquence that is "not created by a stress of emotion, but is a sustained state, a predominating passion — passion always, in this context, implying control".[3]

The work of Margery Kempe, however, has its particular distinction. Such a direct view of the life of the times is rarely found in devotional literature. As an example of autobiography and for the candor with which character is revealed, the *Book* is similarly notable. Although weaker in organization, Margery Kempe at least partially atones for this shortcoming by her much more varied content, which contributes to her style in various ways. Despite losing all sense of chronology, the modern reader would still be more likely to stay with Margery than with Julian.

[1] Read, p. 182.
[2] *Ibid.*
[3] Read, p. 183.

The use of anecdotes and dialogue in the development of her narrative also is strikingly effective in Margery. Her figurative language is stronger at least in the sense of being more natural and homely. Margery's more obvious use of alliteration may be explained by her definite illiteracy. She, more than Julian, may have been in the oral tradition that Chambers said transmitted alliterative poetry. The point that critics of her style appear to have missed, however, is that in all elements where she is weaker — except organization — Margery displays many of the same strengths and techniques shown by Julian: rhythm and balance, rhetorical types of sentence structure, matching of style to thought. Similarly, in weaknesses that Margery possesses — notably monotonous coordination — Julian shares. In the case of Margery, however, it is a lively monotony, like that of the gossip, that has its own perverse attraction and, at least the first time, freshness. The dichotomy of Margery may be said to illustrate Saintsbury's dictum: "All bad language has a positive tendency to vivacity, though also to monotony."[4]

The prose of the late Middle English period has much to offer. If it is true that "with rhythm and structure we have the elements of literary art",[5] the works studied here are important and worthy of intensive study as literature, not merely as examples of medieval piety.

[4] Saintsbury, p. 58.
[5] Read, p. 147.

APPENDIX A

ASSONANCE AND CONSONANCE

It is comparatively rare to find assonance or consonance without some accompanying alliteration, but some examples do occur in which the initial sound of an occasional stressed syllable is sustained by that same sound mainly in unstressed positions. Such examples generally may be considered as assonance or consonance rather than as alliteration. The line between such classifications, however, may be an extremely fine one, and many passages involving considerable assonance or consonance are cited as examples of alliteration because the sound predominates in stressed positions (beginning of word or beginning of accented syllable). The following few passages offer examples of basically unstressed sounds used repetitively enough to achieve some slight emphasis. The basic sound is indicated in parenthesis before the example.

CONSONANCE

Margery:

(r) pur watyr-dropys rennyng doun be her chekys (100/24-25)

(r) & þe Erchebischop ful goodly grawntyd hir al hir desyr, owr Lord rewarde hym hys mede, & delueryd hyr purs wyth hir ryng & hir bedys whech þe Dukys men of Bedforth had takyn fro hir beforn (134/25-29)

(r consonance, g alliteration) cryes be-syden þe grave of þe good Vicary, al rauyschyd wyth gostly comfort in þe goodnes of owr Lord þat wrowt so gret grace for hys seruawnt whech had ben hir confessowr & many tymes herd hir confessyon of al hir leuyng, & ministryd to hir þe precyows Sacrament of þe Awter diuers tymes (147/22-27)

Julian:

(k sound) the first is groundid of our kinde makeying; the second is taken of our kinde (lix/51-52)

(k sound) endless continuant love with sekirnes of kepyng (xlvi/16-17)

(k sound) And be this meke knowing thus throw contritio*n* & grace we shall be broken fro all things (lxxviii/24-26)

(k sound) & he lokyth thereafter & he wil have it, ffor with his grace he makyth us lyke to hymself in conditio*n* as we arn in kynd (xli/43-45)

(f and l) The heyest bliss that is, is to have him in cleerty of endless life, him verily seand, him swetely feland, all perfectly haveand in fulhede of joy (lxxii/6-8)

(l) Than I saw the Lord take no place in his owne house but I saw him rialy regne in his hous & fulfillid it with joy & mirth himselfe endlessly to gladen and solacyn his derworthy frends ful homeley & ful curtesly with mervelous melody of endles love in his owen faire blissid chere, which glorious chere of the Godhede fulfilleth hevyn of joy & bliss (xiv/6-12)

(l) the stinke was so vile & so peynfull & also dredfull, & travellous (lxix/2-3)

(r) This steryng was mikel to forsakyn, & nevertheless mornyng & sorowe I made therefore without reason & discretio*n* (xxvii/9-11)

(r) & it mon now ben sen & felt in mesure be the gracious presence of our Lord whan it is, which presens in al thing is most desirid, for it werkith mervelous sekirness in trew feith & sekir hope be gretness of charite in dred (lv/13-17)

(s, r, l) we have our rewarding & our restyng for our livyng & our travel, & endles overpassing all þat we desiren in his mervelous curtesy of his hey plentivous grace (lviii/28-33)

ASSONANCE

Margery:

my lawys & my comawndmentys so þat þer be no defawte (53/17)

þei seyd nay (74/11-12)

ordeynd a wayne (234/32)

bedred men & women (251/17)

wel helpyn hem-self (74/12)

comendyd hym in hys entent (246/18)

sche is a ryth gret mene to me for þe in þe blysse of Heuyn (210/20)

verily wetyn what peyn it is for to forbere me, & how swet it is for to fele me, & þat þu xuldist be þe mor besy for to sekyn me a-ȝen (205/8-10)

ȝowr scorge and faryth wyth ȝow as a smyth wyth a fyle þat makyth þe yron to be bryte & cler to þe sygth whech be-forn aperyd rusty, dyrke, & euyl colowryd (44/30-33)

hys wyl myt be fulfyllyd (60/5)

as sone as þei come hom to her hostel, þe wederyng fel as sche felt be reuelacyon (101/21-23)

sworyn gret othys & brokyn þe comawndment of owr Lord God (101/17-18)

Julian:

And with this word the person that I spake to waxid al sad & mervelid & anon I was sor ashamid & astonyed (lxvi/19-21)

But whan we sen hym not so, than fele we nede & cause to pray for faylyng, for ablyng of our selfe to Jesus (xliii/32-33)

for we shal sen verily in hevyn withouten end that we have grevously synned in this life, & notwithstondyng this we shal sen that we were never hurt in his love, ne were never the less of price in his syte (lxi/22-25)

these iii ben (lxxx/5)

And in the first reason thus he seith "And þu besekyst it"; there he shewith ful gret plesance & endles mede that he will gevyn us for our besekyng (xli/18-21)

it is ther aforn God with al his holy continuly recevyd, ever spedand our nedys, & whan we shal underfongyn our bliss it shal be gevyn us for a degre of joye (xli/39-41)

And the cause he wil we know is for he wil we be þe more esyd in our soule & pesid in love, levyng the beholdyng of al tempests (xxxii/31-33)

þe creature þat seith & felith þe werkyng (lii/61)

This breking & this helyng our Lord menith be the generall man (lxxviii/28-29)

Than is this the remedy: that we ben aknowen our writchidnes & flen to our Lord; for ever the more nedier that we ben, the more spedefull it is to us to neyghen him (lxxvii/14-16)

wher our Lord apperith, peas is taken & wreth hath no place (xlix/15-16)

fulfillen us in bliss (lxxv/16)

for in manys soule is his very wonyng, & the heyest lyte & the brightest shynyng of the cite is the glorious love of our Lord as to my syte (lvxii/34-35)

APPENDIX B

CONSECUTIVE ALLITERATION

The following examples of consecutive alliteration represent only a sampling from the large number found in Margery's work. Many of Margery's consecutive uses are commonplaces ("many mo", "worshepful woman", "makyn mery") or accidents: "to-Wilsnak-ward" (234/14), but "to-Ierusalem-ward" (44/5). Some very common examples may have been influenced by church activities ("derworthy dowtyr" may have been used in the confessional); others show the Scriptural influence so pervasive in Margery's work: "Woman, why wepist þu" (197/14, cf. John xx.13, 15), "iiij days ded" (253/23, cf. John xi.39), "many-fold mercy" (221/2-3, cf. Neh. xi.10). Despite Margery's lack of originality and the non-exhaustive nature of the listing, these examples may help to indicate how this type contributes to the *Book's* total alliterative impression. The examples have been alphabetized to prevent duplication as much as possible; some make use of both unstressed and stressed sounds, and some go beyond consecutive words to show more alliterative flavor.

alle awngelys (50/8)
And a-non aftyr cam hir good awngel (145/33-34)
ankyr, answeryng (44/24)
bakke brakke (21/29)
bedys byddyng (205/30)
belwys blowyng (90/36)
ben obedient (222/27)
beyng brygth (164/6)
blisful body brostyn (192/38)
blissyd body (192/3)
blissyd body in forme of breed (211/33-34)

body betyn (140/10-11)
born a-bowte (42/32, 171/30)
hys handys wer bowndyn a-bouyn hys heuyd. And þan sche sey sextene
    men wyth sextene scorgys (191/5-7)
Bridis boke (39/24, 47/34)
clerk recuryd (170/6)
clerkys clepyd (116/32)
confessowr cownselyd (151/17-18)
creatur cryed (4/26)
Cristen kyngys (250/13)
iiij days ded (253/23)
dedys doyng (205/32)
derworthy derlyng (52/31, 213/10)
derworthy dowtyr (17/9, 14/38, 26/18, 29/19-20, 50/6, 73/10, 81/26-27,
    etc.)
diuers days (59/9)
dolful deth þat he deyd (148/16-17)
don dew penawnce (176/2)
euyl enformyd (125/17)
euyl entisyng (222/8)
euyr encresyd (192/21)
eyne enduryd (29/16)
fals feith (248/28)
fals feynyd (156/4)
fals flesch (243/21, 244/6, 244/24)
famows frerys in Inglond (148/33)
far fayr (109/30)
fawyn folwyn (44/23-24)
fayr flowerys (126/34, 127/11)
wyth many fayr flowers & wyth many swete spicys (210/31-32)
fleschly affeccyon (70/28, also 161/17)
folwyd forth (189/23-24)
for fro felyng (16/21-22)
fremd folk (119/26)
frendys forsake (157/15)
ful fawyn (173/11)
ful falsly (32/30)
ful fayr (56/24)
ful febyl (127/22)
fyrst felyngys (3/29, 220/13)
gaderyng to-gedyr (124/35)
getyn grace (150/14)
God grawnt (43/13)
gon a-geyn (155/29)

good game (28/16)
goodly grawntyd (134/26)
gotyn grace a-geyn (218/18)
grace God ȝafe (16/11-12, similarly 108/20)
gret game (244/26)
gret gladnes (25/18, 108/2)
gret goodnes (207/33, 250/31-32)
gret goodys (37/7)
gret grace (19/1, 25/16, 40/32, 43/24, 43/29, 51/21, 65/24, 75/20, 166/1)
haddyn hir hom (108/1)
helpyn hem, here my preyerys for hem (253/27-28)
behestyd hym (136/23)
hool hert (218/31)
invyows enmyis (100/23)
kendly cuntre (100/29)
kepars cownseld (8/30-31)
lay a-loone (8/11)
left a-lone (135/11)
Lordys lettyr (136/22, 136/25, 136/37-38)
Lordys lofe (13/3, 42/2-3, 112/28, 113/20, 119/27, etc.)
mad mythy (215/1)
makyth mencyon (59/33, 126/7, 225/20)
mannys meryte (79/19-20)
many-fold mercy (221/2-3, 230/1)
many men merueyled (135/25)
many men mote (249/22-23)
Many mo (54/27, 54/32, 137/10, 177/23, 190/36, etc.)
Me merueylyth mech of þis woman why sche wepith (143/16-17)
mech mone (54/10)
mech mede (180/25)
meche meny (173/28-29, 238/2)
meche multitude (123/13-14)
meke man (41/33)
mennys membrys (145/9-10)
a merowr amongys hem (186/13-14)
Modyrs maydyn (203/9)
a-mongs men (132/37)
mor magnifijd amongys (201/2-3)
mor mede (204/36)
mor myty (220/16)
multiplyed many (133/31)
my mercyful Modyr (218/28)
my Modyr had her in erde (159/30)
mych more mery (13/3-4, 73/21, 123/18-19)

myth mekyn hys hert (150/12-13)
mythist makyn me (184/16)
parisch preste (163/13-14)
perlyows pepil (240/28)
personys compleynyd to þe Prouincyal (168/4-5)
petowsly poyntyd (111/6)
pilgryme purposyng (109/26)
preste compleyned (56/16)
preste prechyn (95/23-24)
prestys presens (127/1)
preste preyd (58/15-16)
preste preysed (56/17)
preuy place (200/29)
propyr persoone (2/3, also 112/33-34)
vnresonably wretyn (4/40)
same cyte (41/2)
Sauyowr sufiyr (185/5)
sayd sone (117/33)
schal schewen (2/6)
sche schewyd (38/31)
schewyd schort cher (247/5)
sekenes scapyd (138/22)
sekyng socowr (2/17)
seyst soth (48/6)
so sodynly a-sundyr (228/33)
so sor (164/36, 234/27, 235/33)
sodeyn sekenes (83/18, 20)
sodeyn sorwe (98/20)
sodeynly sle (21/12, 23/30)
sone consentyng (22/30-31)
xal sone sesyn (230/29)
sor syhyng & sorwyng (176/7-8)
sore a-stoyned (21/21)
souereyn Sauyowr (1/4, 221/1)
sowlys sauyd (142/3)
specialy sent (190/5)
spirit sent (143/30)
stod stille & suffyrd wol mekely tyl it was cesyd and sithyn seyd forth
    hys sermowne (166/4-5)
stod stylle (36/16, 60/14, 120/20)
stonys smale & grete, gresys growing in al erthe, kyrnellys of corn,
    fischys, fowelys (252/5-6)
suffyr despitys & scornys (131/17)
suffyr sorwe (154/35)

suffyrd scornys (245/16)
sumtyme stille (155/37)
swech a sorwe (164/29)
sweche sowndys (87/36)
swech symulacyon (15/14)
swet sauowr (171/13)
swet smellys (51/32, 87/31, 171/17)
swet Sone (50/7, 73/15, 90/21, 196/24-25)
swet spech (73/20)
sympil sowle (182/21, 201/4)
synguler solas (142/25)
syttyn stylle (65/34-35, 217/38)
tunge telle (53/5)
tydingys trewe (230/27)
was wont (169/31-32, 169/32)
waschyn awey (249/3)
wast wel wers (5/22-23)
wel worthy (159/23)
wept wondyr sor (208/11)
wept wondyrly (26/15, also 153/19)
wery weys (241/3)
weryn white (76/14-15)
wesch a-wey (193/33)
wetyst wel þe sunne schynyth al abrod þat many man may se it (31/16-17)
whakyd wondirly (124/24-25)
what wyth wel & wyth woo (234/39)
wil wetyn why I go in whyte (116/29)
Wilsnak, wher is worschepyd (232/10)
womanys witte (228/35)
women wept (130/36)
wonderful werkys (1/13-14, also 22/12)
wondyr why þu wepist so sor whan þu receyuyst me (213/12-13)
wondyr wyde (148/30)
worde wrowt so sor in hir herte (107/32-33)
world wer worthy (250/31-32)
worshepful woman (54/20, similarly 77/33-34, 202/21, 238/9)
went to the worschepful woman, wenyng to a be receyuyd (240/7)
a worschepful woman cam fro London, a wedow wyth meche meny
    (238/2-3)
worthy woman (202/22, 32)
wost wel þat I sen sum-tyme many gret reynys & scharp schowerys, &
    sumtyme but smale & softe dropis (183/5-7)
wot we wel (126/14)
wyfe was worthy (179/23-24)

wykked wyndys (100/23)
wyst wel (12/10, similarly 31/16, 77/5, 85/19, 89/3, 98/4, etc.)
wyth wil (137/6)
wytnessyd wel (100/24)

APPENDIX C

ALLITERATIVE USAGES BY MARGERY KEMPE AND
JULIAN OF NORWICH

Chapter Four and Appendix B show extensive use of alliteration by Margery Kempe. In the following examples, alliteration in both Margery's and Julian's works is listed to give some idea of relative frequency and similarity of use. Although Margery uses alliteration more than Julian, the following listing indicates that Julian's use is not merely confined to alliterating doublets. Many examples are undoubtedly trite commonplaces; but the fact remains that these alliterative groups are present in Julian's work. The following examples — sentences in some cases, short phrases in others — are listed alphabetically with the exception of vowels, which are grouped at the end under "vocalic alliteration" since dissimilar vowels may be involved. Examples involving combinations of sounds will be found after vowels. Although inconsistent with older tradition, sounds in some unstressed syllables have been included here, as they were in Chapter Four, as contributing to alliteration on the basis of both sight and sound. In such cases, however, I have used examples in which the alliterating sound appears in at least one stressed syllable. Examples like Margery's "obstakyl ne obieccyon" (41/25), in which there is little doubt that the first syllable is unstressed in both words, have been omitted (Chaucer several times rhymes *noon obstacle* with *miracle*: KnT 1787, *MchT* 1659, *FklT* 1300).

Some of the entries in Chapter Four and Appendix B may not be represented here: those materials were gleaned from a sweeping, nonexhaustive reading of the entire text. The materials here represent a thorough examination of individual chapters, at least every fifth one, occasionally several in succession. Within each letter group, listings are roughly alphabetical according to what seems to be the key word. Difficulty arises when words such as "God" and "grace", each a key word, appear together; individual groupings tend to break down or be incorporated into other groups. Because of this interweaving of key words, examination of the full listing under a given letter is necessary to view the extent of alliteration, especially in similar uses by both mystics. So that such indications of common tradition may be seen more easily, I have placed the examples from both writers together under each letter. Because prose does not have the measurable lines of poetry, I have had to make arbitrary decisions in some cases where sounds came or did not come "close enough" together to give an alliterative flavor.

B

Julian:
ben al browte up above (xxxv/12-13)
bliss

> be now in bliss (lxxv/6)
> ben in the bliss (lxxxv/6)
> born us to blis (lx/28)
> bringith us to his bliss (lxxx/20)
> broute to his bliss (xlvii/38-39, lxxx/23-24)
> brynen us to bliss (li/139)

blissid, blissful

> blissyd ... be(n) (x/116, lx/24, lxx/7, lxxv/16-17)
> blissid blode (xii/15)
> blissid brest (lx/46-47)
> blisful body (xx/15)
> al blisfully beflowyth (xii/19)
> bright, blissid Lord bare for our sins (x/40-41)
> foule blak dede sheme wherein our faire, bryhte, blissid Lord
>   God is hid (x/66-67)
> blisful beholdyng (xxxii/15-16, lxiv/45, lxxvi/48)
> blisful behest (lxx/31-32)

blood

 the bed al on blode (xii/11)

 blode ascendid up into hevyn to the blissid body of our
  Lord Jesus Christe & there is in him bleding (xii/29-31)

 the pretious blode was bled oute the swete body (xvi/16-17)

 beholding the body plentiously bleding (xii/1)

body

 bodily forth brynging be but litil (lx/57-58)

 in his body mytyly berith (lv/2)

 bolnehede of the body betokenith (lxiv/36-37)

braste her bands (xii/24)

bristinid in brekyng (lx/65)

of the brownehede & blakehede (x/44-45)

in his benignite & in his buxumhede (xlix/25-26)

Margery:

bad hem borwe (35/33-34)

bareyn & bare (2/12)

be

 be not abaschyd (54/13)

 ben obedient (222/27)

 no better be (208/1)

 beyng in bedde (109/6)

 beyng brygth (164/6)

beryn

 beryn a fagot to bren þe (36/15)

 best to beryn (163/11)

 bar a bettyr chylde (195/16)

belschyd, and blomys (126/30)

þi blisse & þe beholdyng (249/11-12)

blissyd ... be(n) (9/1, 16/31, 37/3-4, 60/13, 78/11, 98/6, 164/9, 165/
 18-19, 170/21, 197/9-10, 208/14, 223/10, 225/8, 230/30, 253/6)

blissyd, blissful ... body

 blyssyd body (192/3)

 my blissyd body in forme of breed (211/33-34)

 blisful body brostyn (192/38)

beholdyn þi blisful body (249/29)
blisful Lady bowyd down to hir Sonys body (193/31)
body

body þat he hath bowte (52/8)
body al a-bowtyn (196/29)
beryn owr Lordys body (194/13)
beryn þat precyows body (194/14-15)
blood in þi body (249/9)
born of hir body (101/4)
bond of wedlak to myn husbond, as I am bowndyn (112/16)
book

neuyr boke, neyþyr Hyltons boke ne Bridis boke (39/23-24)
Brides boke (47/34)
browt ... boke (4/14, 126/16)
born a-bowte (42/32)
born þe Sacrament a-boute (107/25-26)
bowndyn a-bouyn (191/6)
bowndyn to obediens (227/2)
brennyng in hir brest (88/31, 88/34)
owte of Breteyn in-to Bristowe (108/24)
broken-back

Richard wyth þe broke bak (77/29)
a broke-bakkyd man (77/1)
brokyn-bak man (44/15)
be buxom & bonyr to do what I byd (87/20)
be buxom & bonowr to my wil & to my byddyng (161/25-26)
be obediens (170/2)
be þe byddyng (3/9-10)
þi byddyng of many bedys (17/26)

C

Julian:

care & keping (lv/21)
chonge-chere

withoute chongyng of chere (xiii/35)

he chongyd his blissfull chere. The chongyng of his blissful
    chere chongyd myn (xxi/11-12)
sodenly he shall chonge his chere (xxi/19)
chongith no chere (lxxviii/13)
chongyng of colour & chere, sometyme more comfortably
    (x/74)
kepith Crist alone al the charg (lxxx/38)
Christs clothing (li/363)
the clertye & the clernes (xliv/22)
color of his clothyng (li/110)
clothyng was a white kirtle (li/195)
comith of the kynd love (lv/16)
because of this gostly comfort (xl/29-30)
ryth so was the comforte shewid: sekirnes & kepyng for al myn
    even-Cristen (xxxvii/13-14)
comprehendith all his cretures (v/47)
for we hold not our covenants ne kepe we our cleness (lxxiii/41-42)
couthest not kepe (lxx/22)
creature that cowde no letter (ii/2)
our curtes Lord that he kepyth (xl/1-2)
curtes Lord comfortith (li/137)

Margery:

occasyon in-to þe Priowrys Cloistyr (164/15)
cawsyd hir to compleyn (98/21)
in charite & in chastite (207/13-14)
in chirche & in hir chawmbre (88/12)
choppyng & chongyng (127/24-25)
clep —
    clepyd & kallyd (11/3)
    clepist al þe cowrt (210/22)
    clepist my Modyr for to comyn (210/9)
cler xuld be so sone chongyd in-to clowdys (164/6-7)
a clerk cam (120/10, 128/9)
clerk recuryd (170/6)
a cloke ful of clowtys (77/9)

clothys, clothyng

 clad in white clothys (76/8)

 clothyn me al in whygth clothys (34/12)

 clothys of whyte & non oþer colowr (32/17-18)

 His cloþes wer al for-clowtyd (76/25)

 for whech cause I haue take my cownsel & my cownsel wil not
 ȝyf me to professe ȝow in so synguler a clothyng (35/9-11)

 He curyd hir in þe schip wyth hys owyn clothys, for ellys sche
 myth a deyd for cold (231/18-20)

come

 cam a good clerke (123/30, 164/27-28)

 as ye kan & comyth (18/5)

 cam & comfortyd (77/29)

 comyn a-geyn & comfortyn (196/8-9)

 cam hir confessowr to hir & askyd (163/10)

 cam hom a-geyn to Lynne, excusyng hir to hir confessowr
 (228/29-30)

 On Corpus Cristi Euyn it lukkyd hem to comyn (234/21)

 be inqwyryng he cam (96/30)

 cownselyn hym to comyn (224/22)

 cuntre þat sche cam fro (229/6-7)

comfort

 þei comfortyd hir whan hir cuntremen wolde not knowyn hir
 (74/21-22)

 comfort of any confessowr (44/10-11)

 comfortyd hym as wel as sche cowde (234/4)

þe qwer wher a cors (53/22)

cowdyst þu wel cryen (161/18)

kendly cuntre (100/29)

her craft & her cunnyng (229/21)

creatur

 cam to þe creatur (5/14)

 creatur cam (34/27)

 Candelmesse Day whan þe sayd creatur be-held þe pepil wyth
 her candelys (198/1-3)

 cawsed þe creatur to wepyn, to sobbyn, & to cryin (197/6-7)

þis cawse he feyned thorw cownsel of hys clerkys, for þei louyd
    not þis creatur (35/32-33)

creatur was clad in blak clothyng (38/20-21)

creatur herd as clerly (195/22)

clerkys askyd þis creatur many hard qwestyons (35/2-3)

creatur was mech comfortyd (42/5)

creatur was comyn (74/33)

creatur in-to þe contre (33/8)

creatur had greet cownsel (6/7-8)

cownselyng þis creatur (42/19)

þe creatur cryed (4/26)

creatur thowt þat sche cryid owt of þe Iewys & seyd, "ȝe
    cursyd Iewys, why sle ȝe my Lord Ihesu Crist?" (192/28-30)

creaturys as wold inqwiryn (46/21)

request of this creatur & compelling of hys owyn consciens
    (6/19-20)

creatur lay in þe qwer (53/29)

Cristys owyn Modyr, cryed not as sche dede, & þat cawsyd hir
    to seyn in hir crying (164/24-25)

Cristen kyngys (250/13)

D

Julian:

dured till day and be than my body was dede fro the middis downe-
    ward (iii/21-22)

Then seid I ... "It is to-day domys day with me." & this I seid for
    I wend a deid; for that day that a man deith, he is demyd (viii/28-
31) dede as to manys dome (1/3-4)

Deed

    deeds that he hath done (i/38)

    to don that worshipfull dede (li/278)

    so long durid the cost & the charge about our redemption in
        dede (xxiii/26-27)

delvyn & dykyn, swinkin & swetyn (li/225)

depe depenes (li/353)

dereworthy blode descendid downe (xii/23-24)

deth of his derworthy son (lii/51-52)
duble deth (lv/54)
done as it was then ordeynid (lxxxv/18)
þe drawyng & the draggyng (li/341-2)
drawith & drinketh (lxxv/7)
drede

>The iij is doubtful drede. Doutful drede in as mech as it drawith
>>to dispeir. (lxxiv/12-14)
>that other is dispeir or doubtfull drede (lxxii/11)
>dwellith a drede (lxxiii/38)

Margery:

daggyd & leyd wyth dyvers colowrs be-twen þe daggys (9/15-16)
day

>Day of Dom (52/12)
>he dede euery day (34/30)
>demenyd þat day (124/10)
>divers days (59/9)
>in dyrkenes as on day-lygth (88/15-16)
>iiij days ded (253/23)

derworthy derlyng (52/31, 213/10, 252/30-31)
derworthy dowtyr (17/9, 50/6, 161/2-3, 213/33)
þe dolful deth þat he deyd (148/16-17)
defye þe Deuyl (248/29)
do

>don to hem in any degre (213/35-36)
>don his diligence (53/14-15)
>don as þow dost (48/12)
>"Do it a-wey, dowtyr ..." (195/9)
>don þis hors drawyn (10/21, 10/26)

doctowr of dyuinyte (3/11-12, 123/21-22, 136/16)
draw

>wold drawe no drawt (10/19)
>Dowtyr, I haue drawe (161/13)
>dowtyr, ȝyf þu wilt drawyn (207/11-12)

dread

>for dreed sche had of dampnacyon (7/19)

I drede me to be deed (100/35)

dredyn þe Devyl (51/9)

drede no grevows peynes in þi deyng, for þu xalt haue thy
    desyre (51/7-8)

"Drede þe not, dowtyr, þer schal no man deyin" (75/31)

he durst for dred (32/29)

ne drynke ne dalyawns (199/27)

dede hir drynkyn (164/33-34, 148/1)

dwellyng in Dewchlond (4/4-5)

F

Julian:

face

His fair face (i/11, li/179)

face was faire browne (li/144)

the fair curtesie that is hevyn afore Gods face (lxxv/46)

Face who is the fairhede of heavyn, flowre of erth & the fruite
    of the mayden wombe (x/97-98)

face of the crucifix (x/1-2, 111/34)

before my face (111/28)

fader(-hode)

fader I stond befor thee (li/293)

aforne þe fader (li/277, 310, 368, 370, 375)

fulfilling of his faders will so he stode afore his fader (li/282-283)

faderhode & moderhede is fulfilled (lx/73)

& therefore we failen often tymes of þe syte of hym, & anon we
    fallen into our self & than fynde we no felyng of ryth, nowte
    but contrarious that is in our selfe & þat of þe elder rote of
    our first synne wyth all that followyn (xlvii/45-49)

faylyng of comforte, for he cowde turne his face to loke up on his
    lovyng Lord which was to hym ful nere in whom is ful comfort,
    but as a man that was febil & onwise for the tyme he entended
    to his felyng ... the first was the sore brosyng the he toke in
    hys fallyng, which was to hym felable peyne. The ii was the

hevynes of his body. The iii was febilnes folowyng of these
two. The iiii that he was blinded in his reason & stonyed in
his mend so fer forth that almost he had forgotten his owne
luf. The v was that he myte not rysen. (li/22-32)

fair

> faire & fele (vi/25-26)
>
> so fer fro faire (x/49)
>
> fair flemand (li/182)
>
> the faire skyn*n*e was brokyn ful depe into the tendir flesh
> (xii/2-3)
>
> ful faire (lxv/47)

fallen be frelte (lxxix/36)

febil(-nes)

> ful febil (li/123)
>
> febilness & fayling (lxiii/50)
>
> febilnes that folowith (li/268)
>
> febilnes folowyng (li/29)
>
> we have of our febilnes & our foly to fallen (lxxvii/3-4)

he fedith us & frethes [*furthereth*, Hudleston; but *MED frethen* =
   "protect", "relieve"] us (lxiii/37)

folow the felynge (xv/35-36)

ful fel & fers (xxxix/51)

for I saw & felt that his mervelous & fulsome goodnes fulfillith
   al our mytys (xliii/42-43)

felt beforn (lxxv/31)

festyn it feyfully (lxx/29)

foule dedly flesh (li/357)

formyth in our feith (lv/22)

aforn enformyd (xlvi/19-20)

so fer forth that onethys I had ony feleing (iii/43)

for in that tyme he shewid our frelte & our fallyngs, our brekyngs
   & our nowtyngs, our dispits & our outcastings & all our wo
   so fer forth as me thowte it myt fallen in this life (lxii/1-4)

fulfill

> fulfilling the noumber that failith (xii/34)
>
> fulfillid of feling (lv/63)
>
> fulfilled with minde & felyng (iii/55)

Margery:

fel fro Goddys face (252/21)
fleth al fals feynyng & falshede (41/30)
forsokyn hir, & ful falsly (32/30)
far fayr wyth me, & I xal far fayr wyth the (109/30-31)
for fayrar, for fowelar (87/19)
ful febyl (127/22)
feynt & feble (38/11)
fele lofe of affecyon to hir gostly fadyr (45/13-14)
on hir feet for þe fervowr of lofe (198/18)
feith
>   fals feith (248/28)
>   defendyn þe feith (250/6)
>   informyd hir in hir feyth (39/21)
be-fel as sche felt (53/28)
fellyn to hir in effect lych as sche had felt beforn (74/30-31)
felyng(-ys)
>   wyth swech felyngys whan it fel not trewe to hir vndyrstandyng,
>   þat hir confessour feryd þat sche xuld a fallyn (55/1-3)
>   fyrst felyngys (3/29)
>   fond hir felyngys (75/32, 170/16)
>   & hir felingys, and a Whyte Frer proferyd hir to wryten frely
>   (6/8-9)
>   Ferthermore her folwyth a rygth notabyl matere of þe crea-
>   turys felyng, & it is wretyn her for conuenyens in-as-mech
>   as it is in felyng leche to þe materys þat ben wretyn be-
>   forn, notwythstondyng it befel long aftyr þe materys
>   whech folwyn. (58/25-29)
fettyn a peyr of feterys & seyd sche xulde ben feteryd, sche was a
    fals heretyke (124/18-19)
fille myn hert ful (192/26)
fleschly er erdly affeccyon (147/34, 161/17)
flowers
>   þo fayr flowerys (126/34)
>   wyth many fayr flowerys & wyth many swete spicys (210/31)
>   defowlyn & deuowryn so fayr flowerys (127/10-11)

flower & fairest (252/29)
fellyng down þe flowerys (126/32-33)
floreschyd wyth flowerys (126/30)
sumdel florischyng & floweryng (127/16)
folk euyl a-feerd (178/2)
fremd folk (119/26)
folwyn
    went so fast þat sche myth not folwyn (233/38)
    fawyn folwyn (44/23-24)
    forseyd creatur folwyd ful of terys (107/28)
    folwyn hys cownsel a-for-tyme (10/7)
fond no defawt (37/1)
defawt he fond (222/15)
bryng me forth mor frwte (48/34)
forth wyth hir felawschep (74/9, 110/24)
fischys, fowelys (252/6)
fedir of fowle (252/7)
Fryday beforn (16-27)
fyer
    fel down to þe grownd, so feruently þe fyer of lofe brent (147/
       18-19)
    a flawme of fyer (88/28, 163/20)
    inflawmyd wyth þe fyre (197/15)
    sparks of þe fyer fleyn (163/17)
    be-forn þe fyer (163/15)
    felyn þe material fyer ʒyf he put hys hand or fynger þerin.
       When sche felt fyrst the fyer of loue brennyng in hir brest,
       sche was a-ferd (88/32-34)
fyndyn but litil frenschep whan ʒe come þer. I pray ʒow, getith
    ʒowr felaschep wher ʒe can, for I was blamyd for ʒowr
    defawte (247/13-15)

G

Julian:

in regard or our gostly forth bringing (lx/58-59)

gevyn a geft (li/58)
so gladd & so gostly (xv/3-4)
glorius godhede (xx/14)
God
> God gave me gostly understondyng (li/10)
> And our Lord God gave me grace (xlvii/16, lxix/13, lxxii/8)
> gefts that God may geve (lx/36-37)
> Gods gift (ii/6; inverted, ii/3)
> This booke is begunne be Gods gift & his grace (lxxxvi/1)
> As good as God is, as gret he is (lxxv/43)
> God is al thing that is gode (vii/17)
> God is the goodnes (lxix/37)
> God is goodnes (xli/27)
> God of his godenes (vi/25, xlvi/52, li/92)
> God of thy goodness give me thy selfe (v/40-41)
> of God & his goodness (v/46, xxxv/39-40)
> goodness of God (i/26, vi/2, vi/32, vi/45, 47, xxxv/42-43)
> propertes of goodness which is God (lix/3)
> grete goodness of God (xl/22)
> God is the holy Gost, & all ben sundry gifts to which he will
> > we have gret regard (lxxx/7-9)
> God hath forgoven (xl/10)
> grace of God (ii/8-9, 37)
> be the grace of God was begonne (xxxv/4)
> greatnes of God (lxxv/36)
> God is the ground (lxxx/6)
> ne only in our kindly ground that we have in God we may not
> > be savid but if we have commyng of the same ground
> > mercy & grace. For of these iij werkyng altogeder we
> > receive all our goodnes, of the which the first arn goods
> > of kynd; for in our first makyng God gaf us as ful goods
> > & also greter godes (lvi/61-67)

gode Lord gave (x/38, lxx/1)
And this be the good which he hath ordeynid to give us from
> without begynnyng (lxxv/22-23)
gret goodnes (xlvi/45)
grete goodness & his grace (lxxix/19-20)

grace

> to geyn grace (x/32)
>
> be grace of the holy Ghost (vii/69-70)
>
> grete plenty of grace inwardly govyn of the holy Ghost (vii/62-63)
>
> grace of God (x/50)

gracious

> gracious gift (iii/54, lxxxiv/14)
>
> gracious ledyng of the holy gost (li/46-47)
>
> gracious werkyng of the holy gost (xl/19, lxxx/5)

gret regard (i/38, lxxx/9)

Margery:

gaderyng to-gedyr (124/35)

be-gan to grutchyn (165/7)

gate hir leue to gon (135/17)

glad & goodly (148/22)

God

> God for (of) hys goodnes (41/22, 74/20, 111/2, 148/27)
>
> God drow not hys grace (231/8)
>
> God wold ȝeue hym grace (5/26, 107/31, 125/8)
>
> Goddys grace (108/20)
>
> grace of God (74/6, 109/26, 223/28, 224/31, 227/38, 246/13-14)
>
> grace of God ȝe wil go (35/12-13)
>
> grace þat God wrowt (werkyth, put) (41/45, 74/25, 96/37-38, 42/10, 148/19)
>
> God of þe grace & goodnes (223/19)
>
> God wrowt greet grace (43/24)
>
> God grawnt (-yd, -yn) (43/13, 164/3, 223/3-4)
>
> ȝyf God wolde grawntyn hym grace (96/25-26)

gon homward a-geyn (194/38-39)

good (-ys, -ly, -nes)

> good to go wyth (32/9)
>
> to gon to a good man (4/30)
>
> grawntyng hym a grett summe of good (4/36)
>
> gret goodys (37/7)

go getyn a-geyn þe booke yf sche myth goodly (5/3-4)

not goodly þat sche xulde gon (226/9-10)

goodness of þe Holy Gost (41/25)

be-syden þe grave of þe good Vicary, al rauyschyd wyth
gostly comfort in þe goodnes of owr Lord þat wrowt so
gret grace (147/22-24)

gret goodnes (250/30, 207/33)

grace

get I grace (193/37)

a-geyn for grace (163/30)

grace for alle good men (212/32)

grace & goodnes (48/13, 208/18, 211/15-16, 224/7-8)

grace of þe Holy Gost (40/17)

grace as þe Holy Gost of hys goodnesse (3/14)

greet grace (40/30-31, 43/29, 51/21, 163/33)

a-geyne to Ierusalem for þe gret grace & gostly comfort (75/
19-20)

gracyows lordshyp to grawnt (36/21)

Gredily þis greuows best (126/33)

gresys growyng (252/5)

gret gladnes (108/2)

3

Margery:

forȝetyng þe frute of hir wombe askyd forȝeuenes (223/5)

ȝevyn hys ȝyftys (41/26)

grettest ȝeft þat God may ȝevyn (46/29)

my ȝyftys & my gracys whech I haue ȝouyn þe (209/35-36)

gret ȝyftys þat I haue ȝouyn (161/10)

H¹

Julian:

hath hast to have us to him (lxxix/44)

---

¹ This letter might not have been sounded in many of the examples listed.
"Eye-alliteration" at least is present.

the hate that hath to our soule (lxxvii/9)
hath non helle (xl/45)
no herder helle (xl/44)
hevyn
    have had in hevyn (lxxv/20)
    to hym in hey hevyn (li/354)
    in hope of the bliss of hevyn while we arn here (lxv/5-6)
heyley & hertily (addition by the scribe)
behold
    And how a soul shall have him in his beholdyng he shal teche
        himselfe (x/89-90)
    to behold hym (xxxv/9)
    how he beholdyth (1/21)
he of his goodnes will shewin hym to man, he shewith him homely
    (li/165-167)

Margery:

hayr
    hast an hayr (17/6)
    an hayr in þin hert (17/7-8)
    weryng of þe haburion or of þe hayr (89/20-21)
held, hold
    how he held of hir (46/22)
    heldyng up hys handys (41/11)
    heldyng up þe Sacrament in hys handys ouyr hys hed (47/16-17)
    holdyn so holy (33/14)
help
    helpyn hem, here my preyerys for hem (253/27-28)
    haddyn gret help (59/13)
    helpyn hem-self (74/12)
herd so hedows (39/6)
hir hert was so ful of heuynes (195/5)
behest
    þu behestyst hym (23/6-7, 136/23)
    he had behested hyr (5/1)
    behestys þat God had be-hyte hir (74/28-29, similarly 230/2)
hir hevyd & hir hodys (9/14)

hevyn

    hand in Hevyn (52/28)

    holy martyres in Heuyn (whan þu heryst of hem) (159/32)

    seyntys in Heuyn whech louyn þe ful hily (50/8-9)

heuynes ocupying hir hert (98/20)

heyl & hool (170/6-7)

hogely to beheldyn (126/32)

home

    haddyn hir hom (108/1)

    bad hir gon hom in haste to hir hostel (101/18-19)

    hyr hom in-to hys owyn hows (112/23-24)

howsyld hir wyth owyn handys (40/22)

hurte hym ne harmyn hym (233/25)

husband

    he þat was husbond (53/22)

    he þat was hir husbond is now in good hele (53/26-27)

    husbond leuyng in good hele (161/13)

so hy & so holy (50/13, 230/21)

J

Julian:

joye that is Jesus (lxxi/7)

we enjoyen in this joy (lv/9-10)

Margery:

joynyd to Ioseph & of þe gostly joynyng of mannys sowle to Ihesu (199/1-2)

K²

Julian:

---

² The *k* in *kn* words was probably sounded at the time both mystics were writing. Although impossible to fix the exact date of the final reduction, phonetic spellings put the *beginning* of the change back to the fifteenth century. See Helge Kökeritz, "The Reduction of Initial *kn* and *gn* in English", *Language*, 21 (1945), 86.

she kepith it ful tenderly as the kind & condition of moderhede will (lx/61-62)

for it is contrarious to our fair kinde. For as sothly as synne is onclene, as sothly is it onkinde (lxiii/16-18)

the wound of very contrition, the wound of kinde compassion (ii/39-40)

Margery:

hir kepars cownseld hym he xulde delyuyr hir no keys (8/30-31)
kepyn
 kepe þi body klene (222/3)
 cotidianly to kepyn (234/19-20)
 vykary kept stylle hys cure (53/20)
wyth a key & comendyng hys wyfe þe key to kepyn (112/25-26)
knelyng
 knelyng on hir knes (124/16, 128/24-25)
 cam a man knelyng (177/30)
 whan he cam sche knelyd down & askyd (109/23)
 creatur was knelyng (206/27)
cownsel xal knowyn (45/27, inverted 224/26, 247/12)
Seynt Kateryn telde what kynred sche cam of (111/33)
comyn of worthy kenred (9/20)
kyrnellys of corn (252/6)

L

Julian:

on the left syde as a laborer (li/375-376)
lay alone (li/33)
ledand in his lawes (lv/1)
me lekid to leven (iii/9)
no licor that is made that he lekyth (xii/16)
lerand his loris (lvii/69)
lerid to longen (xxv/21)
lever a be deliveryd (iii/52)
life
 this life & this langor (lxiv/28)

leden us to endles life (lv/27)

þe life myght ne lenger lesten (xxi/9)

longyth to us in this life (i/47)

in this life for love (lvx/2)

lytyng of the gostly life (lxxi/26)

alike large (i/51, xlii/16)

longyth to learn us (lxxv/12)

Lord

Lord Jesus langring long (xx/1)

led into the Lord (li/185)

let my Lord stonden alone (lxxx/44)

to our Lord & levyn him not alone (lxxx/41)

Lord lokyd downe (xxv/1-2)

Lord lookyth upon his servant ful lovely (li/12-13)

it longyth to þe ryal Lordship (xxx/14-15)

Lord … love (*like*)

it lekyd the Lord (li/231-232)

of al thyng that to us longith, it is most likyng to our Lord (lv/8-9)

his lovand Lord (li/44, 128-129, 130)

love he had to the lord was even like to the love that the lord had to hym (li/202-4)

love of our Lord God, the lother (xl/38)

lovesome & plesant to the lord (li/217-218)

lord lovid (li/215)

to loke up on his lovyng Lord (li/22-23)

love

everlasting love (lii/92, lxxxii/18)

led by love (xlvi/43)

Thus was I lerid that Love was our Lords mening (lxxxvi/24)

lesson of love (vi/68, lxxxii/25-26)

which kind love it never levyth (lx/5-6)

lif, love, & ligte (lxxxiii/5-6)

in this love our life is everlestand (lxxxvi/28-29)

al our hole life in love (xxxix/49)

alone in love (xlviii/18)

longyng in the same love (lxxv/3-4)

Lord himselfe ledith us in the same love (lvi/35)

alyke in love (xliii/37)

blissid lyte of his pretious love (lxx/18, similarly lxxxii/29)

love (*verb*)

lovand & longand (li/139)

it was to have lyved that I might have loved (iii/11)

to loven it & liken it (xlvi/23-24, xxv/37-38)

for he lovith & lekyth us (lxviii/30-31)

it longyth to us to loven our God (lix/35)

longith to his Godhede to be lovid (lxxv/44)

lovely

lovely lesson (xlii/12, lxxix/26)

lovely lokeing that he loked (li/148)

leven ... lovely longyng with our Lord Jesus. For he longyth (xl/26)

lovers lestingly (lxi/14)

this unknowing it is, that lettith most Gods lovers (lxxii/35-36)

low

litil, low & simple (x/34-35, lx/58)

lower dome was lerned (xlv/33)

levyn þe lower dome (xlv/34)

Margery:

long ben labowrd (8/9)

labowryd as long (234/16)

at þe last owr Lady leet hem (194/22-23)

Lady, ȝyf me leue (193/36, 37, inverted 38/2-3, 196/17-18)

at þe last sche toke hir leue (110/7-8)

lay a-loone (8/11)

led ȝow last (247/15)

led hir owt of Lynne (246/34-35, 247/3-4)

leue (*-yn, -yng*)

late hym leuyn (169/36)

to leuyn wyth as is leful (160/15)

hir maner of gouernawns & leuyng, for he trustly beleuyd þat sche was wel lernyd in þe lawe (40/15-16)

lond of leuyng men (225/16-17)

as long as sche leued (4/36, 251/36)
leuyng hir a-lone (75/35, 233/37)
delicyous & delectabyl (244/33)
Lord
leet our Lord (229/22)
leue of ower mercyful Lord (1/11, 18/6-7)
be lordshep & be proces of lawe (60/11)
Lord ... loue
owr Lordys lofe (78/10-11, 100/21, 112/28, 119/27, 236/24)
Lord, for þi lofe (229/26)
lofe of (to) owyr Lord (74/23, 43/19-20, 38/26, 11/1-2, 208/
13-14)
to louyn owr Lord (3/17, 164/38-165/1, 39/32)
leuyth fully þat owyr Lord louyth (42/2-3)
loue
let me to lofe (49/8-9)
of good lofe & leue (225/27-28)
beleuyn þat God louyth (52/15)

M

Julian:

make, made
made me to morn (lxiv/6)
made mention (xxxviii/30)
made myty (lxx/45)
make many menys (vi/5)
man(hode)
of which man I am a member as I hope be the mercy of God
(lxxix/7-8)
man was hurte in hys myte & made ful febil (li/122-123)
manhode for love to suffre more than al man myght (xx/2-3)
it menyth Christs manhood (li/250)
matter
matter of mekenes (lxxix/22)
matter of morneing (lii/58)

I saw matter of myrthe & matter of moning (lxxii/35)

mayde(-en)

    meke mayde (lx/11)

    this swete mayden his blissid moder, our Lady Seynt Mary
(xxv/9-10)

    myldely in the maydens womb (lx/9-10)

meke(-ly, -ness) & *mylde(-ly, -hede)*

    meke & mylde (li/129)

    made (makyth) meke & mylde (xlix/12, 47-48)

    mekely & myldely (li/45-46, lii/86-87)

    myldhede & mekeness (lxiii/42)

    his mervelous mekeness & myldhede by the workyng of mercy
& grace (xxxv/28-29)

    for mekehede of joye mervelyng at the greatnes of God the
maker & of the litilhede of all that is made. For the
beholdyng of this makith the creature mervelous meke
& mylde (lxxv/35-38)

ministre hem to mend (lxv/42)

ne less ne more as it may be seene be our Lords meneing in the
same matter (vii/72)

I have menying of iii manner (lxxi/8)

Moderhede of mercy (lx/3)

made be the moderhede (lx/4-5)

manyfold more (xxxv/49, lxxvii/7)

more of this matter (lv/12)

mor mede (xl/32)

myte no more (lx/32)

full mytyly & full mekely (lxx/19)

Margery:

makyn

    mad gret mone (92/11)

    mad mych of hir (75/15)

    makyn it mete (192/20)

    makyn ful mery (54/24-25)

    makyng hir prayer in hir mende (124/9)

makyth mencyon (225/20, 59/33)

al maner of mekenes (213/30-31)

mech

    mech mone was mad (54/10)

    meuyd in so mych þe mor (78/1)

    as mech as þei myth (78/10)

    meche multitude (123/13-14)

mede & meryte (48/32-33, inverted 72/32-33)

maist not don a-mys, for Goddys cownsel is to be meke (207/12-13)

mend

    to hir mend in þis maner (35/19-20)

    mende of þis mater (53/12-13)

    ministryd to hir mynde (208/19)

    so holy mendys þat sche myth no mesuryn (147/31)

mercy

    mercy & gremercy (41/12)

    many-fold mercy (221/2-3)

    mende of thy many-fold mercy (230/1)

    þe multitude of þi mercy (254/2)

many men merueyled (135/25)

mech more meruayle (48/7-8)

ne a mekar to hys modyr (195/16)

þe modyr to metyn (221/26)

mor

    many mo (54/27, 54/32, 199/10, 249/25, 75/8, 137/10)

    so meche þe mor (161/28)

    meche mor for me (123/26-27)

    meche þe mor mery, for sche had mater (123/18-19)

    meche þe mor, & euyr a-mong owr Lord spak to hir mende (233/21-22)

    mor is ʒowr meryte (43/16)

    mor mynde (51/8, 208/11)

moryn my meryte (249/5)

in remissyon of my synnys & moryng of my meryte (251/38)

myth not mesuryn (197/7)

N

Julian:

never none (x/69, ii/16)
ne myte, ne couthe, ne never non (lx/19-20)

Margery:

neuyr at nede & neuyr forsakyth (76/3-4)
neuyr þe nerar an ende (59/22)
sche knowyth not me ne non of hir neyborwys (177/35-178/1)
A-noon as it was noysed a-bowt þe town of N. (10/34)

P

Julian:

passion

  a parte of his passion: despite, spitting & sollowing, & buffet-
   ting, & many langoryng peynes (x/3-5)
  in the passion of Criste fulfillid with peyne & compassion
   (xxviii/2-3)
  the passion of Criste for most peyne & overpassyng (xxvii/26)
  our Lord shewid the patience that he had in his herd passion.
   And also the joyeing & the likyng that he hath of þat
   passion for love. And this he shewid in example that we
   shuld gladly & wisely beren our peynes, for that is gret
   plesing to him & endless profit to us (lxxii/22-27)
  presious passion (i/17-18)
pety & compassion (xxx/17)
patience for great awe & perplexitie (1/26-27)
man lengith his patiens over the tyme of his living: for onknowing
  of his tyme of passing, þat is a gret profit (lxiv/22-24)
peas her[e] in parte (li/132)
  peyne
  peyne is passand (xv/33-34)
  peynys & passions (xxi/17, xxxi/33, lii/107)
  peynys of Crists passion passen al peynys (xx/32-33)

his peynes were my peynes with compassion (iii/56-57)

in the peyne I might have said with Peter "Lord, save me;
I perish!" (xv/19-20)

in peyn & in prison (xl/13)

payne blamith & punishith (li/136-137)

poynt

we may never full know our selfe into the last poynte, in which
poynte this passand life & manner of peyne & wo shall
have an end (xlvi/9-11)

poynte that may be seen in the passion (xx/11)

al the poynts & propertes (li/106)

presens shuld passyn (1/20)

pretious

the pretious plenty (xii/23, 26, 28)

most pretious as verily it is most plentious (xii/22)

most plentious as it is most pretious (xii/17)

prive

both prive & partie (vii/39)

privy councell in pece (xxx/15)

privy points (vii/67)

the property of pite (xxxi/54)

a piteful propirte (xlviii/31)

Margery:

paciens in þe syn of þe pepyl (48/5-6)

in party of penawns (85/34-35)

compassion

thorw þe beholdyng of þat pete her mende was al holy occupyed in þe Passyon of owr Lord Ihesu Crist & in þe
compassyon of owr Lady, Seynt Mary, be whech sche was
compellyd (148/6-9)

mende of owr Lordys Passion wyth plentyuows terys of compassyon (110/31-32)

compassyon þat þu hast of hys bittyr Passyon (86/14-15)

pety & compassyon (1/18, 1/23, 111/9, 197/18)

pite & compassyon þat sche had of þat petows syght (191/29-
30)

pite, & compassyon of þe Passyon (208/11-12)

compleynt & compassyon (222/20)

compassyon of hir preyng (112/13)

teerys of compunccyon & of compassyon in þe rememorawns of þe bittyr peynys & passyons (245/35-36)

perel

passyd many perellys (233/15)

beyng þer present & seyng þe perel (162/35-36)

put hym in perel (4/29)

perischyn er dispeyryn (230/7)

a persone so plenteuows (246/9)

peyn

[as þu thynkyst] 'Worshepyd be alle þo holy placys in Ierusa-lem þat Crist suffyrde bittyr peyn & passyon in,' þu schalt haue þe same pardon as ȝyf þu wer wyth þi bodily presens (75/25-28)

peynes & passyons (16/34, 75/26)

mor mynde of my Passyon þan on þin owyn peyne (51/8-9)

peyn & ponyschyng (54/35)

peyn þat þei mythyn preysyn (160/8)

peynys of Purgatory (251/28)

lych to a palmyr er a pilgrime (127/6-7)

a pilgryme purposyng (109/26)

supportyn þe in euery place (76/18-19)

as he supposyd, God so greuowsly ponyschyd hym. Sum persone, hauyng knowlach of hys compleynt & compassyon of hys disese (222/18-20)

he supposyd be hir prerys owr Lord sent hym þat ponischyng (222/35-36)

þe Priowr whech was her person, þei he wer powyr (59/17-18)

powyr pepyl (54/9)

poynt

þe lest poynt of blys wyth-owtyn any comparyson passeth al þe joye (39/11-12)

petowsly poyntyd (111/6)

prophecyed in euery poynt (44/16-17)

preche

I preche not, ser, I come in no pulpytt (126/18-19)

leyd Seynt Powyl for hys party a-geyns hir þat no woman
    xulde prechyn (126/16-18)

þe persun cesyd a lityl of hys prechyng & seyd to þe pepil
    (165/11-12)

he plesyth me mech wyth hys prechyng & schew hym thy
    preuytes (38/14-15)

precyows

precyows body aperyd (192/5-6)

precyows body for peyne (192/15)

presens of þat precyows body (194/9)

preste

Preste, þu þi-self art þe pertre (127/15)

prestys in þe same place (147/36-37)

preste, trustyng in hire prayers (5/8)

þe prestys presens (127/1)

preyid for þe same preste (147/36-37)

preuyn hyr paciens (123/19)

preuyng her feith & her pacyens (229/15)

prey(-er)

partabyl of her preyerys (250/11)

compleynyd to þis creatur & preyde hir to prey (110/6)

supportyd be ȝowr preyers (41/18)

preyers, a prest cam to hir & preyde hir to prey for a woman
    whech lay in poynt of deth (53/29-31)

prey to God for hym & purchasyn hym grace (5/7)

pomp & pryde (2/12, 5/33-34)

hir pride ne hir pompows aray (9/10)

þe principal day of pardon (246/32-33)

profit

plesawns & profite (223/7)

most plesawns to God & profyte to hir owyn sowle (124/10-11)

prechyn my word in erth þat þei myght profityn (212/32-33)

a-propyrd myght & power (210/36)

proym to expressyn mor openly (5/30-31)

purchasyn

purchasyn hir mor pardon (75/21-22, 245/32)

placys to purchasyn hym pardon (224/14-15)
whan þer is gret pardon of plenyr remyssyon, for to purchasyn
grace, mercy, & forȝeuenes for hir-self, for alle hir frendys,
for all hir enmys, & for alle þe sowlys in Purgatory. & þer
was a lady was comyn fro Rome to purchasyn hir pardon
(79/25-30)
purposyng to passyn (223/25)
in purpose, hys vnwetyng, to preuyn (97/28-29)
put in ple (59/9)

Q

Margery:

enqwiryd of þe preste þe cawse (127/7-8)
kanst neuyr a-qwityn (211/2)
aqwityn hys costys (247/19)

R

Julian:

raggid & rent (li/340)
redy to be raggid & rent (li/198-199)
ryth rechly clad (li/370-371)
rayhid him & dyte him ful redy (lx/14-15)
reverently redy (li/12)
rialy regne (xiv/7)
never risen nor removen (lxxxi/13-14)

Margery:

reden it & wrytyn it (5/7-8)
mad redy & arayd (108/25)
ronnyn down wyth reuerys (192/39)

S

Julian:

swete sacraments he susteynith (lx/39)

our savior & our salvation (xxx/2)

sayand swetely (xl/13)

se (-n), saw

> thei myght seen & knowyn the same that I saw (viii/26-27)
>
> suppose the same that seyen me (ii/22-23)
>
> sen in the xvi shewing wher it seith (lv/34-35)
>
> seen owr selfe so foule (xl/4-5)
>
> sothly ther was none seen (li/4)
>
> sen this sothnes (1/31)
>
> for he will be sene & he wil be sowte (x/32)
>
> to sen in God that synne (1/22-24)
>
> saw with bodily sight (x/1)
>
> saw him assigne (xlv/22)
>
> saw sothly (li/167)
>
> for I saw him sowte (x/13)
>
> thus I saw him & sowte him (x/19)
>
> And thus to se this overpassing noblith was myn under-stondyng led into God in the same tyme that I saw þe servant fallen (lii/55-57)
>
> for I saw the Lord sitten as a man & I saw neither mete ner drynke wherwith to servyn hym. This was on mervel. Another mervel was that this solemn Lord had no servant but on, & hym he sent owte (li/218-221)
>
> And this was a singlar joy & bliss to me that I saw him sitten, for the sekirnes of sitting shewith endles dwelling (lxviii/5-7)
>
> saw the Lord sitten solemnly and the servant stondand reverently (li/189-190)
>
> sothly I saw þat our substance is in God (lvii/71)
>
> for I saw full sekirly that our substance is in God. And also I saw that in our sensualite God is; for the selfe poynte that our soule is mad sensual in, the selfe poynt is the cite of God ordeynid (lv/28-31)
>
> And also in this same shewing where I saw that I shuld synne there was I leryd to be dredfull for unsekirness of myselfe (lxxix/12-14)

sekyn, suffrin, & trusten (x/79)

& hope sothly that al those that seke this he shal spedyn, for they
    sekyn God. Al this that I have now seid & more þat I shal
    sey after is comfortyng ageyn synne. For in the thred shewyng
    when I saw that God doeth al that is don, I saw no synne
    (xxxiv/24-28)

seming of the scorgyng (xii/2)

sensualite, suffrid for the salvation (lv/61)

servant

    In the servant is comprehendid the second person (li/246-247)

    servant standyth (li/11)

    The servant that stode aforn the Lord I understode that it was
        shewid for Adam (li/117-118)

    stondyng of the servant (li/112-113, 309, 324)

    Be the nerehede of the servant is understode the son, & be the
        stondyng on the left syde is understod Adam (li/251-253)

    sendyth hym to a certain place to don his will, the servant not
        only he goeth, but suddenly he stirtith (li/14-15)

semly to servyn (li/173)

I assented to set (iii/33)

þat is to sey, now þat þu seest it. This was seid not only for the
    same time, but also to setten thereupon þe ground of my
    feith (lxx/22-25)

Also God shewid that synne shal be no shame but worship to man
    (xxxviii/1-2)

sit (sat)

    it seith he sittith in our soule (lvii/64)

    sittith in his noblest set (li/367)

    sittith solemnly (li/10-11, 116)

    no such syttyng as to my syte (li/379-380)

    the place that the Lord sat on was symple (li/140)

shall be swith sodeyn (x/115)

son

    stondith not the son (li/368, 375)

    I saw the son stondyng, saying in his menyng (li/292)

    son syttith on the ryte hond syde be syde (li/378)

if this be soth then were it good to synne (xl/31)

sothly that we synne (1/8)

soule

    safe in body & soule (x/27)

    In which shewing I saw & understode ful sekirly that in every
        soule that shal be save is a Godly wille that never assent
        to syn*n*e (liii/11-13)

    soul seith (xl/37)

    the same grace that the soul sekith (vi/36)

    sekyng of the soule (x/78)

    without assent of the soule, in whych God assignyth no blame
        (xix/28-29)

    a sily soule (v/37)

    the simple soule understode (xlvi/48)

    rest in soule & softnes in consciens (xl/9)

    & sothly as I understond in our Lord menyng, wher the blissid
        soule of Crist is, ther is the substans of al the soules that
        shal be savid be Criste (liv/6-8)

    suffer the soule (x/86)

    ful swete to the soule that seith by grace. Al the sowlys that
        shal be savid in hevyn without ende be mad rythful in the
        syte of God (xxxv/37-40)

    soule to ben his owen cyte (li/170)

þe more spede to our selfe (xxx/10-11)

it is spedeful to some soulis (xv/22)

all swich that is spedfull (lxxx/32-33)

despite, spitting, & sollowing (x/3-4)

sterid by the same grace to sekyn with gret desire to se him more
    blissfully (x/16-18)

stondith he swemely (lxxx/38-39)

never cesyn ne stintin (lxiii/27)

understond(-yng)

    understondyng wold servyn (li/107-108)

    understondyng in the simple stature as she was whan she con-
        ceivid (lx/12-13)

    understond I sothly (xl/21)

    stonyd in his vnderstondyng (li/123)

    understond the ministratio*n* (lxxx/24)

    And also the more understondyng this swete word, our Lord

God spekyth to al mankynde that shal be save (xxv/14-15)
ryght so he was most strong & myghty to suffir. And for every
mannys synne that shall be savid he suffrid, & every mannys
sorow & desolation he sawe & sorowid for kyndenes & love.
For in as mekyl as our lady sorowid for his peynes, as mekyl
he suffrid sorrow for her sorow & more, in as mekyl as the
swete manhode of hym was worthier in kynd. For as long
as he was passible he suffryd for us & sorowyd for us, & now
he is up rysyn & no more passibyl, yet he suffryt with us. And
I beholdyng al this be his grace saw þat þe love of hym was
so strong whych he hath to our soule, that wilfully he ches it
with gret desyr & myldly he suffrid it with wel payeyng
(xx/17-30)
which is sensualite, suffered for the salvation (lv/61)
þe sweppys & the scorgis (li/340-341)
swe(e)te
same understondyng in this swete word wher he saith (lx/50-51)
sharp smyting al about the sweete body (xii/3-4)
swete open syde (lx/47)
syte was full swete (lv/49)
swinkin & swetyn (li/225)
syte that I had both of the Lord & þe servant it semyth that he was
anew, that is to say new begynnyng to travellyn, which servant
was never sent out aforn (li/212-214)
synne(-rs), *synnefull*
strange to him be synne, dispeir, or slowth (lxxx/43)
as synne is suffrid to pursue rythful soules, And whan synne
hath no longer leve to pursue, than shal the werkyng of
mercy secyn & than shal al be broute to rythfulhede &
therein stondin (xxxv/43-46)
syte of our synne (lxxviii/41)
be the same dome I understode þat synners arn worthy sumtime (xlv/28-29)
sen himself synnefull (lxxviii/30)
in the syte of God, the soule that shal be save was never dede
(l/4-5)

Margery:

Sacrament
    receyuyd þe blissyd Sacrament (209/29-30, 231/11)
    sumtyme whan þu receyuyst þe precyows Sacrament (212/25-
        26)
    steryng & mevyng of þe blyssed Sacrament, desyring to se
        mor Sacreys (47/22-23)
    thorw þi Seruyse seyyng & þe Sacramentys ministryng (127/
        16-17)
sithyn he sey hir sad & sobyr a-now (179/2-3)
so sadly & streitly (192/1)
forsake
    forsakyng hys seruawnt (8/13, 76/4)
    forsoke hys seruyse (10/32-33)
    forsake hys synne (23/5-6)
schakyd & schoderyd (192/37)
schame & schenschep of Sathanas (252/20-21)
þe mor scharp þat he is to ȝow, [þe mor] clerly schinyth ȝowr sowle
    in þe sygth of God (44/34-35)
schewyd schort cher (247/5)
schille schrykyngys (107/13)
sche schuld be dampnyd, for sche was not schreuyn (7/10-11)
sche answeryd schrewdly & schortly & seyd (9/19-20)
for seeknes and alle scornys, for all spitys & all wrongys (251/33-34)
it semyth hym to sittyn (211/9)
seylyng ouyr þe see (221/18)
se(-n), sey (saw)
    sche sey sextene men wyth sextene scorgys (191/6-7)
    semeliest man þat euyr myth be seen (208/8)
    seyng dysese on euery syde (22/17)
    seyng alle þis aduersytes comyng on euery syde, thowt it
        weryn þe skowrges of ower Lord þat wold chastyse hir for
        hir synne (11/4-7)
    seen wyth mannys eye, clad in a mantyl of purpyl sylke,
        syttyng up-on hir beddys syde (8/16-18)
    sey þe synne (48/6-7)

Than sche, consyderyng þis wondyrful chawngyng, sekyng socowr
(2/17)

sent hem swech stormys (229/16)

sent fro be-ȝonden þe see (4/33-34)

sett & seruyd (97/21)

settyn hys stody (221/29)

seyin (*verb*)

schuld seyin a sermown (227/20-1)

þow seyst soth (48/6)

seyd to hir in hir sowle (108/36)

seyd vn-to hir spyrite (53/13, 54/13)

seyd (*adjective*)

he seyd to þe seyd creatur (108/17-18, 159/21)

the seyd creatur had a sone (221/16)

þe sayd creatur had sorwe (229/22-23)

... ser", seyd þe sayd creatur (128/21-22)

þe seyd creatur, seyng & wel vndirstondyng þat hir confessowr
vndirstod not (97/30-31)

[while] þe Erchebischop takyn hys see, þe seyd creatur stod
(124/36)

slawndyr

slawndryd hir, scornyd hir, & despysed hir (120/16-17)

perelys wer sesyd, sum men slawndyrd (164/10-11)

slawndyr & speche (51/15)

slep

sodeynly, sche wist not how sone, sche was in a maner of slep.
& a-non in þe syght of hir sowle sche sey owr Lord
standyng (208/19-22)

wyth a maner of slep, & sodeynly sche sey, hir thowt, owr
Lady in þe fayrest syght þat euyr sche say, holdyng a fayr
white kerche in hir hand & seying to hir, "Dowtyr, wilt
þu se my sone?" & a-non forth-wyth sche say owr Lady
han hir blissyd Sone in hir hand & swathyd hym (209/18-
23)

sob(-bing)

sobbyng so sor þat vn-ethe sche myth stondyn (198/17)

syhyngys, & sobbyngys (199/17)

sche met a semly man & wept & sobbyd ful sor in þe manhod
    of Crist as sche went in þe stretys (86/34-36)
so sodeynly a-sundyr (228/33)

son

    thynkyst þe same of þe Sone (211/16)
    Sone owr Sauyowr (198/4)
    se thy sone of Seynt Iohn (193/3)
    Good sone, I beseche ȝow (97/18)
    my Sone & me asondyr (194/19)
    sone consentyng (22/30-31)
    xal sone sesyn (230/29)

sore

    sattelyn as sor (212/30)
    so sor whan þu receyuyst me (213/13)
    so sor for hys synnes (108/12)

sorwe

    cesyth of ȝowr sorwyng (193/23, 195/12)
    sodeyn sorwe (98/20)
    swech a sorwe (164/29)
    sorwe in þe synne (48/8-9)
    gret sorwe for þi gostly fadyrs synnys in special (212/22-23)
sothfast & sekyr in þe forseyd creatur (60/16-17)
mor sotyl & mor softe & mor esy to hir spiryt (209/13-14)
mor sotyl in vndirstondyng (209/7)

souereyn

    souereyn sauyowr (1/4, 221/1)
    leue of hys souereyn to spekyn wyth þe sayd creatur (170/7-8)
    belouyd souereyn, Crist Ihesu, whos melydiows voys swettest
        of all sauowrys softly sowndyng in hir sowle, seyd (98/24-26)

sowle

    saue hir sowle (54/1)
    speke wyth hym in cownsel & schewyn hym þe secretys of hir
        sowle (33/33-34)
    sowle is mor sekyr (89/11)
    Holy Wryt seyth þat þe sowle of a rytful man is þe sete of
        God, & so I trust, syster (43/11-12)
    receyuid me into thy sowle (213/17)

receyuyn me to þe saluacyon of thy sowle (213/30)

seyd in hir sowle (119/28)

seying to hir sowle (87/17-18)

sowle be-for þe Sone (87/14)

sor in hir sowle (98/33)

sorwys þat þu hast for þe sowlys (160/6-7)

spak on-to hir sowle (50/4)

spechys & dalyawns þat owyr Lord spak to hir sowle (42/13)

art in silens & sufferyst me to speke in thy sowle (89/24-25)

a sowle stabyl & stedfast (42/28-29, negative 42/30)

"Syr", seyd þe creatur, "drede ȝe not, for I vndyrstond in my
      sowle … "(59/36-37)

strengthyd in hir sowle (36/29)

sylens in hir sowle (86/19)

thryd of white sylke in thy sowle (210/34-35)

synful mannys sowle (249/10)

receyuen swech spechys (74/31-32)

spechys in hir sowle cawsyd hir to sobbyn (233/34)

speke (*spak*)

sithyn sche spak so sadly a-geyn syn & her mysgouernawns
      þat þei wer in sylens (109/18-20)

as sone as þe seke woman þat was alienyd of hir witte saw hir,
      sche spak to hir sadly (178/7-9)

speke wyth her but seldom (4/22)

my spyrit xal speke (17/34)

ly stylle & speke to me (17/29)

þe spiryt of God þat spekyst in my sowle (76/11-12)

not consentyng but scharply answeryng a-geyn, sche, sumdel meuyd
    wyth scharpnes of spiryt, seyde, "Now sithyn …" (221/31-
    222/2)

fel in gret sekenes, & sche was steryd in hir sowle for to kepyn hym
    in Goddys stede (147/2-3)

stille

satt al stille (97/26)

softly & stilly (139/31)

stod stylle (36/16, 60/14, 120/20)

swownyd & lay stille (191/23)

stonys smale (252/5)

strength wold seruyn (8/37)

suffyr

> sche suffryd meche despite, meche repref, many a scorne, many a slawndyr (137/3-4)
>
> sufferd sche many scornys (135/22)
>
> suffred hir to sey (37/11)
>
> it suffyrd & felt, þei sorwyd & mornyd & syhyd ful sor (192/15-16)
>
> suffyrst me wilfully to spekyn (89/17)
>
> suffyrn me speke to þe in þi sowle (210/7)
>
> strong for to suffyr (119/36)

of summe to be sauyd (54/33-34)

þei partyd a-sundyr, & sone aftyr þe same ȝong man passyd ouyr þe see (222/6-7)

"... syr, I xal not sweryn", sche seyde, "for I xal spekyn of God & vndirnemyn hem þat sweryn ..." (126/1-3)

swet(-nesse)

> swet smellys (51/32, 87/31)
>
> my swet Sone (50/7, 191/21, 192/25, 196/24-25)
>
> forsakyn my swete Sone (196/7-8)
>
> swete spicys (210/31-32)
>
> no sauowr ne swetnesse (199/34)
>
> swetnesse of spech þat owyr Lord spak on-to hir sowle (50/3-4)

sygth

> saue only þe sygth (43/31)
>
> staryng to mennys sygth (9/17)
>
> sterrys & awngelys in þi syght (252/11-12)

synne

> of hys synne & relesyng of þe sekenes (223/6)
>
> soget to syn (41/29)
>
> sweryng & oþer synnes (36/11)

T

Julian:

techyn (*taught*)

taught in this tyme (xxxv/5-6)
techyn me & tellyn me (1/43)
techyth is trew (xlv/36)
trew teching (lxx/36)
trew love that techith (xl/34)
kepe þe therein & comfort the therewith & trost thou thereto (lxx/11-12)
looke thereupon and comfort thee therewith (iii/29-30)
continuant contrarieste (xlviii/12-13)
truely trosting (lvii/70)
than atwix these two (x/62)

Margery:

trespasyd & takyn (222/33)
teerys
  plentyuows teerys of contricyon (2/21-22)
  terys turmentyn (43/7)
  turnyd by þe teerys of thyn eyne (212/28-29)
  many tymes wyth teerys of thyn eyne (52/4-5)
tell
  telle me, & I xal takyn hym (197/17)
  tellyn þat tale (126/23-24)
  telde me þe werst talys (126/22)
  ne tunge telle (53/5)
obteyn & getyn her intent (59/30)
thynk swych thowtys (17/27)
toke hys toos (208/23)
tretys schal tretyn (1/12-13)
trewly
  I telle þe trewly it is trewe (47/33)
  I telle þe trewly þes wyndys & tempestys (230/28)
  þat trewly trostith (76/4)
chastysed wyth many tribulacyons & horrybyl temptacyons (39/2-3)

W

Julian:

waste

    all these may wasten & weren away (vi/46-47)

    wasten our wreth (xlviii/56)

    westith & destroyith our wreth (xlix/11-12)

wele & wo (i/21, xix/24, lii/9, lxi/62, lxxvi/30, inverted xv/25, lv/13)

wetyn (wiste, wit, wot, etc.)

    wete it now wele (lxviii/12)

    wele I wete (viii/9-10)

    wel wetyn (xxx/17)

    I weste wele whyl I beheld (xix/2)

    I wiste wele (xix/15, xvii/57)

    witt it now wele (lxx/19-20)

    I wote wele (xxv/5)

    wel I wote (li/131)

    he wil we wetyn (xxxii/5)

    he wil we wetyn þat it is his wil (xxxiv/6)

    willing to wete (i/46)

    wotist what I would (ii/33-34)

    þat wot it ne shal wetyn it (xxxii/66)

will (verb)

    whan he wille, and suffrith us in wo (xv/30-31)

will (noun)

    it is his will þat we wetyn (lxv/26)

    my will & my worship (li/209-210, lxiv/18-19, lxv/39-40)

    man werkyth evermore his will & his wership lestyngly with-
        oute ony styntyng, & what this worke is was shewid in
        the firste (lxiv/1-3)

    worship when it is thy will (li/294-295)

within & without (lxx/34, 36) (vowel alliteration but also prefix
    repeated)

in witt & wisdom (lviii/27-28)

wretchid world (li/260)

worthynes of the heyest worshipful kyng (xx/7-8)

not as wounds but as worships (xxxix/34-35)

wallowing & wrythyng (li/346, 356)

waylith, & writhith (li/18)

wene we that God were wrothe with us (xl/5)

Margery:

wast wel wers (5/22-23)
waschyn awey (249/3)
in wel & (ne) in wo (17/21, 87/22)
what wyth wel & wyth woo (234/39)
wepyn
    weyke j-now of wepyng (162/24-25)
    no wondyr þow þu wepe (211/32)
    wondyr why þu wepist (213/12)
    wynnyst many sowlys fro hym wyth þi wepyng (51/13-14)
    wepen whan sche wold & slawndered þe werk of God (2/23)
weryn white (76/14-15)
wetyn (*wiste, wot, etc.*)
    wel to wetyn (247/8)
    wetyn wel (195/20, 211/38)
    wost wel (89/3, 213/20, 227/1)
    wot(e) wel (77/5, 126/14, 210/16, 210/23, 211/11, 225/40, 227/10)
    wote wel sche wolde I wer (228/7)
    wyst ful wel (9/12, 98/4, 223/26, 234/27-28)
    wist not wel what (128/8)
    wist wel a woman (233/26)
    not wyst of the werld (40/19)
    wetyn hir wylle (33/29-30)
wex ful of whelys (222/11)
whakyd wondirly (124/24-25)
went wil in a wode (126/25-26)
wistly
    as wistly as it is not in my power to wepyn (249/16)
    as wistly as it is not my wil ne myn entent to worschepyn
        (248/26-27)
    as wistly as I wolde (249/26)
witte & wisdom (128/29)
it was a womanys witte (228/35)
woman wondryd (111/14)
woman in þis world (195/15-16)
hys wonderful werkys (1/13)

word þat is wretyn (47/34)

world

    world knew al my wikkydnes as þu dost, þei wolde merueylyn
        & wonderyn (250/29-30)

    worshepys of the world (11/8-9)

    I wolde þat al þis worlde wer worthy (250/31-32)

    wretthyd world (11/4)

    wretchyd wordelys exile (100/30)

worshep(-ful)

    o day in þe weke for worschep (162/11-12)

    a worshepful woman (54/20, 170/10-11)

    worshepful wyfys (77/32-33)

worthy(-ly)

    wel worthy (159/23)

    as þu hast mad of vnworþi creaturys worthy, so make al þis
        world worþi (250/32-33)

    worthily wyth al maner of worschep (211/37-38)

    worthy & worshepful clerkys (3/21, 164/33)

    vnworthy wretche (229/33)

weryn wroth (109/16-17)

wrytyn þis booke & neuyr to be-wreyn it (4/35-36)

wrytyn it betyr wyth good wylle (4/20)

wyfe

    weddyd wyfe (87/18)

    weddyn a wyfe (213/21, 223/10-11)

    rith wel of good wil wyth hys wife (123/28)

    wyfys desyr & to wetyn whedyr hys moder wolde (224/21)

    wyfys whech woldyn (49/2)

    wifys þer arn in þis worlde (212/15-16)

wykkydnes as wistly as I was neuyr so wykkyd (207/34)

wyl (verb)

    I wyl þat þu were clothys of whyte (32/17)

    wher he wyl (40/18)

    wher he wyl, & of vnworthy he makyth worthy (41/26-27)

wyl

    was in wyl (1/16)

    þi wil of chastite as þu wer a wedow (161/12)

    it wer þi wille I wolde (225/8)
    what was hys wille (109/23-24)
    þe wille & þe werkyng (229/8)
    werkyn my wil (210/4)
    wyth good wyl (10/9-10, 41/31, 123/35, 178/27)
fayr wynde & wedyr (110/25, 229/13)
wykked wyndys (100/23)
as wytnessyd wel (100/24)

VOCALIC ALLITERATION

Julian:

all in ease (v/27)
& al to one end (lxxv/9)
and if I aske any thing (v/42-43)
And to al this I had non other answere (lxv/40)
upright vnderlenand (iii/23)

Margery:

alle
    alle þe ale was lost euery brewyng aftyr oþer (10/1)
    al þe day aftyr (127/23)
    al hir lyfe aftyr (8/4)
    alle þat arn in Heuyn & in erth (253/8)
    to alle þat askyn (253/12)
    alle þe awngelys (49/32)
    alle awngelys & alle seyntys (50/8)
The ankyr, answeryng a-ȝen (44/24)
And a-non aftyr (207/3)
answer
    answer to certayn artyculys (40/24)
    at hir answer (123/35)
    was hir auoket and answeryd (148/20)
awter & askyd (164/35)
& eche of vs of oþeris (250/12)

enmy
> of alle her enmijs (250/8)
> or ellys of ʒowr enmy (18/8)
> hys enmy had envye (5/24)

euer(y)
> euery euyn & morwyn (77/28-29)
> eye is euyr up-on þe (161/5)
> hir eyne wer euyr to-gedirward (206/28-29)

boþe of on & of oþer (45/2)

onyment þat þei myth a-noyntyn (196/18)

ALLITERATIVE COMBINATIONS

Julian:

(b,g)

eyther we abyden a better tyme or more grace or a better gyfte
> (xlii/29-30)

(b,p)

the toknys of the blissid passion & the plentious sheddyng of his
> pretious blode (viii/5-6)

(b,s)

blissid brest be his swete open syde (lx/46-47)

(d,s)

delvyn & dykyn, swinkin & swetyn (li/225)

(f,d,s,p)

One is the drede of afray that cummith to a man sodenly be
> frelte. This drede doith good, for it helpith to purge man as
> doeth bodily sekenes, or swich other peyne that is not synne.
> For all swich peynys helpe man, if thei be patiently taken.
> The ij is drede of peyne wherby man is sterid & wakid fro
> sleepe of synne. He is notabil for the time to perceivyn the
> soft comfort of the holy Gost, till he have vnderstonding of
> this drede of peyne of bodily deth & of gostly enemyes. And

this drede stirrith us to seken comfort & mercy of God, & thus this drede helpith us & abileth us to have contrition be the blisfull touching of the holy Gost. The iij is doubtful drede. Doutfull drede in as mech as it drawith to dispeir (lxxiv/2-14)

(g,l,f,s)

& this wrowte & shal be be the grace of the holy gost so long til we shal dey in longyng for love. And than shal we all come into our Lord our selfe clerely knowand & God fulsomely havyng, & we endlesly ben al had in God, hym verily seand, & fulsumly feland, hym gostly heryng, & hym delectably smel-lyng, & hym swetely swelowyng (xliii/54-60)

(h,g,s)

& how I hope be the grace of the holy Gost I shal sey as I saw (xliv/6-7)

(l,n,s)

kingdomes longand to a Lord. And whan it had sen al the noblyth beneathyn, then merveling it was sterid to seeke aboven (lxvii/24-26)

(m,f)

Mercy be love suffrith us to faylen be mesur, & in as mech as we faylen, in so mekyl we fallen, & in as mekyl as we fallen, so mekyl we dyen (xlviii/21-24)

(m,f,k)

he kepith us mytyly & mercifully in the tyme þat we arn in our synne & monge all our enemies þat arn full fel upon us. & so mekil we arn in the more peril, for we geven him occasion therto & kno not our owne nede. The iii is how curtisly he kepith us & makith us to knowen that we gon amyss. (lxxviii/7-12)

(m,l)

But here shewid our curtes Lord þe moneing & the morning of the soule, menand thus: "I wote wele thou wilt liven for my love merily & gladly suffrand all the penance that may com to the,

but in as mech as thou livest not without syn*n*e þu woldest
suffre for my love all the wo, all the tribulatio*n* & disese that
myte come to the ... "(lxxxii/1-8)

(m,p)

him reverently thankyng & prasyng of our makyng, mytily prayeing
to our Moder of mercy & pite, & to our Lord þe holy Gost of
helpe & grace. For in these iij is all our life — Kynde, Mercy
& Grace, whereof we have mekehede, myldhede, patiens, &
pite (lix/36-41)

(m,s,p)

mekely make we our mone to our dereworthy moder, & he shal al
besprinkle us in his precious blode & make our soule ful soft
& ful myld & hele us ful faire be proces of tyme (lxiii/22-25)

(m,n)

no man*n*er of myslekyng, no wanting of wil (lxiv/16-17)

(r,d,h)

he reysid up the gret rote out of the depe depenes, which rythfully
was knit to hym in hey hevyn (li/352-354)

(s,h)

it plesyth most God & sonest spedyth, for our soule is so specially
lovid of him that is heyest that it overpassyth the knowing of
all creatures (vi/51-54)

(w,s)

in witt & wisdam we have our keping as anempts our sensualite,
our restoryng, & our savyng (lviii/27-29)

(w,s,p)

I weste wele whyl I beheld in the Cross I was seker & save; ther-
fore I wold not assenten to put my soule in perel, for beside
the Cross was no sekernes (xix/2-5)

Margery:

(c,g)

creatur was þus gracyowsly comen a-geyn (9/7-8)

(c,ch,w)

clene & chaste in al hir gouernawns as fer as þei cowde knowyn
      in cher, cuntenawns, in worde, & in werke (114/18-20)

(f,s)

fadyr of þe sayd persone folwyd þe sone (225/18)

(g,c)

glad of hir comyng & gretly comfortyd (178/10-11)

(g,l)

grawntyng hym good lofe & leue (57/11)

(l,m)

Lord Ihesu, þis maner of leuyng longyth to thy holy maydens
      (48/35-49/1)

(l,s)

lost his bodyly strength & lay stylle (39/8)

(p,g)

to þe preste wyth rygth glad cher, preyng hym to do hys good wyl,
      and sche schuld prey to God for hym & purchasyn hym grace
      (5/5-7)

(p,s,w)

Hys name & hys perfeccyon of prechyng spred & sprong wondyr
      wyde (148/29-30)

(s,w)

Syr, ȝe xal welyn sum day þat ȝe had wept as sor (125/6)

(w,s,c)

Whan þas good women seyn þis creatur wepyn, sobbyn, & cryen
      so wondirfully (78/6-7)

(w,s,h)

worde wrowt so sor in hir herte (107/32-33)

(w,sh,s)

þu wost wel þat I send sum-tyme many gret reynys & scharp
      schowerys & sumtyme but smale & softe dropis (183/5-7)

BIBLIOGRAPHY

Bacon, Leonard, "The Book of Margery Kempe", *The Saturday Review of Literature*, XXVII (November 4, 1944), 12.

Barnet, S., M. Berman, and W. Burto, *A Dictionary of Literary Terms* (Boston, Little, Brown & Co., 1960).

Bennett, H. S., "Margery Kempe", *Six Medieval Men & Women* (Cambridge, University Press, 1955), pp. 124-150.

Betts, Henry, *Some Secrets of Style* (London, George Allen & Unwin Ltd., 1932).

"The Book of Margery Kempe", *Times Literary Supplement*, October 10, 1936, p. 805.

Bosworth, Joseph, and George Waring, *The Gospels: Gothic, Anglo-Saxon, Wycliffe, and Tyndale Versions*, 4th edition (London, Gibbings & Co., 1907).

Bracker, Frederick, "Understatement in Old English Poetry", *Publications of the Modern Language Association*, LII (1937), 915-934.

Brodeur, Arthur G., *The Art of Beowulf* (Berkeley and Los Angeles, University of California Press, 1959).

Brooks, B. G., "Margery Kempe", *The Nineteenth Century and After*, CXXXII (July, 1942), 30-32.

Brown, Carleton (ed.), *Religious Lyrics of the Fourteenth Century* (Oxford, Clarendon Press, 1924).

Brown, Carleton (ed.), *Religious Lyrics of the Fifteenth Century* (Oxford, Clarendon Press, 1939).

"Catholic Mystics of the Middle Ages", *Edinburgh Review*, CLXXXIV (October, 1896), 298-321.

Chambers, R. W., *On the Continuity of English Prose* (Early English Text Society, No. 191A.) (London, Oxford University Press, 1957). Also found in the Introduction to Nicholas Harpsfield's *Life of Sir Thomas More*, edited by E. V. Hitchcock and R. W. Chambers. (The Early English Text Society, No. 186, 1932.)

Chaucer, Geoffrey, *Canterbury Tales*, edited by John M. Manly (New York, Henry Holt & Co., 1947).

Chaucer, Geoffrey, *Poetical Works*, edited by F. N. Robinson (Cambridge, Mass., Houghton Mifflin Co., 1957).

Cholmeley, Katherine, *Margery Kempe: Genius and Mystic* (London, Longmans, Green, and Co., 1947).

Ciardi, John., "How Does a Poem Mean", *An Introduction to Literature* (Cambridge, Mass., Houghton Mifflin Co., 1959).

Coffman, G., "The Book of Margery Kempe", *Speculum*, XVII (1942), 138-42.

Colledge, Eric, *The Mediæval Mystics of England* (New York, Charles Scribner's Sons, 1961).

Davidson, Donald, *American Composition and Rhetoric* (New York, Charles Scribner's Sons, 1959).

Fifield, Merle, "Alliteration in the Middle English Lyrics", unpublished Ph.D. dissertation, University of Illinois, 1960.

Hamilton, Clarence H., "A Psychological Interpretation of Mysticism", Private edition distributed by the University of Chicago libraries. Ph.D. dissertation, University of Chicago, 1914.

Harford, Dundas, "Richard of Caister, and his Metrical Prayer", *Norfolk and Norwich Archæological Society*, XVII (1910), 221-244.

Hodgson, Phyllis, *Deonise Hid Diuinite* (Early English Text Society, No. 231) (London, Oxford University Press, 1955).

Hussey, S. S., Review of "The Chastising of God's Children and The Treatise of Perfection", *Modern Language Review*, LIII (1958), 231-232.

Inge, W., *Studies of English Mystics* (London, John Murray, 1907).

James, William, *The Varieties of Religious Experience* (New York, Collier Books, 1961).

Jones, Rufus M., *The Flowering of Mysticism* (New York, Macmillan Co., 1940).

Joseph, Sister Miriam, *Shakespeare's Use of the Arts of Language* (New York, Columbia University Press, 1947).

Julian of Norwich, *Revelations of Divine Love*, edited by Dom Roger Hudleston, 2nd edition (London, Burns Oates & Co., 1952).

Julian of Norwich, *Revelations of Divine Love*, edited by George Tyrell (London, Keegan Paul, Trench, Trübner & Co., 1902).

Julian of Norwich, *Revelations of Divine Love*, edited by James Walsh (New York, Harper & Brothers, 1961).

Julian of Norwich, *Revelations of Divine Love*, edited by Grace Warrack, 4th edition (London, Methuen & Co., 1911).

Julian of Norwich, *The Shewings of Lady Julian*, edited by Dundas Harford, transcribed and edited from Brit. Mus. Addit. 37790, 3rd edition (London, H. R. Allenson, 1925).

Julian of Norwich, *A Shewing of God's Love*, edited by Sister Anna Maria Reynolds (London, Longmans, Green, and Co., 1958).

Kempe, Margery, *The Book of Margery Kempe*, edited by W. Butler-Bowdon (New York, Devin-Adair Co., 1944).

Kempe, Margery, *The Book of Margery Kempe*, Vol. I, edited by S. B. Meech and H. E. Allen (Early English Text Society, No. 212) (London, Oxford University Press, 1940).

Klæber, Fr. (ed.), *Beowulf and the Fight at Finnsburg*, 3rd edition (Boston, Heath & Co., 1950).

Knowles, Dom David, *The English Mystics* (London, Burnes Oates & Washbourne, 1927).

Kökeritz, Helge, *Guide to Chaucer's Pronunciation* (New York, Holt, Rinehart, and Winston, 1962).

Kökeritz, Helge, *Shakespeare's Pronunciation* (New Haven, Yale University Press, 1953).

Kökeritz, Helge, "The Reduction of Initial *kn* and *gn* in English", *Language*, XXI (1945), 77-86.

Krapp, George P., *The Rise of English Literary Prose* (New York, Oxford University Press, 1915).

Kurath, Hans, and Sherman Kuhn (eds.), *Middle English Dictionary* (Ann Arbor, University of Michigan Press, 1954).

Lawlor, John, "A Note on the 'Revelations' of Julian of Norwich", *Review of English Studies*, N.S. II (1951), 255-258.

Leuba, J. H., *The Psychology of Religious Mysticism* (London, Keegan Paul, Trench, Trübner and Co., 1925).

Lewis, C. S., *The Allegory of Love* (New York, Oxford University Press — Galaxy Book, 1958). First published 1936.

Loane, G., *A Short Handbook of Literary Terms* (London, George Allen & Unwin Ltd., 1923).

Mackinnon, E., "Studies in Fourteenth Century English Mysticism", unpublished Ph.D. dissertation, University of Illinois, 1934.

McCann, Dom Justin, "The Book of Margery Kempe", *The Dublin Review*, CC (1937), 103-116.

Moliniari, Paul, *Julian of Norwich* (London, Longmans, Green, & Co., 1958).

Morgan, Margery, "A Talkyng of the Love of God", *Review of English Studies*, N.S. III (1952), 97-116.

Mossé, Fernand (ed.), *A Handbook of Middle English*. Translated by James A Walker (Baltimore, The Johns Hopkins Press, 1952).

Oakden, J. P., *Alliterative Poetry in Middle English*, 2 vols. (Manchester, University Press, 1930-35).

Owst, Gerald, *Literature and Pulpit in Medieval England*, 2nd revised edition (New York, Barnes and Noble, 1961).

Read, Herbert, *English Prose Style* (Boston, Beacon Press, 1961).

Reynolds, Sister Anna Maria, "Some Literary Influences in the *Revelations* of Julian of Norwich", *Leeds Studies in English and Kindred Languages*, Nos. 7-8 (1952), pp. 18-28.

Rickert, Edith, *New Methods for the Study of Literature* (Chicago, University of Chicago Press, 1927).

Saintsbury, George, *A History of English Prose Rhythm*, 2nd edition (London, Macmillan & Co., 1922).

Schipper, Jakob, *A History of English Versification* (Oxford, Clarendon Press, 1910).

Scott, John H. and Zilpha Chandler, *Phrasal Patterns in English Prose* (New York, Ronald Press, 1932).

Shibata, S., "Notes on the Vocabulary of the *Book of Margery Kempe*", in *Studies in English Grammar and Linguistics in Honour of Takanobu Otsuka* (Tokyo, Kenkyusha Ltd., 1958), pp. 209-220.

Shipley, Joseph T. (ed.), *Dictionary of World Literature* (New York, Philosophical Library, 1943).

Tempest, Norton R., *The Rhythm of English Prose* (Cambridge, Eng., University Press, 1930).

Thompson, W. M. (ed.), *þe Wohunge of Ure Lauerd* (Early English Text Society, No. 241) (London, Oxford University Press, 1958).

Thomson, J. A. K., *The Classical Background of English Literature* (London, George Allen & Unwin Ltd., 1948).

Thomson, J. A. K., *Classical Influences on English Prose* (London, George Allen & Unwin Ltd., 1956).

Thouless, R. H., *The Lady Julian* (London, Society for Promoting Christian Knowledge, 1924).

Underhill, E., "Margery Kempe", *The Spectator*, CLVII (October 16, 1936), 642.

Undset, S., "Margery Kempe of Lynne", *The Atlantic Monthly*, CLXIV (1939), 232-240.

Wilson, R. M., "Three Middle English Mystics", *Essays and Studies 1956*, N.S. 9. (London, John Murray, 1956), pp. 87-112.

White, Helen C., "Margery Kempe of Lynn", *Commonweal*, XXXIX (1943), 164-166.

Williamson, George, *The Senecan Amble* (London, Faber and Faber Ltd., 1951).

Zeeman, Elizabeth, "Continuity in Middle English Devotional Prose", *Journal of English and Germanic Philology*, LV (1956), 417-422.

Zeeman, Elizabeth, Review of "A Litil Tretys on the Seven Deadly Sins", *Modern Language Review*, LII (1957), 581-582.

INDEX